THE

CHRISTIAN WORLD OF

C. S. LEWIS

THE
CHRISTIAN WORLD OF
C. S. LEWIS

by

CLYDE S. KILBY

Wм B. Eerdmans Publishing Company
GRAND RAPIDS, MICHIGAN

To C. K. B.

$4.00

PREFACE

IT WAS ALMOST A QUARTER CENTURY AGO THAT I PICKED UP AT my college book store a little volume by an Oxford don named C. S. Lewis. It was called *The Case for Christianity,* and when I sat down to read it I realized that a new planet had sailed into my ken. Unlike Lewis when he discovered the works of George Macdonald, I felt neither holiness nor Joy in this book — these were to appear later — but a mind sharp as a scalpel and as intent as a surgeon upon the separation of the diseased from the healthy. I discovered a writer who like a philosopher claimed that the unexamined life is not worth living, yet who with the humblest Christian gave that life a Living Center. My impression was of a man who had won, inside and deep, a battle against pose, evasion, expedience, and the ever-so-little lie and who wished with all his heart to honor truth in every idea passing through his mind. And now, some forty books later, I have no reason to change my basic impression of the man.

There are critics who accuse Lewis of word-juggling and a diabolical cleverness used to promote what they call an outdated fundamentalism. Some dismiss him as little more than a popularizer. I think he would willingly have acceded to the charge if popularizer is meant in its original sense of one who hopes to influence (for good) the mass of ordinary people. Lewis himself speaks of "the divine popularizer Boethius." But the charge is by no means applicable to him if it means the entertainment of the vulgar, the cheapening of values to win a clientele, or the effort to pad one's pockets. The truth is that Lewis holds up a higher standard of literary discipline than most writers and a higher standard of Christian discipleship than most clergymen — standards which bespeak the very antithesis of popularization.

As a derisive term, popularizer may be intended to indicate someone deficient in knowledge but glib in style, someone incapable of original thought who is nevertheless clever in re-phrasing and illustrating the ideas of his betters. Lewis's reputation as a scholar in realms other than religion provides evidence of his vigorous intellectual originality. As to style, Lewis is undoubtedly a master. D. S. Savage declares that a great writer discovers that method which is precisely suited to himself and to his subject and actually creates a vehicle for his unique purpose. Any sensitive reader becomes aware of this quality in Lewis, not alone in the fictional works where metaphor, allegory, symbol, and myth are used but also in the seemingly opposite style of some of Lewis's expository prose which, despite its apparently unstudied directness, turns out on examination to be filled with strength and grace.

Lewis is indeed a stylist. But so were Gibbon and Addison and Carlyle. There is a sense in which style becomes not simply the "dress" of thought but its body, as de Quincey argued. When Dr. Johnson said that hell is paved with good intentions and Lowell remarked that the gift without the giver is bare, they were not enunciating things theretofore unknown in the world. They were simply giving perfect expression to well-known truths. Lewis repeatedly states that Christianity is the very last subject on which to attempt originality. Instead, he says, he has sought to set forth "plain Christianity which no Christian disagrees with," to "restate the primeval moral platitudes." Of his *Problem of Pain* he says, "If any parts of this book are 'original,' in the sense of being novel or unorthodox, they are so against my will and as a result of my ignorance." The value of Lewis's books lies in the depth and freshness of his observations and the permanency of his expression.

I hope that my study may be of value to three classes of people. First, a guide to those who know little or nothing of Lewis and wish to choose some of his books. Secondly, a help to those who have read and yet not fully understood his books. Thirdly, to those who have been reading and perhaps re-reading him for years, an evaluation of the breadth and scope of his work as a whole. Let me say an additional word concerning the second group. I have talked with numerous people who have "discovered" Lewis and been much benefited by his books, yet who have invariably felt they missed a portion of what he had to say. This is of course as it should be with any writer worth reading in the first place. While I do not pretend to have exhausted Lewis's meanings, I hope I have been useful in extending them.

My main purpose is simply to evaluate Lewis's Christian works one by one, to compare them with each other and sometimes with books by other writers, to discover the themes which make up the main body of his writing, and to consider the consistency of Lewis's works as a whole. While I have not wished to violate Lewis's obvious desire to keep the details of his private life from the public, I have occasionally added some meaningful detail which has appeared in obscure sources or from my correspondence with him. It will be noted that I give considerable space to summaries of books, more space of course to those which require it. Yet I have always intended my summaries to be interpretations as well. One critic has said that some of the Narnia books are without Christian implications. I do not so read them and hence even these simple stories I have briefly summarized as well as discussed.

While it would be impossible for me to mention all those who have "talked Lewis" with me through the years, I should like to give credit to a few. Professor and Mrs. Frank Bellinger, Dr. Arthur Holmes, and Mr. Robert Siegel read the manuscript in whole or part and made valuable suggestions for improvement. The members of two seminars on Lewis which I conducted at Wheaton College brought up and answered important questions concerning Lewis the scholar or Lewis the Christian. I am indebted beyond my footnote acknowledgments to the doctoral dissertations mentioned in my appendix, especially to the dissertations of Corbin S. Carnell and Marjorie E. Wright, both these scholars having been former students of mine. Most of all, I feel a deep debt of gratitude to Dr. Lewis himself for answering, sometimes at length, my queries of him.

I am grateful to the following publishers and authors for permission to use quotations: Geoffrey Bles for quotations from *They Asked for a Paper;* Faber & Faber Limited for a quotation from Charles Williams's *Place of the Lion;* Harcourt, Brace and Company for quotations from *Surprised by Joy, Reflections on the Psalms,* and *Letters to Malcolm: Chiefly on Prayer;* Harper & Brothers for a quotation from D. E. Harding's *The Hierarchy of Heaven and Earth;* Macmillan Company for quotations from *The Great Divorce, That Hideous Strength, The Abolition of Man, The Silver Chair, The Last Battle,* and *The Weight of Glory,* as well as briefer quotations from other books; The National Anti-Vivisection Society of London for a quotation from *Vivisection;* Wm. B. Eerdmans Publishing Company for quotations from *The Pilgrim's Regress;* the University of California Press for quotations from Charles Moorman's *Arthurian Triptych;* the *Atlantic Monthly* for two quotations from an article by C.E.M. Joad; the *Saturday Evening Post* and the author for a quotation from an article by Eric Hoffer; and the *Nation* and the author for a quotation from an article by Philip Siekevitz.

I also express my gratitude to periodicals in which brief portions of this book have appeared: The New York *Herald-Tribune,* The Chicago *Daily News, Christianity Today,* and *His.*

—C.S.K.

CONTENTS

Preface   5

   I SEARCH FOR JOY   11

  II HELL AND HEAVEN   37

 III PAIN AND LOVE   65

 IV MYTH OF DEEP HEAVEN   79

   V THE KINGDOM OF NARNIA   116

 VI PSALMS, MIRACLES, AND ORTHODOXY   147

VII THEMES IN LEWIS   173

Appendix   191

SEARCH FOR JOY

UNTIL A SHORT TIME BEFORE HIS DEATH IN NOVEMBER, 1963 Clive Staples Lewis was the distinguished occupant of the Chair of Medieval and Renaissance Literature at Cambridge University. He was among the best literary critics of his period. At the same time he was a Christian and the author of more than a score of books concerning his faith. Furthermore, he managed the difficult feat of successfully integrating his scholarship and religion. Add to these things the gifts of a lively imagination, a vigorous and witty mind, and a brilliance of language and you discover why his books have sold widely and why his audience is steadily on the increase.

Following the train of an argument by Lewis, says the *Guardian,* is "like watching a master chess player who makes a seemingly trivial and unimportant move which ten minutes later turns out to be a stroke of genius." Our generation has seen only too much of a diabolical cleverness turned to the destruction of old values. Lewis's supreme cleverness was turned rather to the defense of those values. Dabney A. Hart, who attended Lewis's lectures at Cambridge, thought that the reason they were always crowded was simply that "what he gave could not be found in books, neither the wealth of detailed information nor the vitality of his synthesis of it." Kenneth Tynan, one of Lewis's students, said that he had "more knowledge at his finger tips" than anyone he had ever known, and Dom Bede Griffiths, one of Lewis's colleagues at Oxford, believed that Lewis had "the most exact and penetrating mind" he had ever encountered. David W. Soper

11

says that so great a judge as Etienne Gilson has called Lewis a "pure theologian" and expressed joy in his works. "I am grateful to Lewis," says Edmund Fuller, "for some of my richest experiences of mind and heart."[1]

It is possible that Lewis was the unique illustration of a man whose greatness resided in a capacity to be honest. In a world where a genuine naiveté, despite all our talk about it, is almost nonexistent, Lewis was the example of a naive man. He described one of his teachers as a person "without a particle of affectation," and the phrase is appropriate to Lewis himself. One critic sarcastically charged him with possessing the mind of a child. This was correct, though not as the critic meant it. "When I became a man," he wrote, "I put away childish things, including the fear of childishness and the desire to be very grown up." He was derisively called a romanticist, a charge he confessed before it ever was made. It was true in the sense that Lewis had open eyes and had not, like most of us, lost his capacity for wonder at the way of things. The fact that God was made flesh disclosed to Lewis a sanctity in the commonplace and everyday.

Lewis was even called vulgar, and he did at times seem to match his own description of Mr. Badger in *The Wind in the Willows* as an "extraordinary amalgam of high rank, coarse manners, gruffness, shyness, and goodness." If at times he was a little hard to approach, it was nevertheless the common testimony of many visitors that once in his presence they found nowhere a more genial, courteous, and thoughtful host. The supposition that he was gruff needs to be put alongside Lewis's conviction that perfect love dispenses with modesty. In *The Screwtape Letters* he describes one strategy of hell as creating in people a false sense of modesty. Screwtape tells his fiendish understudy Wormwood to fix in his subject's mind the notion that humility con-

---

[1] The Hart quotation is from a dissertation called "C. S. Lewis's Defense of Poesie"; those of Tynan and Griffiths from a dissertation called "The Dialectic of Desire: C. S. Lewis' Interpretation of *Sehnsucht*," by Corbin S. Carnell; that of Soper from "An Interview with C. S. Lewis," *Zion's Herald*, January 21, 1948; that of Fuller from *Books With Men Behind Them*.

sists in trying to believe genuine talents to be less valuable than they really are.

My impression is that few people ever faced the delusive nature of selfishness more thoroughly than Lewis, and if he sometimes was franker than the rest of us it was because he had succeeded better in breaking the charm of a deceptive delicacy. He not only escaped the face-saving devices common to our generation but in innumerable instances turned them upside down before us in order to demonstrate what dupes they make of us. What his detractors do not understand — or maybe what they understand only too well — is that Lewis had come out on the other side of a door most of us never manage to enter. He once described himself as a "converted pagan living among apostate Puritans" and a man who had taken as long to acquire inhibitions as others have needed to get rid of them.

Surprised by Joy

Lewis's *Surprised by Joy* he calls "the shape of my early life." It is less an autobiography in the ordinary sense than an account of his religious ups and downs from childhood — of the almost complete lack of religion in his early experience, of his childhood prayer to the Magician God whom he wished to heal his dying mother and then go away, of his first hectic efforts in boarding school to create a satisfying spiritual realization, of his glad retreat into atheism, and then of the long and tortuous return through nature, spiritualism, and philosophy to Theism and finally to Christianity.

He was born on November 29, 1898 at Belfast. His father, Albert James Lewis, was a solicitor and his mother, Flora Augusta Hamilton Lewis, a descendant of clergymen, lawyers, and sailors. On his father's side there was sentiment and passion, on his mother's irony and coolness yet a capacity for happiness. Lewis's picture of his father is a masterpiece. Someone should bring the many details of this Tristram Shandy together into a single essay. He had, says the son, a gift for confusing an issue or misinterpreting a simple fact. "Tell him that a boy called Church-

13

wood had caught a fieldmouse and kept it as a pet, and a year, or ten years later, he would ask you, 'Did you ever hear what became of poor Chickweed who was so afraid of the rats?' For his own version, once adopted, was indelible, and attempts to correct it only produced an incredulous, 'Hm! Well, that's not the story you *used* to tell.' " Lewis's mother died before he was ten, but she had already started him in French and Latin. Lewis and his only brother, three years his senior, were left alone in the large house and spent endless hours in their respective imaginative worlds of Animal-Land and India.

He learned *Sehnsucht,* longing, from looking out of the nursery windows at the Castlereagh Hills, but there were no genuine religious experiences. The house was rich in books and the brothers read widely. They also wrote and illustrated for their private pleasure their own childish fantasies. They lived almost totally in their imaginations. One day as young Lewis stood beside a currant bush in flower there suddenly and mysteriously arose in him "as if from a depth not of years but of centuries" the memory of an earlier happy morning. Though it happened in an instant of time, he felt that "in a certain sense everything else that had ever happened to me was insignificant in comparison." It was the beginning of his search for Joy.

At ten, throttled by an Eton collar, bowler-hat, and uncomfortable shoes, Lewis was sent to school in hated England under the tutelage of Oldie, who flogged his boys with and without excuse but taught them to think logically. At twelve he went to Campbell College, not far from the Lewis home in Ireland, but his stay was cut short by a spell of illness which gave him six happy weeks on his own.

From thirteen to fifteen he was back in England at a small preparatory school he calls Chartres. Here at last he began to love the English countryside, but here also he lost his faith, his virtue, and his simplicity. At Oldie's school he had begun to read the Bible and pray, but, strangely, prayer was one of the things that led him to atheism and, he says, might have driven him mad if pursued as he was attempting it. In his efforts to avoid the hypocrisy of simply "saying" his prayers he acquired

14

the opposite extreme of long, weary stretches when by sheer will-power he struggled to acquire a "realization," a stirring of the affections. Other things which led him to atheism were the occultism imparted to him by a matron at the school, the spell of a dancing mistress on whom he had cast lustful eyes, a natural pessimism, and particularly the reading of Lucretius, H. G. Wells, and Sir Robert Ball.

At fifteen he won the classical scholarship to "Wyvern" College, located in the same English town as Chartres. Though Lewis's brother had attended Wyvern and liked it, he himself concluded that this school, like most other such colleges in England, produced not the understanding and fraternal man described in its catalogue but rather "a bitter, truculent, sceptical, debunking, and cynical *intelligentsia*" dominated by the social struggle and priggishness. Only a few students succeeded in remaining outside the rigid student hierarchy of Bloods, Punts, and Tarts and the "furnace of impure loves" which was prevalent. One of these was an Irish earl who always carried a revolver and played a form of Russian roulette by loading one cylinder and pointing the weapon toward a student's head and counting off as he pulled the trigger. One of the few valuable assets of Wyvern was Smewgy, a hard but courteous teacher who could say, "You will have to be whipped if you don't do better at your Greek Grammar next week, but naturally that has nothing to do with your manners or mine." He taught his boys to be scholars without being pedants. In religion Lewis at this time suffered the conflict, as he says, of maintaining that God did not exist and being angry with Him for not existing.

From sixteen to eighteen Lewis prepared for university entrance under the tutorship of a tall, lean, and shabbily dressed but ruthlessly dialectical man named W. T. Kirkpatrick in Surrey. Despite a stunning rebuke from Kirkpatrick in the first moments of their association, Lewis loved his lanky teacher and, free from the games and other school routines he had unwillingly participated in, found this the happiest period of his life. He read abundantly in literature of all sorts, including much of Homer and other Greek authors in the original. His atheism was strengthened by Kirk-

15

patrick's own, for his teacher was an old-fashioned "high" atheist who doted on *The Golden Bough* and Schopenhauer and who at a later time would have made an excellent logical positivist.

All along since Chartres, Lewis had been living not one life but two. One was filled with the bustle of ordinary pleasures and miseries while the other was secret, imaginative, and full of longing for Joy. During his illness while at Campbell he had first found delight in fairy tales and fallen under the spell of dwarfs. His earlier discovery of Arnold's *Sohrab and Rustum* was the prelude to the heartbreaking ecstasy of the pure "Northern-ness" which engulfed him when he came upon the account of Siegfried and the twilight of the gods and the great world of Norse mythology. Under Smewgy he had indirectly discovered not more Northernness but the volcanic power and fire of Mediter-ranean myth. And of course there was plenty of King Arthur and early Britain. All these myths reawakened in him a great love for nature and music, at least the music of Wagner. Joy, "that central music in every pure experience," pressed its illimitable claims upon him and spread its glory in unbearable waves to the roots of his being. Yet the time came when Joy disappeared and only the memory of it teased him. His very impatience to retrieve it seemed to frighten it away. He found that neither sexual indulgence nor any other experience was a substitute for it.

Meanwhile his atheism grew bolder and Christianity came to mean ugly architecture, ugly music, and bad poetry, and God a great "transcendental Interferer." He wanted to tell God and everybody else that his innermost being was marked No Admit-tance. At this time he says he was made up of two separate ele-ments: one the longing for Joy, the other a fixed and certain belief in scientific materialism. Then he discovered in Yeats and Maeterlinck men who while disbelieving Christianity yet thought that there was a world behind, or around, the material world, and he was temporarily persuaded to a belief in magic and oc-cultism.

It was at this point that he, like Browning with his *Old Yellow Book,* came upon a soiled copy of George Macdonald's *Phantastes* in a bookstall. Browning's description of his own transport over his discovery applies equally well to Lewis as he sat down to read:

A spirit laughs and leaps through every limb,
And lights my eye, and lifts me by the hair.

Alongside the romantic elements in the novel, Lewis found something new, a "bright shadow" that he later discovered to be the voice of holiness. "It was as though the voice which had called to me from the world's end were now speaking at my side. It was with me in the room, or in my own body, or behind me. If it had once eluded me by its distance, it now eluded me by proximity — something too near to see, too plain to be understood, on this side of knowledge." Always in the past Joy had been separate from the ordinary world; in Macdonald he found, to his surprise, that the bright shadow transformed all common things while itself remained unchanged. His imagination was baptized. It was the beginning of the road back.

At eighteen he took the scholarship examination for Oxford and was elected. But a war was in progress, and the day he was nineteen he found himself in the front-line trenches in France. A brief illness gave him three weeks in an army hospital, where he first began to read G. K. Chesterton and loved him in spite of his religious element. He was wounded in April, 1918 by a British shell falling short of its German target. In January, 1919 he was discharged from military duty. He ridicules his experience of taking sixty German prisoners of war; what happened, he says, is that they simply appeared with their hands up and ready to surrender.

Back at Oxford, he began to make friends who were to influence his future. The first was A. K. Hamilton Jenkin, who taught him how to rejoice in the existence of each thing, "to rub one's nose in the very quiddity" of objects and experiences. Another was Owen Barfield, an anthroposophist, who became Lewis's "anti-self" and with whom he argued night after night and on long walks. These and others Lewis found to be men of high principles. He met also a dirty and tragic Irish parson who had lost his faith but was avidly eager to prove human survival after death. This monomania to carry some kind, any kind, of self

17

beyond the grave disgusted Lewis with the whole conception of immortality. Just when the New Psychology was causing him to doubt his whole experience of Joy, some of his closest friends began to turn Christian. With Barfield in particular he debated violently and learned much. It was he who destroyed forever in Lewis the easy belief in "chronological snobbery," or the conception that whatever has gone out of date is thereby automatically to be discredited. He also convinced Lewis that abstract thought can give indisputable truth and is therefore a different sort of thing from experience of the senses. Finally Lewis was forced to conclude that logic itself participated in a cosmic *Logos*. He also became convinced of a cosmic Absolute but did not assume it would ever get personal.

Lewis was twenty-three when he finished Greats and, because he could find no position, decided to remain for a fourth year at Oxford. Almost immediately he was drawn to a brilliant young man named Nevill Coghill and was shocked to discover him a Christian and thoroughgoing supernaturalist. At the same time it dawned on him that all the authors on whom he could really feed — Macdonald, Chesterton, Dr. Johnson, Spenser, Milton — saw things through Christian eyes. Even the most religious of the Pagans — Plato, Aeschylus, Virgil — had some of the same quality. They had "roughness and density of life." He still thought Christianity only a myth, a good philosophical framework on which to hang Absolute Idealism.

He became a temporary lecturer for a year and was then elected a Fellow of Magdalen College in 1925, when he was twenty-six years old. Christians now began to appear all around him — men like H. V. D. Dyson and J. R. R. Tolkien, the latter both a Roman Catholic and a philologist, two things he had been warned never to trust. He re-read Euripides' *Hippolytus* and Joy returned to exalt his heart. On the intellectual side he read Alexander's *Space, Time and Deity* and learned the all important principle that we do not think a thought in the same sense in which we think that Herodotus is unreliable. A thought is not simply a thing inside one's own head and isolated from its object. Introspection can only find what is left behind and

18

cannot operate while the original thought exists. It is a terrible error to mistake the track left behind for the thing itself. Immediately Lewis knew he was looking in the wrong place to find the Joy he had long sought, that his hope to find some mental content on which he could lay his finger was wholly futile, for this was and would always be simply the "mental track left by the passage of Joy." Not only must Joy look to its object, but a desire owes all its character to its object, for the object is the very thing which makes it desirable. He had always been wrong in thinking that he desired Joy itself. "All the value lay in that of which Joy was the desiring," an object clearly outside both his mind and body.

Now teaching philosophy at Oxford, Lewis began to have real troubles with the Absolute. He lectured on a philosophical "God" but distinguished it from "the God of popular religion" and insisted that there could be no personal relation with Him. But now two hard blows struck him. He read G. K. Chesterton's *Everlasting Man* and was shaken by its theistic rationale. Shortly afterwards the toughest of all the atheists he had ever known sat beside the fire in Lewis's room and said, "Rum thing. All that stuff of Frazer's about the Dying God. Rum thing. It almost looks as if it had really happened once." Lewis thought that nobody could be safe from God if this man were not.

There followed a time in which all the strands steadily platted themselves into an invincible whole in Lewis's inner being. It seemed to him that God was as surely after him as a cat searching for a mouse. "You must picture me," he says, "alone in that room in Magdalen, night after night, feeling, whenever my mind lifted even for a second from my work, the steady, unrelenting approach of Him whom I so earnestly desired not to meet. That which I greatly feared had at last come upon me." It was in the Trinity Term of 1929 that he capitulated. As he knelt down in prayer and admitted that God was God, he felt himself "the most dejected and reluctant convert in all England."

It was conversion to Theism only, not Christianity and not belief in a future life. They came later. "I was driven to Whip-

19

snade one sunny morning. When we set out I did not believe that Jesus Christ is the Son of God, and when we reached the zoo I did." It was thus that the Hound of Heaven overtook and conquered his prey.

Surprised by Joy closes with its author thirty-one years of age. Afterwards he continued on the twin paths of academic scholarship and Christian writing. At twenty-one, under the pen name of Clive Hamilton, he had published *Spirits in Bondage,* a book of youthful lyrics on nature, romance, and certain other subjects that he would treat more fully later. Though five years earlier he had felt the enigmatic quality of holiness in Macdonald's *Phantastes,* many of these poems portray God as nonexistent or at least disinterested in the affairs of men. At twenty-eight, also under the pen name, he published a long narrative poem called *Dymer.* The hero, a young man who had borne all he could of reason and science in a totalitarian state, revolted, walked up and struck his teacher dead, and left in search of better things. He went through a whole galaxy of strange and romantic experiences reminiscent of Macdonald's *Lilith* and *Phantastes* and finally lost his life to a wild beast, yet not actually a beast but a "wing'd and sworded shape" brimming with life. In the preface to a later edition Lewis says that his hero was a man escaping from illusion who was first made joyful and then found he could not repeat his youthful rapture. The unhappy consequences of his rebellion and especially the murder of his teacher brought him to despair and the same sort of despair which had been Lewis's own six years before the poem was written. This shock forced Dymer to accept reality. But then the shabbiest of bribes was offered him, "the false promise that by magic or invited illusion" there might be a short cut back to happiness. Though he succumbed to the bribe, he was not really deceived, and was finally able to defy the magician who had tempted him and thereafter to face his own destiny.

The first of Lewis's many Christian books was *The Pilgrim's Regress,* published in 1933. *The Allegory of Love,* first of his scholarly works, came out in 1936 and won him the Hawthornden

Prize. In 1946 St. Andrews University in Scotland awarded him
the honorary Doctor of Divinity degree. He continued as Fellow
at Magdalen College, Oxford, until 1955, when he went to
Cambridge. For three years he made regular broadcasts on religious topics over the British Broadcasting Corporation, and some
of these have been rebroadcast via the Episcopal Hour in the
United States. During the Second World War he was asked by
the Royal Air Force to visit air bases and lecture on theology.

Many even of Lewis's enthusiasts thought of him as a confirmed
bachelor who feared and perhaps despised women. When my
wife and I visited him at Oxford some years ago even the gateman
at Magdalen acknowledged that there was "some truth" in his
reported antipathy.[2] Yet I know of an American girl who a
little later was invited to lunch by him and treated magnanimously.
Lewis really never was an outlaw from feminine society. He
says that he and his brother were "civilized" by the good graces
of Lady E., his mother's first cousin, and her well-mannered household.

In 1957 Lewis was married to an American named Helen Joy
Davidman Gresham. Both she and her former husband William
L. Gresham had been brought up during the cruel, bitter years of
the Depression in a generation which, as she says, "sucked in
atheism with its canned milk."[3] Both not only became atheists
but enthusiastic communists. Talented as a writer, she joined the
staff of the *New Masses* and attempted to hew to the absolute line
of Marxism. Her husband had spent fifteen months fighting for
the underdogs in Spain. Later he became an alcoholic and neu-
rotic and finally tried unsuccessfully to kill himself. In a brief
time of relief he had written a successful novel describing the
savage and violent world he envisaged. Thanks in part to the
books of C. S. Lewis, both had professed a belief in Christ. "With-

---

[2] Perhaps his opinion is summed up in his remark about how his good
friend Owen Barfield impressed him in their early acquaintance: He
found Barfield "as fascinating (and infuriating) as a woman."

[3] The succinct and inspiring personal accounts of both Joy Davidman
and William Lindsay Gresham are told in David Wesley Soper's *These
Found the Way.*

21

out his works, I wonder if I and many others might not still be infants 'crying in the night,' " said she. "His books exposed the shallowness of our atheist prejudices; his vision illumined the Mystery which lay behind the appearances of daily life," said he.

But the Gresham marriage began to go on the rocks, and the time came when he fell in love with another woman. There was a divorce which she did not contest. Later she went to England, and previous to her marriage to Lewis acted as a sort of secretary to him.

Not long after she and Lewis were married it was known that she had an advanced case of cancer with prognosis of at best only a few months of life. They invited a minister to come and lay hands on her and pray. In June, 1958 Lewis wrote me that she had made "an almost miraculous recovery and is at present very well indeed." She returned to excellent health, and the X-ray specialist called it a miracle. She was able to take long woodland walks with her husband and carry on a normal life. She had always wanted to go to Greece, and the two made the trip together and had a wonderfully memorable time. She died July 13, 1960, after their return to England. She was forty-five. Lewis became the guardian of David and Douglas Gresham, her teen-age children.

A small volume in 1961 called *A Grief Observed*[4] is Lewis's outpouring of despair and sorrow following his wife's death. He describes her as possessing a lithe, quick mind which was extremely sensitive to cant and hypocrisy and a soul "straight, bright, and tempered like a sword." He tells of their happiness and even gaiety together even after all their hope for a second miracle was gone, also of his numb despair following her death. "Her absence is like the sky, spread over everything," he wrote.

This book reveals an element of Lewis not heretofore apparent in his writings, that is, a profound emotional depth and, despite his long bachelorhood, a deep capacity for conjugal love. It also reveals, especially during the early part of his bereavement, an outspoken resentment toward God which is like Job's cry,

---

[4] Published under the pen name N. W. Clerk, later issued under Lewis's own name.

Therefore I will not restrain my mouth;
I will speak in the anguish of my spirit;
I will complain in the bitterness of my soul,

and which reminds one of some similar outcries in Lewis's *Spirits in Bondage,* published long before he became a Christian. In one instance in *A Grief Observed* he confesses that his bitter words against God the night before were "a yell rather than a thought." Like Job also, he feels at the end of the struggle that his forthright charges have brought about a kind of spring cleaning to his soul.

Lewis himself suffered a long illness during the winter of 1961-62. Unable to teach, he returned to his beloved house at Headington Quarry, Oxford, where he slowly recovered. His brother, Major W. H. Lewis, also a writer, and Walter Hooper, an American for whom Lewis had come to hold a high regard, lived with him and assisted with correspondence and other tasks. In 1962-63 he returned to Cambridge, but, after another nearly fatal illness in July, 1963, he resigned his chair. Throughout the autumn he retained his hearty sense of humor and was as brilliant in conversation as ever until the final heart attack which marked his rapid decline.

Lewis consistently withstood invitations to go abroad for lectures. He was, in fact, no traveler, preferring to remain home and walk the little hills and valleys of England. "I like monotony," he once said. He had small respect for the automobile. "The truest and most horrible claim made for modern transport is that it 'annihilates space'. It does. It annihilates one of the most glorious gifts we have been given." In his autobiography he repeatedly emphasized his physical clumsiness, perhaps over-emphasized it actually. His one great love was swimming, preferably in the ocean. Next to that perhaps came walking and next to that sitting before a comfortable fire or in a pub talking.

In a true Wordsworthian sense Lewis was a lover of nature and solitude. When he walked he refrained from smoking in order not to miss the full odor of nature. He described what he regarded as an ideal day. It would consist of breakfast at eight, study and writing from nine until one with perhaps a cup of tea at eleven. After a one-o'clock lunch there would be a walk, preferably alone because talking "blots out the sounds and silences of the out-door world." If a friend went along, it must be a case of two bodies with but one soul, when a simple halt would be sufficient proof that some image of earth and sky was shared. The arrival home at four o'clock would be the signal for tea but now in solitude with only some "gossipy, formless book that can be opened any-where," like Boswell, *Tristram Shandy, The Essays of Elia,* or *The Anatomy of Melancholy.* From five until seven there would be more work, then the evening meal and afterwards talk, lighter reading, and bed at eleven.

Lewis's antipathies were in a few instances quite pronounced. He had little use for newspapers, which he believed create a taste for vulgarity, sensationalism, untruth, and the habit of fluttering from subject to subject without discrimination. He hated collectivism of every species and seemed in particular to enjoy pot shots at the inequalities of the British income tax. He had little good to say about what he called modern education, by which he meant that in which the old verities are scrapped in favor of laxness, experimentalism, chronological snobbery, and busyness. Our world, he said, is "starved for solitude, silence, and privacy: and therefore starved for meditation and true friendship." He thought that perhaps half of all the happiness in the world comes from friendship, not the artificially stimulated friendship of organizations existing for the purpose but friendship generated among a few people brought together to do something that they like in common. He was always on the side of the unadjusted man and of sales resistance to slick advertising and everything else that leads to a bland, jejune existence. He favored the common man over the intellectual snob. In general he was fearful of men in authority, even religious authority. There are few things he eschewed more than pride, especially pride masquerading in religious or psychological attire.

At regular intervals the word went out that Lewis had become a Roman Catholic. Actually he remained in the Church of England to the end of his life, "not especially 'high,' nor especially 'low,' nor especially anything else." He was not satisfied with the excessive "good taste" in the Church of England and thought that the Roman church, the Orthodox faiths, and the Salvation Army have all retained a certain gusto that his own church could well re-acquire. His objection to Roman Catholicism was the ordinary Protestant one, that of addition of doctrines not in the Bible, such as transubstantiation, the immaculate conception, worship of the Blessed Virgin, and papal infallibility. Yet he felt that Protestants are about as busy in subtracting from the Gospel as Romans are in adding to it. He felt more at home with Catholics than with some extreme Anglo-Catholics who have "passed into a worse state of ecclesiastical rigor mortis."[5] Yet it was in an Anglo-Catholic church that Lewis experienced his first real contact with Christ.

Since *The Pilgrim's Regress* is direct allegory and might well be called the further spiritual adventures of C. S. Lewis, it is appropriate to summarize and discuss it at this point.

The Pilgrim's Regress

In this novel John, a boy born in Puritania, discovered at an early age that there were many things he could not do because the Landlord would not like them. One day John was forced to put on uncomfortable clothes and go with his parents to visit the Steward. He was totally confused about the Steward's explanation of the Landlord and his rules, but he saw clearly one thing: the Landlord was a person to be feared and at all hazards avoided. About the same time John gazed into a woodland near his home and heard sweet music and saw, momentarily and far away, a calm sea and an enchanting Island that created in him an intense longing, such a longing that he could do nothing else than start out in search of the Island.

The first morning after his departure from home he met big, red-headed Mr. Enlightenment, who invited John to travel westward in his neat little trap drawn by a fat pony. Mr. Enlightenment was a fine talker, but John declined an invitation to go with him to his home city of Claptrap. Although Mr.

⁵ David W. Soper, "An Interview with C. S. Lewis," *Zion's Herald*, January 14, 1948.

Enlightenment described it as magnificent, all John could see was a vast sprawl of ugly huts. Mr. Enlightenment had made John happy by assuring him there was no Landlord.

John next came upon a traveler named Mr. Vertue who was to accompany him most of the long journey westward. Vertue prided himself on his independence of soul, yet he disciplined himself more thoroughly than anyone John had ever met. As they went along they met Media Halfways, who invited them to visit her father in the city of Thrill, off to the south of the main highway. Vertue refused but John, taken with Media's looks, went and was entranced with old Mr. Halfways' music until the hobnailed step of Gus Halfways came along to dissipate the enchantment.

Next day Gus seated John in a horrible machine and they roared north of the main road to the city of Eschropolis where John met the Clevers but finally made a remark which infuriated them and was forced to run for his life. Lost in an icy rain, John was arrested for trespassing on the territory of the Spirit of the Age. He was fettered and thrown into a dirty prison in the rocks. After some days the jailer, who turned out to be Sigismund Enlightenment, son of Mr. Enlightenment, got angry with John and bloodied his mouth but also kicked him out of the prison. Outside, John was arraigned before the Spirit of the Age, a giant large as a mountain, when a tall figure muffled in a blue cloak came riding up on a great black stallion. When the giant learned she was Reason, he quickly offered her a passport through his territory, but instead she spurred her horse onto the giant and thrust her sword into his heart, and the Spirit of the Age settled down into what he had seemed at first, simply a great hummock of rock. Before John and Reason left, she broke down the prison door and invited all the prisoners to come out. They wailed and insisted on remaining just as they were.

John and Reason traveled together and she taught him many things before she directed him back to the main road. At sunset, as he continued westward, John came upon Vertue, who had been trudging steadily along. Just then John was alarmed to

26

discover that the road ended abruptly on the edge of a precipice overlooking a great canyon seven miles wide.

Vertue was attempting to persuade John down and across the canyon at all hazards when Mother Kirk appeared and told them that neither could get over without her help. But ·Vertue and John refused her offer and turned northward along the canyon hoping to discover a crossing on their own. They stayed overnight with Mr. Sensible and his servant Drudge, and Drudge decided to go along with Vertue and John when they started farther north next morning. They discovered that the canyon widened, the land became more desolate, and the weather grew colder as they went along. Drudge informed them that there was no chance whatever of descending into the canyon from that part of the world.

When John grew faint, they knocked at a little shanty beside the road and were invited inside by three pale young men. Next day Vertue went still farther north, and when he came back reported on his harrowing experience there. He had found the country barren and inhabited only by red and black dwarfs, vassals of one Savage, who was married to Grimhild, Mr. Halfways' elder daughter. Vertue warned the pale men of Savage's warlike intentions and told them that they must acquire some of that powerful man's enthusiasm if they hoped to withstand him. But none of them seemed to be greatly disturbed.

After this, John and Vertue set out southward along the canyon. In the cold and darkness they got separated, and next morning John found that his friend Vertue had become blind. He led him gently back to the main road, where again they refused the aid of Mother Kirk and set off to explore southward for a way across the canyon. They came into a lovely country clustered with primroses and opening into increasingly beautiful landscapes. The first house they reached was that of Mr. Broad, a Steward, who had long been the close friend of Mr. Sensible. He entertained them at tea on his lawn and sent them on to Mr. Wisdom's, where they remained for some time enjoying the delightful countryside and calm, indolent days. One night John was awakened by the younger members of Mr. Wisdom's house-

27

hold and invited to a sumptuous meal and a gay party on the moonlit lawn. Next morning he found the young people so quiet and sincere that he could not determine whether they were conscious of the previous evening or not.

That afternoon John found that Vertue's eyesight was restored, but after a disagreement between them Vertue went off angry and John attempted to follow him up the steep side of the canyon. John became lost and in his despair called out for help and was cared for by a mysterious person. Later in a cave in the cliffside he came upon the hermit History, who revealed to him many things he had never known before. Then Reason, with her sword in her hand, took charge of John and carried him to the floor of the canyon, where he found his friend Vertue in the presence of Mother Kirk. Both found it necessary, if they would cross the canyon, to throw off their rags and dive naked into a pool before them, which they nervously did. They went down a long way and up through catacombs to the other side, where they found many other pilgrims, all of whom took their way westward beside a clear river which ran through lovely vistas down to the sea, and there John could see his Island. Yet because it was not to be reached from where they were, he and Vertue were given a Guide to lead them all the way back to Puritania, for indeed John's Island was not an island at all but rather the other side of the eastern mountains where the Landlord lived, mountains which John once dared not look at because of his dread of that Landlord. On the return journey John and Vertue saw many unusual and instructive things and fought two fierce dragons. John discovered that his parents had long since crossed the brook eastward, but his sorrow was assuaged when the Guide told him and Vertue that before night they also should go over toward the Island which was not an island but the home of the Landlord Himself.

Since a number of people who have read *The Pilgrim's Regress* carefully are still puzzled by portions of the allegory, I shall venture some suggestions as to its meaning. The story is obviously patterned on that of Bunyan, being a journey "from this world to the next." Like Bunyan's, the account is set forth as a dream in which the hero undergoes perilous adventures, representing a man in search of a great preoccupying passion.

Geographically the main road leads as straight as an arrow from Puritania to the great canyon, but there are numerous roads to the north and south. Inhabitants to the south tend to be genial, friendly, and easygoing, those to the north hard, determined, and disciplined. Their distance from the main road suggests Lewis's conception of the relative degree of their theological or philosophical error. The *Mappa Mundi* accompanying the story indicates some territories about which we hear little or nothing and may indicate the scope of the plot as originally projected by its author. Most of John's deviations take him north of the main road until he finally crosses southward at the rim of the canyon.

The Island coveted by John represents the longing for God which Lewis believes to inhabit every man's soul, a signpost pointing toward Him. The cry of the heart for a great and permanent satisfaction is so persistent that a man's whole life consists in greater or less degree of the search for it. Like John, he may fear and even hate God, yet the gnawing remains and no adequate substitute is possible. The Landlord lived within sight of John's home and might have been discovered there had not John's education and consequent obstinacy prevented.

John had been brought up to understand diametrically opposite things about God, for instance, that He is kind and good yet will not hesitate to send one to hell. The rules are of course God's laws and the Stewards are ministers. Our pretense that all is well, often lasting to the grave itself, is represented by the masks put on by John's parents and friends as they accompany his disreputable Uncle George down to the brook of death. Yet Uncle George was so nervous that his mask would not stay on, that is, for the first time in his life he faced a reality capable of destroying his pretense.

The naked brown girl was John's first substitute for God and their children perhaps the complications of sin. Lewis says in

29

Surprised by Joy that he himself found a loose sexual life a false substitute for Joy. Mr. Enlightenment bombarded John with isolated fragments of "scientific" evidence to prove there was no Landlord. Claptrap, his home city, he thinks magnificent, yet to John's common sense it appeared a most undesirable place. These things suggest Lewis's opinion of the source and quality of much "evidence" against Christianity. John again parallels Lewis's own experience in temporarily becoming a happy atheist. Looking backward toward the home of the Landlord in the eastern mountains, John, now assured there is no Landlord, was able to patronize God as the embodiment of beauty.

Vertue represents the man who establishes his own disciplined standards and tells God to let him alone. Again like Lewis at one stage of his life, Vertue prizes independence and sees God as the great Interferer. Vertue would rather go to hell than acknowledge any authority above his own. It is noteworthy that Lewis makes Vertue stick to the main highway even while John goes off seeking his Island and gets into trouble. Vertue teaches John one important lesson that keeps reappearing throughout the story: there is a world of difference between wanting and choosing. Vertue is himself a chooser and John a wanter. Yet the time comes when Vertue collapses under his tightlipped discipline of choosing and John must plead with him simply to *want* something. I think that perhaps Lewis wishes his reader to see John and Vertue as types of monists who are both wrong in their procedure. The merely moral Vertue with his precise conduct and dearth of feeling comes to the impassible canyon at the same time as the emotional John who tries any experience which he thinks may lead to his Island.

Media Halfways and her father are, as their name suggests, a compromise between the grossness of outright carnality and the life of dedication to Christ. They represent people who substitute aesthetic experience and other compromises for God.

Lewis's picture of Gus Halfways and Eschropolis are unmistakably clear. The Clevers are the hard-boiled and soulless moderns who love modernity and revolt for their own sake. They are people who have learned from certain modern psychologies to get rid of their inhibitions and who in doing this make a fetish of the immoral and the brutal. They are tensely eager to perform the rites of their emancipation from every kind of normalcy. John's simple remark that they were out of date so enraged them that they attacked him — i.e., uptodateness is what certain people cherish so much that any denial of it is a denial of all they are. John discovered that most of the Clevers were writers in the employ of Mr. Mammon, an adequate comment on Lewis's opinion of "emancipated" authors. In *The Problem of Pain* he says that "the 'frankness' of people sunk below shame is a very cheap frankness."

Equally engaging is Lewis's depiction of the Spirit of the Age, John's jailer Sigismund Enlightenment, and the people imprisoned. Sigismund is of course Sigmund Freud and the imprisonment the power exercised by the domination of popular psychoanalytical teachings. Sigismund confidently assured John that all his visions of the Island were nothing more than his repressed lusts for the brown girls. Lewis tells in his autobiography how his search for Joy had lured him many times into undisguised erotic reverie and how he came to the point of vilifying all his images of Joy because, as he then supposed from his study of psychology, he had "seen through" them.

This phrase "seen through" explains Lewis's meaning in the horrifying experience John went through in the prison. He discovered that whatever the Spirit of the Age's eyes looked upon became transparent and turned John's fellow prisoners from human beings into viscera, brains, intestines like a coil of snakes, and lungs panting like sponges. When John turned downward from the gruesome sight, he saw only the workings of his own inwards and concluded that he was in a hell as bad as any concocted by the Landlord. Lewis thus expresses his own unabated horror at conceptions which reduce man simply to his glandular or physiological makeup.

The same idea is continued in Sigismund's sardonic analysis of the prisoner's food while they ate it. He would remind them they were eating corpses and give them minute details of how the animal was slaughtered. Finally, when Sigismund joked

31

about the milk they drank as simply one of the secretions of the cow, John suddenly began to laugh and then to ridicule the simple failure of the jailer to distinguish milk from sweat or dung. Like the Clevers, Sigismund could brook no interference with his favorite belief and struck John in the mouth but also opened the prison door and threw him out. Lewis means that one good reasonable look at the claims of radical psychoanalysis and related philosophies is enough to release a victim from their ridiculous assumptions. The same is suggested by the appearance of Reason outside the prison and her destruction of the Spirit of the Age.

But when Reason broke down the doors of the jail, the prisoners refused to be liberated. They only wailed and said, "It is one more wish-fulfilment dream" and resolutely remained in their dark, noisome, and stinking quarters, suggesting that none are so blind as they who will not see. A similar irrationality was practiced by the dwarfs toward the end of *The Last Battle* when they refused to believe in Aslan after they had been fooled by the ape.

Reason led John away from the icy coldness and stench he had experienced into a place warm with the first accents of spring. As they went along she explained to him the difference between the archtype and ectype, model and copy. She told him that though his love for the brown girls and his love for the Island were similar they were by no means the same. The Island was the archtype and must not be mistaken for the ectype or copy. She taught him also that true philosophy and theology are the younger sisters of reason.

When John complained about the highway ending in a great precipice, Mother Kirk told him that the Landlord did not make it that way and began to explain how it was originally. Then ensued an account of Eden and the Fall in which Satan is represented as a land-grabber who actually owns all the territory occupied by the Clevers, Mr. Mammon, and the Spirit of the Age. Mother Kirk explained how the rules became necessary after the taste of mountain-apples infected all growing things in the land.

The allegory of Vertue's and John's refusal of Mother Kirk's help is obvious. It represents people who are intent on getting over the canyon of salvation by their own efforts.

The account of John's and Vertue's trip north along the rim of the canyon is somewhat less ingenious, I feel, than what has preceded. Mr. Sensible is a talkative man filled with grandiose but superficial notions. His garden is his pride, though he grows there nothing but radishes in soil only a half-inch deep over solid rock. His food really comes from Mr. Mammon, Eschropolis, old Mr. Halfways, Horace, Epicurus, Rabelais, and the like. Sensible returned thanks at his table but assured his guests that the Landlord was only a "tradition." John slept very cold in this house, which was called Thelema: Let every man be persuaded as he will and follow that persuasion. Mr. Sensible is quite a thoroughgoing contrast to Mr. Wisdom who appears later on.

The pale men are new aspects of Anglicanism, Classicism, and Humanism.[6] Lewis tells us that the men representing these respective positions are T. S. Eliot, Irving Babbitt, and George Santayana. (The reader should remember that this book is dated 1933.) Perhaps the most important thing to be noted is that Anglicanism regards God as a fact, Classicism has no interest in the matter, and Humanism is sure He is a fable, yet all three are united against the idea that there is any goodness or decency whatever on their side of the canyon.

Savage and the red and black dwarfs represent Marxism, Fascism and other tough movements bent on conquering the world. Vertue reported that Savage thought the three pale men the supreme fools who polished the brass while, according to their own claims, the ship was already sinking. Savage liked the wind from the north pole because it made a man of one, suggesting Lewis's notion of the bleakness of communism but also its danger. The warning to the three pale men that they should

---

[6] In his preface to the third edition Lewis says, "Barth might well have been placed among my Pale Men, and Erasmus might have found himself at home with Mr. Broad."

strengthen themselves if they expected successfully to fight Savage is very obvious, yet it is equally obvious that none of them will do anything about it. As for Mr. Neo-Classical, he was convinced that Vertue had dreamed the whole experience and that no people lived farther north than he and his two brothers.

As Vertue and John set out southward, Vertue confessed his doubts about the correctness of his devotion to a life in which the imposing of his will on his inclination had become an end in itself. He had always thought it excellent training but now he had begun to ask what the training was for. He could not afford to be moved by any pleasure which might lie ahead and neither by any dread that might lie behind, for those were matters of the emotion rather than of the will. Finally he assured John he could find no reason ever to rise from the stump on which he was sitting. John urged him to want something, but he could not. I think that Lewis here is insisting that to live by the principle of duty alone, without the warmth of a great hope and a great expectation, is blindness. Man is a unit and he dismisses all elements of his unity except one, such as the will, at his peril.

Lewis tells us plainly that Mr. Broad represents broad-church modernist Christianity. Friendly and cheerful, Mr. Broad nevertheless could only give John the flabby suggestion that the seeking for his Island was the finding of it, and when pressed refused to say positively whether one must actually cross the canyon or not.

John and Vertue's visit to the house of Mr. Wisdom is the most difficult part of the novel. Wisdom represents philosophical idealism as Lewis experienced it not long before his conversion. When questioned, Wisdom explained the errors, as he believed, of the people both north and south of the main road. The southern people, he said, err in supposing east and west real places and the Landlord a real man. The northern people err equally in thinking these things mere illusions. His own belief was that things were not an illusion but an appearance, a true appearance and one always to be desired but never actually hoped for. In *Surprised by Joy* Lewis says that he and his Oxford friends came to a point where they "could talk religiously about the Absolute:

34

but there was no danger of Its doing anything about us." This Absolute had something of the quality of heaven, yet it was a heaven that one could never get to. The valley to be crossed from Wisdom's house was, on the oldest maps, marked the Valley of Humiliation. Perhaps Lewis wishes us to understand that the one thing not known to him and his friends was simple humility.

John was much surprised when he discovered that the food enjoyed by the younger people in secret was furnished by Half-ways, Mammon, and other unexpected sources, even some things from the Savage dwarfs as well as some from Mother Kirk. These young people represent idealistic philosophers who borrow, apparently without knowing it, from sources they would not always care to acknowledge.

From here on the allegory is quite self-explanatory. The rags which John and Vertue were forced to take off before baptism represent efforts at self-help. When John said he could not dive, Mother Kirk told him the art of diving was not doing anything but only ceasing to do, that is, becoming wholly dependent upon Christ's sacrifice.

The Guide back to Puritania I take to be the Holy Spirit. His telling them that they would find the old road very different perhaps means that the Christian view puts everything in a new perspective. His explanation that John's Island was really not an island at all but rather the other side of the eastern mountains where the Landlord lived has by this time in the story become clear. John's deep longing was always a misunderstood longing for God. The dragons John and Vertue had to fight doubtless signify their learning obedience and further humility.

Although this is one of Lewis's most difficult books, it will reward anyone who is willing to stay with it, and will in fact grow increasingly meaningful as one contemplates the spiritual significance of such remarks, for instance, as Mother Kirk's that she is the daughter-in-law of the Landlord, that is, the Church as the Bride of Christ. Packed into the novel are not only philosophical and theological truth but also much warmth of soul. John's search for the Island becomes as paramount and joyously pervasive in *The Pilgrim's Regress* as the pursuit of the Grail in the Arthurian legends. More successfully than any other of Lewis's books, even *Surprised by Joy,* it makes clear his meaning of *Sehnsucht* or the longing which haunts every man and entices him toward God.

There are times when this novel bears favorable comparison with its great model, and I think that Lewis's depiction of the overwhelming desirability of the Island exceeds Bunyan's motivation of Christian. On the other hand, there are times when Lewis's story is weakened by excessive exposition, as at the house of Wisdom. The study by Dabney A. Hart points this out. I think I would take some exception to Dr. Hart's additional remark that at the climax of John's return journey Lewis "tries to compensate for his lack of an adequate image to express the spiritual experience by using passages of verse to heighten the tone."[7] My own impression is that the verse fits very admirably into the story.

Two apologies made in later editions of *The Pilgrim's Regress* should be mentioned. One expresses Lewis's regret for the bitterness of some of his criticism. It is indeed a book in which the author's understanding of other people's errors appears far more clearly than his love for those people. He sounds at times like an angry young man drawing a caricature, as when he has Mr. Enlightenment say that making a guess often enough turns it from a guess into a scientific fact and when Mr. Mammon reports that every single one of the Clevers writes for him or has shares in his land. The other apology is for the summary sentences at the top of pages. It is not at all that Lewis wished to puzzle his readers but rather that he was fearful people might suppose allegory simply a trick to say obscurely what might have been said more clearly in plain exposition. What he means is that a worthy fiction will always rise into a dimension of its own and transcend any mere one-to-one tie with ordinary reality.

---

[7] "C. S. Lewis's Defense of Poesie," a doctoral dissertation at the University of Wisconsin, p. 190.

II

HELL AND HEAVEN

LEWIS'S FICTION MAY BE CONVENIENTLY CLASSIFIED INTO THE space trilogy, the Narnia stories, and a group of novels dealing in one way or another with hell and heaven. *The Screwtape Letters* and *The Great Divorce* clearly fall into this last category. *Till We Have Faces* is discussed here not so much because one or two of its scenes are located in hades as because it illustrates how far the hellish sin of selfishness masquerading as love can subvert the activities of an entire life. I also include *The Problem of Pain* because pain and punishment are described by Lewis as mainly devices which, by reminding man of God's reality, help him to escape hell.

The Screwtape Letters

One of the most popular of Lewis's books is *The Screwtape Letters*. From the time of its publication in 1942 this satirical classic has been continually reprinted. When the first American edition appeared, Leonard Bacon called it an "admirable, diverting, and remarkably original work . . . the most exciting piece of Christian apologetics that has turned up in a long time . . . a spectacular and satisfactory nova in the bleak sky of satire."[1] A new edition in 1962 includes an added chapter called "Screwtape Proposes a Toast" and also a revised and significant preface.

St. John Ervine says that to William Booth "hell was as actual . . . as the Whitechapel Road, and much more horrible." So

[1] *Saturday Review of Literature,* April 7, 1943.

also is hell to C. S. Lewis, and, thanks possibly to Lewis's emphasis, so is it to a good many recent theologians. But Lewis says it is important to remember that in *The Screwtape Letters* he had in mind not speculation about the nature of hell but rather the wish to throw light on men's lives. He also says that the composition of this book was the most distasteful of his experience because he was forced to project himself while speaking through Screwtape into "dust, grit, thirst, and itch" while all "beauty, freshness, and geniality" had to be excluded.

In this witty, brilliant story Screwtape, an Under Secretary to the High Command of Hell, writes letters of instruction and warning to his nephew Wormwood, a junior tempter in charge of a young male "patient." There are other hellish characters: Glubose, in charge of the patient's mother; Slumtrimpet, in charge of the patient's fiancée; Slubgob, head of the Tempters' Training College; Toadpipe, secretary to Screwtape; and also Scabtree and Triptweeze. Hell has not only a Training College and an Intelligence Department but a House of Correction for Incompetent Tempters and also a headquarters where are kept the dossiers on the vast array of patients. In the preface to the new edition Lewis adds a note on the source of his names, saying that Screwtape probably arose from such phonetic associations as *Scrooge, screw, thumbscrew, tapeworm,* and *red tape,* and Slubgob from *slob, slobber, slubber,* and *gob.* What he does not say is that he probably got Wormwood from the book of Revelation.

Wormwood is in trouble from the beginning because he has failed to prevent his patient from becoming a Christian. Screwtape suggests many devices for reclaiming the patient's soul. He must prepare for the time when the first emotional excitement of conversion begins to fade. He must turn the patient's thoughts while in prayer from God to his own moods and feelings. When the patient prays for charity, let him start trying to manufacture charitable feelings in himself. Wormwood must stir up irritations between the patient and his mother. He must be persuaded to think of devils as comic creatures in red tights and tails. He must be caused to believe that his "dry" periods are signs God is unreal and the idea must be inculcated that religion is good "up to a point." He must be introduced to smart, superficially intellectual and skeptical people who will teach him to despise "Puritanism" and love religious flippancy.

For a time Wormwood reported gleefully on his success but then had to confess that his patient had experienced repentance and renewal. Screwtape warned him of the blunders he had committed and ordered a strong renewal of efforts. The patient was to be made to confess that he is humble, the surest way of destroying his true humility. He must be persuaded to shoulder the future with all its cloud of indefinite fears rather than live in a simple, immediate dependence on God. He must be attacked at the point of his chastity. He must be made spiritually resentful and proud. If possible, he must be brought to love theological newness for its own sake and think of the "historical Jesus" rather than the Jesus of the Gospels. The patient's prayer life must be rationalized so that if the thing he prays for does not come to pass he will see it as proof that petitionary prayers simply do not work or if it does come to pass as nothing more than the operation of nature. When it is discovered that the patient is in love with another Christian, Wormwood is instructed to begin planting seeds of domestic hatred that will mature ten years afterward.

Despite Screwtape's repeated warning that the patient must be kept alive, with a view to a more favorable time for further attacks, he was killed while acting as an air raid warden. Screwtape closed his letters with a note of despair on the failure of the Intelligence Department of hell to learn more of God's secrets and a note of bitter promise literally to swallow up his bumbling nephew.

In the preface to the original edition Lewis had said that Screwtape might at times tell lies, and in his last letter to Wormwood it is easy to get the impression Screwtape knew all along that hell's reality was false when compared with heaven's. One actually feels sorry for Screwtape when he describes to Wormwood the joyful experience of the patient on the instant of his death when all his doubts fell away and, as he saw heaven, realized that it was this which had haunted him since infancy, which had been "that central music in every pure experience." One can feel Screwtape's own longing as he tells Wormwood, "What is blinding, suffocating fire to you, is now cool light to him, is clarity itself, and wears the form of a Man . . . . He is caught up into that world where pain and pleasure take on transfinite values and all our arithmetic is dismayed." Indeed, Screwtape parenthetically confesses that he is "tempted" to give up hell for heaven. Could any writer make clearer how infinite he believes the love of God to be?

In this book both human and divine conduct are seen from the viewpoint of hell. One of the best things is the devil's-eye conception of God, who is observed as one with none of the high dignity and austerity of hell but rather as "irredeemably vulgar" and bourgeois-minded, one fond of platitudes and the ordinary. He is a hedonist who invented pleasure and filled the world full of happy things like eating, sleeping, bathing, playing, and working. Hell hates God's undignified stooping to communication and fellowship with a man on his knees. Hell's Intelligence Department, though it has worked hard to do so, has never been able to discover one great fact about God, that is, His disinterested love for verminous man and His wish to make every man more individual, more himself in the right sense, rather than, as is the custom in hell, simply to absorb him. "When He talks of their losing their selves, He only means abandoning the clamour of self-will; once they have done that, He really gives them back all their personality, and boasts . . . that when they are wholly His they will be more themselves than ever." Whereas in hell there is nothing but competition and terrorism, the swallowing up of all whom by shrewdness and power one is able to overcome, God loves distinctiveness. Hell's unity is dominated by a constant lust to devour, but God aims at the paradox of infinite differences among all creatures, a world of selves in which the good of any one self is not competitive but rather the good of all other selves, like that of a great loving family.

God loves "otherness," but hell hates it. Like Filostrato's wish in *That Hideous Strength* to destroy the forest trees at Belbury and put metal ones in their place, hell can hardly stomach God's interest in organisms, in ordinary matter with all its selfhood and freedom. The devil has not had the great advantage which God has had, that is, becoming flesh and entering into the experiences of men and things. Hell hates God's complex and dangerous world pervaded with choices, a world which God has inseminated with all sorts of realities that carry their hidden winsome reminders of Himself, such as beauty, silence, reverence, and music — hell hopes one day to make the universe one unending Noise.

Lewis's ingenious and realistic picturing of the devious workings of the human soul make up one of the finest things in *The Screwtape Letters*. Despite his inability to understand the motives of heaven, Screwtape knows the heart of a man only too well. He tells Wormwood that his patient is pretty safe while he is praying for his mother's "spiritual" life but not when he begins to pray for her daily and actual needs. He instructs Wormwood how to create a situation between the patient and his mother in which something said for the express intention of offending can yet create a grievance when offense is taken. Wormwood is to make his patient's mind while at church flit back and forth between "the body of Christ" and the oily-faced groceryman hurrying up to offer him a hymnbook. The patient is to be caused to enjoy bawdy and blasphemous ideas from sophisticated friends on Saturday evening while congratulating himself on his deeper spiritual life and then to enjoy kneeling beside the grocer on Sunday while congratulating himself on his urbanity, and thus, "while being permanently treacherous to at least two sets of people, he will feel, instead of shame, a continual undercurrent of self-satisfaction." Looking to the time when his patient will be married, Wormwood is to plan a situation in which the husband will feel obligated to argue in favor of his wife's supposed wishes and against his own, while the wife does the opposite. Thus they can be brought to do what neither really wants while each feels a happy self-righteousness and retains a claim to better

41

treatment next time and a grudge at the easy manner in which the sacrifice has been accepted.

One of the great strategies of hell is to remove all genuine naturalness from a man's life, make him give up whatever he really likes in favor of the "best" people, or the "right" food, or the "important" books. Hell gets one of its greatest satisfactions from hearing a patient say, on its arrival there, "I now see that I spent most of life in doing *neither* what I ought *nor* what I liked." An honest argument about religion is regarded by Screwtape as undesirable, and a war between nations much more so, for these things may bring people to a realistic condition of mind. What is wanted instead is a mild, contented worldliness that takes a man from one year's end to the next. It is quite all right for the patient to imagine doing good things provided Wormwood can succeed in keeping them out of his will. There is no objection to the patient's feeling sympathy or duty so long as he never acts upon it. "The more often he feels without acting, the less he will be able ever to act, and, in the long run, the less he will be able to feel." The ideal of hell is to bring a man to the place, like Wither in *That Hideous Strength,* where not even the last moments before damnation mean anything. Preferably let him know with perfect clarity that some action of his might save him, but let him remain drowsily unable to make this knowledge real enough to act upon even while hell itself waves its ghastly flag over his head.

With such a view it is not surprising that Lewis advocates an active Christianity. A Christian is to attend church, serve the poor, take part in civil life, and help in establishing a just society. He is to obey God implicitly and in daily trials see God's hand. He is not to waste time and not to take part in church squabbles. Lewis cites Coleridge's remark that he prayed by merely "composing his spirit to love" as a horrid example for any but a very matured Christian. Rather, a man should get down on his knees to pray, and he is to pray when the law of undulation, the natural cyclical ups and downs of the spirit, brings him into a a period of dryness and God seems far away. All of life is to be an active engagement in spiritual growth; indeed birth and death are meaningless apart from such a calling.

I mentioned earlier that hell was an actuality to Lewis. In the preface to the new edition of *The Screwtape Letters* he explains his belief more exactly. [He is sure that the devil is not, like God, a power self-existent from eternity and God's opposite, since God alone is uncreated. Like most theologians, he regards evil not as a thing-in-itself but rather the absence of good. There can be no such thing as "perfect badness" because when you take away from badness such good elements as intelligence, will, memory, energy, and even existence, there will be nothing left.] Lewis says that he believes in devils because he believes in angels, for a devil is simply a corrupted angel. Both good and bad angels are pure spirits but the latter have abused the free will given them of God and thus become what they are.

But he goes on to add that he does not necessarily believe in devils as they are depicted symbolically in art and literature. Indeed, he feels that some of these symbols are pernicious. The angels of Fra Angelico "carry in their face and gesture the peace and authority of Heaven," but by the nineteenth century angels in the plastic arts had become "soft, slim, girlish, and consolatory" and avoided voluptuousness only by their complete insipidity, something very contrary to the Scriptural angels whose visitation was so alarming that they had to preface their message by the words, "Fear not." The literary symbols, says Lewis, are even more dangerous. Milton's devils, by their "grandeur and high poetry," have created the wrong image. The worst symbol of all is Goethe's Mephistopheles. "It is Faust, not he, who really exhibits the ruthless, sleepless, unsmiling concentration upon self which is the mark of Hell. The humorous, civilised, sensible, adaptable Mephistopheles has helped to strengthen the illusion that evil is liberating." Since humor is impossible apart from a sense of proportion and the ability to see oneself from the outside, a humor like Mephistopheles' is simply antipodal to hell. On the contrary, hell is a place where "everyone is perpetually concerned about his own dignity and advancement, where everyone

43

has a grievance, and where everyone lives the deadly serious passions of envy, self-importance, and resentment." One thing hell cannot endure is ridicule of itself.[2]

Lewis explains how he cannot agree with Milton's devils who hold "firm concord," since concord suggests friendship and a being which can love has obviously not yet become a devil. Hence Lewis's own attempt to show hell's cooperation to be based on fear, greed, and mastication of one's enemies. "Everyone wishes everyone else's discrediting, demotion, and ruin; everyone is an expert in the confidential report, the pretended alliance, the stab in the back." All else is a mere crust on the surface, and when it gets punctured the black hatred spills out. (Lewis exploited the same situation at the human level in the Belbury crowd in *That Hideous Strength*.) Screwtape's inadvertent statement that God loves man was promptly shown by his underling Wormwood to the Secret Police with the notion of pressuring Screwtape, who kept quiet about it until he had a return twist on Wormwood and then threatened him with the House of Correction in deep hell.

The Great Divorce

Though *The Great Divorce* consists of a visit to the environs of heaven, it is mostly a picture of souls from hell who refuse the offer to go in. This book illustrates the doctrine found all through Lewis that the innumerable choices of life inevitably condition a soul for eternity and that these choices are a perfect reflection of the will of the individual. Either a man says to God, "Thy will be done" or God is finally forced to say to a man, "*Your* will be done." The rule is that everything grows to be more and more "itself."

---

2 Compare D. H. Harding's remark: "In Hell we are all admirably practical and down-to-earth; we do not find life fun, but take it and ourselves very seriously. But I suspect that all Heaven is light-hearted and merry, that the skies are one broad smile, and the blessed galaxies are even now shaking their fiery manes with laughter, while Satan is profoundly shocked at their lack of gravity and earnest common sense." *The Hierarchy of Heaven and Earth*, p. 128.

The story is told in the form of a dream with Lewis himself as the dream-visitor in a busload of bullying, resentful, cynical, and, above all, selfish men and women who travel from the Grey City of hell to the glorious purlieus of heaven and, with one exception, turn down the warm invitation of the pure spirits there to enter.

Hell consists of a city laid out into astronomical distances because its ghostly citizens are so quarrelsome that they keep moving farther and farther from each other. The same selfishness which has taken them to hell has continued its work of isolation until some are many light years from the center.[3] It is a place of endless twilight and filled with fear. The faces of its people are all fixed, "full not of possibilities but of impossibilities, some gaunt, some bloated, some glaring with idiotic ferocity, some drowned beyond recovery in dreams; but all, in one way or another, distorted and faded." Instead of flames and devils, hell possesses a very active Theological Society and other "attractions." It is a place where you can have a new home and other material things simply by thinking of them. The only hitch is that your house will not keep out the rain and your commodities will not be anything you can really bite or drink or sit on. Wishful thinking is the rule and the place is without essential reality.

When the bus had reached its destination within view of the glorious light and color of heaven, the passengers left it and were greeted by radiant people whose solidity made all the bus passengers so transparent they could hardly be seen. One by one the visitors were invited in, and the book consists mainly of their excuses for declining that invitation. The first was extended to the ghost of an employer by a Solid Person who had once worked for him and had committed a murder. It happened that both murderer and murdered were now residents of heaven.

---

[3] In Jean-Paul Sartre's *No Exit* hell is confined to a single room but the torment derives from the same element — completely selfish people forced to live together forever.

The ghost was astonished that he was forced to live in the pigsty of the Grey City while a murderer reached heaven. "Look at me, now," he said. "I gone straight all my life. I don't say I was a religious man and I don't say I had no faults, far from it. But I done my best all my life, see? I done my best by everyone, that's the sort of chap I was. I never asked for anything that wasn't mine by rights. If I wanted a drink I paid for it and if I took my wages I done my job, see? . . . I'm asking for nothing but my rights . . . . I'm not asking for anybody's bleeding charity." The Solid Person replied, "Then do. At once. Ask for the Bleeding Charity." Like Vertue in *The Pilgrim's Regress,* he told the Solid Person he would rather be damned than forsake his self-righteous independence and stalked off angrily on his way back to the bus.

The next was an apostate preacher who magisterially denied the reality of hell and heaven and who on earth had sidetracked belief in the Resurrection and everything else supernatural not because he had ever honestly faced these things but because the denial of them would gain him popularity over others who preached a "crude salvationism." After some lengthy semantical sparring, he quickly rejected the invitation into heaven when he remembered that he was to speak to his Theological Society and present an "interesting" new angle to a verse of Scripture.

Another was the Hard-Bitten Ghost who had been everywhere and found everything a trap for tourists and a flop, even hell itself; another well-dressed woman ghost loved her appearance more than she loved heaven, even though her finery looked ghastly in the reflected light of heaven; another was a garrulous grumbler almost at the point of becoming a grumble; another a famous artist who showed some signs of willingness to come into heaven until he discovered that his artistic reputation was unimportant there; another a wife who was willing to remain in heaven only on condition she be allowed to take up again the management of her husband, a management which by her overweening social ambition had driven him on earth to a mental breakdown and death; another a woman whose life was selfishly taken up with mourning for a deceased son while she neglected her living daughter and husband.

One of the most meaningful cases was that of the tall, thin, and seedy actor who seemed to be leading on a chain another ghost the size of an organ-grinder's monkey. Yet when the Solid Person extended her heavenly invitation it was not to the tall actor but rather the little ghost who, as it turned out, was actually leading him. The Solid Person, who had been his wife on earth, earnestly asked his forgiveness, yet through the small ghost, which in turn pulled the chain and caused the actor to give a high flown but hypocritical reply. As the conversation proceeded, the sweet compulsion of the Solid Person sometimes made it appear that the small ghost, all that was left of the man's true self, would conquer the actor which continued to strike attitudes over it. Yet finally when the actor got the upperhand and began to declaim about its self-respect and to assert a maudlin self-pity, the little ghost grew rapidly smaller to the size of a kitten and then to invisibility. Afterwards the Solid Person had to ask the actor where her real husband had disappeared to. She discovered he had been totally swallowed up in his pretenses.

Of all the bus passengers only one accepted the invitation inside. He was a ghost who carried a little red lizard of lust on his shoulder and was always trying to get it to stop its ceaseless whisperings in his ear. A colossal angel came up to him and offered to destroy the lizard if he would allow it. After much tormenting persuasion the ghost desperately asked for the deed to be quickly done. The angel took the writhing, biting reptile, broke its back, and flung it on the ground. The ghost was himself left shaken and reeling as a result of the experience, but shortly he began to become solid like the other inhabitants of heaven and at the same time grew to a size little smaller than the angel. While this was taking place the lizard also took the form of a great silvery white stallion with mane and tail of gold. After flinging himself at the feet of the angel in a gesture of gratitude, the new Solid One jumped on the back of his steed and was off toward the heights of heaven like a shooting star. The very earth beneath the horse's hooves sang its joy.

Toward the middle of *The Great Divorce* one of the Solid People who had the double appearance of an old weather-beaten shepherd and an ageless and enthroned spirit came and offered, like Virgil in Dante, to guide Lewis. It was George Macdonald. After explaining his indebtedness to Macdonald's books, Lewis delightfully accepted him as companion and began to ask questions. Lewis learned that where they then stood might be called the Valley of the Shadow of Life, even as the streets in the Grey City were the Valley of the Shadow of Death.

To the question whether there is really a way out of hell into heaven, Macdonald answered somewhat enigmatically that both good and evil when full grown become retrospective. Heaven will "work backwards" and turn even agony into glory for the saved, and in the same manner spread backward into the past of the damned and contaminate their pleasures into sin. For instance, the artist who "sacrificed all for his art" will, at the judgment, see that his art itself, by uprooting God from his life, was hellish and that actually he never lived anywhere but in hell. But hell can be called a state of mind only in the sense that "every state of mind, left to itself, every shutting up of the creature within the dungeon of its own mind" is, finally, hell. Heaven, however, is not so but rather reality itself. Damned souls are what they are because they always choose something less than Reality, Joy, God.[4] They do not find God because finally they prefer something else. Those who really seek find. Even a worthy activity may become a substitute for God — yes, a man can get so excited about proving the existence of God that he reaches the point of caring more for his apologetic than for God. Another can

[4] One of the characters in Charles Williams's *The Place of the Lion* discovers that choice and being are one. He observed that will was simply the determination to choose something, but what was choice? "How could there be choice, unless there was preference, and if there was preference there was no choice, for it was not possible to choose against that preferring nature which was his being; yet being consisted in choice, for only by taking and doing this and not that could being know itself, could it indeed be; to be then consisted precisely in making an inevitable choice." P. 114.

48

occupy himself so completely with the spread of Christianity that he forgets Christ.

Macdonald went on to say something more about hell which is illustrated by Lewis in the character of Weston in *Perelandra*. In one sense, says Macdonald, hell is hard to talk about because it is almost nothing. The road to hell begins with, say, a grumbling mood. The possessor of that mood knows it simply as a mood and he himself very distinct from it. By criticizing the mood he can prove his separate identity.[5] But the time may come when the mood and the man unite. A man no longer is a grumbler but only a grumble. There is no "you" left either to criticize or to enjoy the mood. Weston had so long and completely committed himself to his spiritualism that the evil spirit finally took possession of him. "The forces which had begun, perhaps years ago, to eat away his humanity had now completed their work. . . . Only a ghost was left — an everlasting unrest, a crumbling, a ruin, an odour of decay." He was really not Weston.

Lewis asked Macdonald whether the misery in hell ought not to destroy the joy in heaven. To do so, Macdonald replied, would be to give hell a veto over heaven. Though it may sound good to say that one will accept no salvation that leaves anybody in the outer darkness, it is a sophistry which will "make a Dog in a Manger the tyrant of the universe." God will cure the disease which submits to a cure, but He will never let the disease of hell infect heaven, else it would not be heaven at all but hell. Furthermore, a damned soul is actually almost nothing, being all shrunk up in itself with clenched fists and fast shut eyes and small enough to hide itself in an invisible crack in the earth.

The last question which Lewis asked Macdonald was about his universalism, i.e., whether all men will be saved. Macdonald replied that all answers to such a question are deceptive. One thing, said he, is sure — a man may choose eternal life or death. Time means moments following each other, moments in which choices are made. Time is like a man looking through the

---

[5] This is partly what St. Paul meant when he said, "For that which I do I allow not: for what I would, that do I not; but what I hate, that I do." Romans 7:15.

wrong end of a telescope — he sees small and clear something which he would not otherwise see at all. The thing he sees is freedom of choice, "the gift whereby ye most resemble your Maker and are yourselves parts of eternal reality." This is the answer within time. The other point of view, that of eternity, is not revealed to man. The attempt to see God's eternal way except through time destroys one's knowledge of freedom. A dimension unknown to man has simply been added and this makes any man's opinion of universal salvation nothing more than speculation.

The question of universal salvation is bothersome to Lewis, as indeed to many Christians, yet *The Great Divorce* clearly shows the cleavage between heaven and hell with eternal destiny contingent upon the soul's own choice. In the preface he insists that the universe presents man with an unavoidable "either-or." The world is not one in which all roads lead to a center but rather one where each road shortly branches into two and those two into four and where a decision must be made at each fork. "If we insist on keeping Hell (or even earth) we shall not see Heaven: if we accept Heaven we shall not be able to retain even the smallest and most intimate souvenirs of Hell." Evil will never develop into good; evil must be undone. Death is always necessary to rebirth. In *The Problem of Pain* Lewis puts the case against universalism very clearly. "I would pay any price," he says, "to be able to say truthfully 'All will be saved'. But my reason retorts, 'Without their will, or with it?' If I say 'Without their will' I at once perceive a contradiction; how can the supreme voluntary act of self-surrender be involuntary? If I say 'With their will', my reason replies 'How if they *will not* give in?' "

I have already mentioned Lewis's objection to Milton's and Goethe's depiction of devils as urbane, civilized, and even humorous. His own effort, on the contrary, is to show heaven as the place of solidity and reality. Heavenly creatures are the very opposite of ghost-like. Heaven's reality is so infinitely greater than hell's that it makes men so transparent they can hardly be seen. Macdonald told Lewis that there is joy enough in the little finger of a saint "to waken all the dead things of the universe into life." Heaven is a place where truth can be tasted like honey, the land of Eternal Fact, where a liquid love and brightness flows into and back out of everyone, where "the light's the thing," and where going farther in and higher up entails an ever-lasting experience of increasing joy and reality.

Both *The Screwtape Letters* and *The Great Divorce* deserve the wide reading they have had. In both, contrary to the more philosophical *Pilgrim's Regress,* Lewis deals with matters quite directly practical to the Christian life — selfishness, the moral law, gluttony, sex, bad habits, hypocrisy, choices, and problems of the family. Theologically both books point to the inadequacy of substitutes for Christ. While avoiding the urbanity of Milton's and Goethe's devils, he has managed to give Screwtape and Wormwood reality and to convey a thoughtful conception of what hell might be like. He makes it very clear that neither of these novels is intended to teach any doctrine about the actual details of the after-world.

W. H. Auden has commended the power of *The Great Divorce* to entertain and instruct but finds some minor faults with it. One is that, despite the example set by Dante, it is not theologically in order to present the historical character Napoleon as a lost soul. Auden does not seem to have the same objection to the others mentioned by Lewis, i.e., Tamerlane, Genghiz Khan, Julius Caesar, and Henry V. (In "Screwtape Proposes a Toast," Lewis adds Messalina, Casanova, Farinata, Henry VIII, and Hitler.) My own judgment is that, taken in context, the relegating of Napoleon to hell is less a theological than a creative error.

At the beginning of this chapter I suggested that my reason for including *Till We Have Faces* here was its depiction of the atrocious sin of selfishness masquerading as love, a condition which would have pleased Screwtape no end and which would have made its chief character Orual one of the returning bus passengers from heaven in *The Great Divorce.* Indeed Orual's situation is quite similar to that of several of the passengers,

51

particularly the woman whose vanity made her cherish the memory of her dead son to the exclusion of any kindness to her living daughter and husband. It is also the account of a lifetime of antagonism to God.

Till We Have Faces

Orual, Queen of Glome, decided to write down her case against the gods after she discovered what a dastardly trick she felt they had played on her as a means of punishing her. One part of their trick was to have it reported that she had a hateful jealousy of her sister Psyche, whereas Orual was sure she loved Psyche more than anybody else in the world. The other part of the trick was the report that she had clearly seen Psyche's palace across the river, whereas all she had seen was a glimpse of it and that on a misty morning.

In order to make her case against the gods plain, Orual goes back to tell the entire story of her life. She was a princess whose mother had died young. Her father, a brutal king, married a second time and his wife died in childbirth of Psyche, who grew up not only a girl of exceeding beauty (by contrast with Orual, who was so ugly of feature that she finally adopted the habit of always wearing a mask) but one who came to be revered as a healer of disease by the barbarous people of Glome. The goddess of Glome was Ungit, a shapeless stone worshipped with blood sacrifices. After a great drought, a plague, and the threat of enemies in surrounding nations, the priest of Ungit and the people of Glome concluded that a sacrifice to appease Ungit was necessary. The lot fell upon Psyche and, amid elaborate ceremonies, she was taken to the top of the Grey Mountains and there left chained to a tree. Symbolically she became the bride of the Shadowbrute or Ungit's son, the god of the mountain.

In her cutting sorrow over the event Orual was comforted by Lysias, nicknamed the Fox, a Greek slave who had long been the teacher of the princesses and who had inculcated, particularly in Orual, his Stoic and rationalistic philosophy.

Some days after the sacrifice Orual, accompanied by a faithful soldier Bardia, slipped away from her court and went to the Grey Mountains to pay her last respects to her sister and bury Psyche's bones if an animal had slain her. But Orual and Bardia found no bones. Farther down the other side of the mountain, in a particularly beautiful spot, they were amazed to find Psyche herself. A stream separated them from her. She greeted them warmly and helped Orual across to her. To Orual's excited inquiries Psyche explained that after the people left her chained to the tree the Westwind came and carried her to this new land where unseen hands served her exquisite food, gave her splendid clothing, and provided a glorious palace as her permanent abode. Orual came slowly to the shocking realization that either Psyche was lying or else she herself could not see the things described. Most shocking of all was Psyche's simple assertion that she now had a husband who came to her nightly but who had commanded her not to see his face.

Slowly the determination arose in Orual that, despite Psyche's joyful acceptance of her situation, she must rescue her sister. But her efforts were fruitless and Orual recrossed the river frustrated and forlorn. Had she not always loved Psyche with all her heart and been like a mother to her? She could not understand. Early the next morning Orual went down to the stream for a drink and, as she raised her head from the stream, beheld the very palace which Psyche had tried so hard to show her on the previous day. In a moment, however, the palace had dissolved into the morning mist.

On the way home Bardia, and later the Fox, explained these events as the result of natural causes. They believed Psyche had been rescued from the tree by an evil mountaineer who had somehow persuaded her to believe in him. How else, they said, could one account for the fact that her "husband" did not want her to see his face? Finally resolved that something very evil had occurred to Psyche, Orual returned over the mountains determined either to rescue her sister or else kill her and herself. She believed anything would be better than the degradation to one so high-born and beautiful as Psyche. She crossed the stream once more, found Psyche, and lengthily tried to persuade her to

53

return to Glome. To all this Psyche repeated her simple explanation that she was happily married and eager to remain as she was. At last totally exasperated, Orual thrust her dagger clear through her own arm as a sign to Psyche that she intended to rescue her at all hazards. To save Orual's life Psyche reluctantly agreed to light a lamp that night after her husband came to her bed.

After dark Orual watched eagerly from the other side of the stream. She finally saw a light illuminate the darkness and was momentarily happy in the thought that Psyche soon would cross the stream, explain that she had found her husband an imposter, and urge Orual to take her home. Instead there was lightning and thunder and a great storm, in the midst of which Orual saw a man with a face of great beauty standing on the far side of the water or perhaps on the water itself. He told Orual that Psyche must now go weeping through the world, and Orual heard the receding voice of her sister going off into exile.

Orual then returned to Glome believing that the gods intended some dire punishment for her. But none came, and she settled down to the long, unhappy existence which she felt was to be hers. Upon the death of her father she succeeded to the throne. She fought a successful duel with Argon of Phars, led a crusade against the country of Essur, and as the years passed became a completely successful queen. She made friends with the new priest of Ungit, who had now become imbued with Greek learning and had less of the old pungent air of holiness than his predecessor. In time the Fox died of old age. Now an old woman herself, Orual decided on a visit to the neighboring countries. It was in one of these that she made an accidental discovery which was the cause of her decision to write her case against the gods. She came upon a clean little temple in the forest where flowers and fruit instead of blood were offerings and learned from the priest in charge that it was for the worship of Psyche, under the name of Istra. Actually he told her the original myth of Cupid and Psyche. Orual, supposing it her own biography, was struck by what she considered the falsity of some of the most important facts. One was that Orual really did not love Psyche but was jealous of her. Another was that Orual had actually seen Psyche's palace as clearly as Psyche herself saw it. Wondering how many other sacred stories were twisted into falsehoods of this sort and bitter in the thought that this was the gods' way of punishing her, Orual decided to write a book to expose their trick.

In the second part of the novel Orual has a series of dreams and visions. In one she is forced to dig far below the earth and there looking into a mirror discovers that she is actually Ungit, selfishly "gorged with men's stolen lives." Horrified, Orual then attempted suicide but a god's voice told her she could not thus escape Ungit. "Die before you die. There is no chance after," the voice said. Thereafter Orual tried to change her ugly soul into a fair one, but after strenuous effort concluded she could never cease being Ungit. The only ray of happiness she could imagine was that she had at least loved one person truly, that is, her sister Psyche.

She had hardly begun to comfort herself in this idea before other visions occurred. In one she was required to fill a bowl with water, yet the water she must obtain was located in the center of a mountain covered with high crags from which loose rocks fell all the time and inhabited by innumerable serpents and scorpions. In another she was carried inside a mountain where she found a vast concourse of the dead, before whom she was ordered to read her charges against the gods. When she began she discovered herself reading not the logical case she thought she had written but a vile scribble full of savagery. She had to confess that she had very well known for forty years that the gods are real and Psyche's palace was real and that she hated the gods simply because they had stolen Psyche's love from her. The basic difficulty, she concluded, is that there is no room for both men and gods in the same world. Gods are a tree in whose shadow men cannot thrive. "We want to be our own. I was my own and Psyche was mine and no one else had any right to her . . . . She was mine. *Mine.*" Suddenly Orual was interrupted by her judge and found she had been reading the same account over and over. She realized also that this was her true voice. Shocked, she found

55

also that the complaint was the answer to her supposed case. She saw then why the gods do not speak to people openly or let people answer them. She saw that her life motives had been wrong from the start, that her "case" against the gods was not true, and that the gods could actually have no communication with men as long as they heard "the babble that we think we mean." Orual then asked herself the leading question of the novel, namely, how the gods can meet men face to face until men have faces.

Next the Fox came forward to Orual and abjectly confessed that all his Greek teachings were little more than a prattle of maxims, thin and clear as water, that he had fed her on words only, that Ungit was closer to the truth than his easy logic ever was, and that Ungit more nearly identified the way to the true gods.

But now the tables were turned and Orual must hear the charge of the gods against her. The Fox led her to a beautiful cool chamber the walls of which were covered with painted stories which came alive as one looked at them. All of them were pictures of Psyche's labor at tasks which Orual herself had been charged in visions to do but at which she had failed. Last and greatest of these was Psyche's journey to the Deadlands to get beauty from Death herself and bring it back to Orual so that she would be beautiful. If Psyche's journey was to be successful, she must disregard people who would try to lure her from her task. To Orual's astonishment she discovered that those who would entice Psyche were the people of Glome, the Fox, and finally Orual herself. Ignoring the earnest appeals of those who tempted her to turn away from her task, Psyche finally returned with the casket of beauty and gave it to Orual. Orual fell at the feet of the now gloriously beautiful Psyche and confessed that her former supposed love for her had been totally selfish. "Never again will I call you mine," she declared, "but all there is of me shall be yours."

Orual was now silenced by joy, feeling that she had come to the utmost fullness which the soul can contain, when suddenly she realized that some far greater event was about to happen. Awed and trembling voices were heard saying, "He is coming. The god is coming into his house. The god comes to judge

Orual." She held tightly to Psyche's hand as she felt a terror, an overpowering sweetness piercing her through and through like arrows. The surroundings glowed with the flush of his approach. "The most dreadful, the most beautiful, the only dread and beauty there is, was coming." It was the god of Grey Mountains whom the people of Glome had called the Shadowbrute. How different he was from their conception. Orual dared not look up, but in the lovely pool of water before them she saw her own and Psyche's figures reflected and they were equally beautiful. She who had been the ugliest of women was now unutterably beautiful. "You also are Psyche," said a great voice, and this was the "judgment" of the gods.

Orual, now near death, found herself able to speak truth at last. She had formerly insisted that the gods had no answer to her case against them. "I know now, Lord," she said, "why you utter no answer. Before your face questions die away. What other answer would suffice? Only words, words . . ."

Before I discuss what I consider the main themes of the novel, I should like to say something about a few of the characters. It must be kept in mind, however, that Lewis wishes his reader to regard the novel not as allegory but as myth. Although Lewis says that he looks upon Psyche only as an example of one who is making the best of her pagan religion rather than as a symbol of divine love, it is very easy to see her as such as symbol. She manifests tender, sacrificial love. She goes out willingly to serve the poor, tries to heal the sick, forgives her enemies, thinks maybe she was born to die sacrificially, is called "Accursed," becomes the perfect sacrifice, submits willingly to an undeserved death brought on by the demands of priests and people, is chained to a Holy Tree on the mountain, prays agonizingly there, sees herself a "ransom for all Glome," and feels she is going back "home." After her experience on the mountain this sacred character is less typified, but toward the end of the novel Psyche again seems to symbolize the divine love as she performs the great labor of going to hades and there obtaining from Death the casket full of beauty. This casket she brings back to Orual

57

and thus Orual, instead of the awful retaliatory penalty she expected from the gods, is given a great beauty to replace the ugliness of her life. That is, Psyche, or divine love, did for Orual what Orual could never do for herself.

When I asked Lewis about this view of Psyche as a symbol of Christ, he replied: "Psyche is an instance of the *anima naturaliter Christiana* making the best of the pagan religion she is brought up in and thus being guided (but always 'under the cloud,' always in terms of her own imagination or that of her people) towards the true God. She is in some ways like Christ not because she is a symbol of Him but because every good man or woman is like Christ."[6]

Orual is the central character of the book. Within her own framework her love for Psyche was true and tender, but as we read the novel we see that her love becomes more tyrannically possessive and finally turns to hatred after Psyche went out of her possession, a fact which Orual is at last forced to confess. It is like that of parents who become upset when their child proposes to be a foreign missionary. The child is *theirs* and they are outraged. She becomes typical of those who usurp relatives, friends, and things generally and ultimately discover that there is no room in the universe for anything other than their possessiveness, no room even for God.[7] Orual is in general the sort of person described in the last portion of the chapter called "Affection" in *The Four Loves,* one who needs to be needed. She also represents the sort of person who says, "Show me God and I will believe." Orual actually had enough evidence of the supernatural, but she was too much absorbed in herself. Though she knew that the gods existed, she had *willed* otherwise. She had said, "My will, not thine."

One character in *Till We Have Faces* is sharply identifiable. Lysias the Fox is a Greek rationalist who as pedagogue to Psyche and Orual attempted carefully to inculcate reason and nature as sufficient explanations of all phenomena. As in *That Hideous Strength* Lewis deprecates the smug omniscience of a certain kind

[6] Letter dated February 10, 1957.
[7] This idea also was given me by Dr. Lewis in the letter mentioned.

of science, here he does the same for a well-oiled brand of philosophical naturalism. Even before his abject posthumous confession, the Fox was at times inconsistent and uneasy as to his facile logic. There was no place in it for tears, yet he sometimes wept; there was no place in it for joy and lilt, yet he loved his occasional indulgence in poetry and song. At last he was forced to confess that though his rationalism was clear it was also as thin as water. Vertue, in *The Pilgrim's Regress,* was like the Fox in stolidly following a system which looked excellent on the surface but had a worm at the roots.

At least two of the minor characters are valuable as examples of conduct. Bardia is like the man who lives the good and worthy moral life and unthinkingly accepts religion as he finds it. He bows politely to Ungit but carefully avoids too close a connection with the goddess. Arnom, the new priest of Ungit, indoctrinated by the philosophy of Lysias, cleared Ungit's temple of blood sacrifices and prepared a beautiful Greek-like statue to take the place of the faceless Ungit. But the people would have nothing to do with this modernized and rationalized religion. Here it appears that Lewis is saying that, though of course neither is correct, a corrupted religion of blood is better than a religion which charms the mind and aesthetic sense and rejects blood.

An important idea in the novel is that men substitute words for worship. Instead of falling down before God to utter "the speech which has lain at the center of your soul for years," men are inclined to evade as long as they can. In his novel *Lilith,* George Macdonald describes a great dance in a moonlit forest attended by sensual and murderous people who are without faces. As a spectator looks on this fearful sight he is forced to ask himself why they are thus. "Had they used their faces, not for communication, not to utter thought and feeling, not to share existence with their neighbors, but to appear what they wished to appear, and conceal what they were, and, having made their faces masks, were they therefore deprived of those masks, and condemned to go without faces until they repented?" In *Till We Have Faces* Lewis seems to say that the only valid relationship between men and God is one in which man speaks back to Him the everlasting yea of repentance and thus discovers the only cure for glibness, prattle, mere words, facelessness.

This vast, involved book does not yield its meaning easily, not because Lewis has failed to make his ideas clear but rather because he has combined so many of them into a single complex story. There are at least three main themes: 1) a rationalistic versus a Christian interpretation of the universe, 2) Orual's case against the gods and the gods' case against Orual, and 3) the significance of the great myths of mankind.

The last paragraph of the novel indicates that the story is specifically addressed to people like Lysias who believe that the only god is the god within and who feel able to explain all events as the result of natural causes. That is, the book is for people who deny anything supernatural, those who think, as Lewis said in *Miracles,* that nature and reason are "the whole show." Though he was gentle, kind, and temperate, the Fox held that the gods were simply the lies of the poets, i.e., *merely* mythological,[8] and that man has no essential personality after death. When Orual told him about seeing Psyche after her supposed death, the Fox had a ready explanation: some wandering vagabond found Psyche chained to the tree and released her. Psyche's idea of being in a better world was, said he, simply her demented ravings growing out of her excruciating experience as Glome's sacrifice to Ungit. The vagabond, taking advantage of her condition, had persuaded her to think him a god and met her only in the dark so she would not see him for what he was. To Orual the Fox became a pillar of wisdom by his ability to make rational explanations of everything. Yet, as I have said, he sometimes indulged, a little shamefully, in things of the heart. His "Island" was far more vague than John's in *The Pilgrim's Regress* but it was real enough to create longing.

---

[8] I.e., mythological in Niebuhr's sense of (in Lewis's words) "a symbolical representation of non-historical truth." On the contrary, Lewis thinks that mythology is more properly described as "an account of what *may have been* the historical fact."

As to Orual's case against the gods, she insisted that if there really are gods they ought to reveal themselves, not remain in mystical shadows and dark, bloody places of worship like that of Ungit. Using arguments taught her by the Fox, she asked why the gods, if they exist, should be secretive and mysterious. Why could they not make their message to the citizens of Glome just as simple and clear as the Greek's? Orual despised the odor of holiness coming from the house of Ungit and emanating from the old priest. Later she became persuaded that there may be gods but that they hated and were determined to punish her, also that they had stolen Psyche away from her. After her father's death, she became the strong-willed and busy queen and succeeded pretty well in excluding the gods from her thoughts. It was only shortly before her death that they returned to trouble her and finally to make only too clear their case against her.

They reminded her that most of her life they had been whispering to her and she had simply refused to acknowledge it. She had twice had a direct glimpse of the supernatural — one on that misty morning when she saw Psyche's palace, and again the night of the storm when she saw the shining face of a man with its look of measureless rejection of her after she had persuaded Psyche to test her lover. And something pervasive and constant in her life had always told her, even while she was accepting it, that the Fox's denial of the gods had somehow a false note in it. Her very fear and hatred of the holy odor of Ungit's house told her too. Also that feeling she had experienced that her life was in two halves, one following the Fox and the other intuitively following the gods, and the two halves leaving her separated from any secure tie with reality.

Orual's reading of her case against the gods was at the same time their case against her and their answer to her. They needed only to remain silent. Argument, Screwtape told Wormwood, was a dangerous thing because it might lead a man to God. Orual argued herself to that point. The Fox had once said that the art and joy of words came from saying the very thing you meant. Yet now Orual felt how glib that observation was. When she had uttered the speech lying for forty years at the center of her soul, she found there was less of art and joy in it than of idiocy. She had only uttered the babble she thought she meant. Now she understood why the gods refused to speak openly to men or let men answer them. How could the gods meet people face to face until people had faces? St. Augustine put it another way that was much the same, "Thou hast made us for Thyself, and we shall never rest until we rest in Thee."

Then Orual was given to see the meaning of her dreams and visions and how the same agencies may produce opposite effects according to whether one has a selfish or a loving heart.[9] That vision of walking over burning sands with her empty bowl and searching for the water of death was proof of two things: she must go to the Deadlands before she could live, yet the water of death was wholly inaccessible to her. How different it was with Psyche under the same circumstances, for the eagle came and took her empty bowl and brought back the water. The same eagle sent by the gods which willingly served Psyche was the one that called Orual to trial and judgment. That vast pile of seeds which Orual had failed so miserably in sorting was her attempt to be her own god; how easy it was for Psyche when the ants were sent to help her accomplish the same task. Those golden rams which knocked Orual flat when she tried by her own efforts to obtain their fleece, did they not for Psyche willingly leave their fleece caught on the thorns so that Psyche could joyfully gather it? Last and most meaningful of all, had not Psyche succeeded where Orual had failed in going to the Deadlands and bringing back the casket of beauty? Had not, in fact, the people of Glome, the Fox, and Orual herself, done all they could to prevent it — the very casket of beauty that was to take away Orual's lifelong ugliness? Orual discovered that she was dependent upon the visit of another to the Deadlands. Like David in Browning's "Saul," after what seemed a century of anguish and darkness

---

[9] A similar illustration involves the dwarfs near the end of *The Last Battle*. Aslan gave them the most sumptuous food and wine, but in their evil state of mind they supposed they were eating old turnips and raw cabbage and drinking dirty trough water.

Orual experienced "angels, powers, the unuttered, unseen, the alive, the aware."

The third theme in *Till We Have Faces* involves by far the best illustration in all of Lewis of what he means by myth and particularly how the great myths of the world provide monitions of a Perfect Sacrifice and a need for Death and Rebirth. I believe Lewis means to say that myth, as we now find it, is like the lumpish and almost unrecognizable image of the fertility goddess Ungit. It seems to have no face and yet has a thousand faces, including a hidden face. If we will but look at it closely enough we shall find it revelatory of the fundamentally theistic stuff of which the universe is made. The Cupid and Psyche myth on which *Till We Have Faces* is based is itself an example, modified by Lewis for his special purposes. Although the worship of Ungit had many evil aspects, its basic assumptions, "water-spouts of truth from the very depth of truth," were correct — the assumptions that man should worship, that he is dependent on the gods for rain and for life itself, that blood is the correct sacrifice, that one person may have to die for all the people's sins, and that consolation is to be found in the temple.

To make his meaning even clearer, Lewis presents a myth within a myth. Orual, visiting in the foreign land, found that her own and Psyche's experience had transmuted itself into myth and, as she then supposed, quite a corrupted myth. Orual tried to set the priest right but gave up when she discovered that the "story and the worship were all one in his mind." Orual herself failed then to realize, even as a principal in the myth, that its theme was after all a religious one. Another story within the story likewise suggests the nature of myth. Orual had to dig downward through one room after another, yet each smaller and darker, until she came to a very small room indeed, yet a room made of "living rock" with water trickling down the walls of it. The first myth within a myth suggests how certain themes such as that of sacrifice tend to spread from one country to another, the second that to discover the essential truth of myth one must go, if he can, to the depths of it. It was in the room of living rock that Orual saw herself in the mirror and realized that she was Ungit. "Drenched with seeings," Orual for the first time comprehended her lifelong selfishness, saw Glome as a web and herself "the swollen spider, squat at its center, gorged with men's stolen lives." But it was only by going deep through successive layers that she came to the living substance which enabled her to comprehend. While digging the rooms, she was told they were far below any dens that a fox could dig, that is, the thin abstractions of the Fox were left far behind before Orual could ever come to the real truth. Psyche, on the other hand, had intuitively the gift of seeing through to the centricity of the myth. Even from childhood she had longed for West-wind — what the unenlightened in Glome called the Shadowbrute — and wished to marry him. When that time arrived she discovered him neither brute nor shadow but a real and loving husband and a person so glorious that before him she became ashamed of being a mortal.

Though *Till We Have Faces* has not been nearly so widely read as some of Lewis's other books, he himself regarded it as his best. The considerable number of strands in it and the intricacy of their merging are discouraging to a reader who is not already cognizant of the rewards from a close study of Lewis. My discussion by no means exhausts the novel, and anyone sufficiently interested will do well to consult the section of Dabney Adams Hart's doctoral dissertation covering this novel.[10] The study points out, for instance, the many contrasting themes of the story, such as those of barbarism and enlightenment, beauty and ugliness, appearance and reality, barrenness and fertility, and love and hate. It calls attention also to the doctrine of substitution in *Till We Have Faces,* something perhaps learned from Charles Williams, by which one person suffers the pain of another, such as Orual's having Psyche's pain in her side. I take it that Orual's "becoming" both Ungit and Psyche are also possible examples.

---

10 "C. S. Lewis's Defense of Poesie," an unpublished doctoral dissertation at the University of Wisconsin, pp. 257-278. Marjorie E. Wright's unpublished dissertation "The Cosmic Kingdom of Myth" also has various worthwhile comments. I suggest particularly pp. 55-56, 114, 152, and 155. The latter dissertation was written at the University of Illinois.

III

PAIN AND LOVE

THE CASE FOR DISBELIEF IN GOD BECAUSE OF PAIN AND EVIL
in the world was so succinctly put by the late Professor C. E. M.
Joad of the University of London that I should like to use it in
beginning this chapter. "For many years," said Dr. Joad, "the
problem of pain and evil seemed to me to offer an insuperable
objection to Christianity. Either God could abolish them but
did not, in which case, since He deliberately tolerated the
presence in the universe of a state of affairs which was bad, I
did not see how He could be good; or He wanted to abolish them
but could not, in which case I did not see how He could be all-
powerful."[1] It is a problem which has at some time disturbed
every thoughtful person.

Dr. Joad went on to say that he had accepted the Christian
view of pain as a fact not incompatible with a benevolent
God, and stated why. Since C. S. Lewis has said that Dr. Joad's
summary is very close to his own position in *The Problem of
Pain,* I shall cite him again: "It was of no interest to God to create
a species consisting of virtuous automata, for the 'virtue' of
automata who can do no other than they do is a courtesy title
only; it is analogous to the 'virtue' of the stone that rolls down-
hill or of the water that freezes at 32°. To what end, it may
be asked, should God create such creatures? That He might be
praised by them? But automatic praise is a mere succession of

[1] This and the following quotation are from the *Atlantic Monthly,*
August, 1950.

65

noises. That He might love them? But they are essentially unlovable; you cannot love puppets. And so God gave man free will that he might increase in virtue by his own efforts and become, as a free moral being, a worthy object of God's love. Freedom entails freedom to go wrong: man did, in fact, go wrong, misusing God's gift and doing evil. Pain is a by-product of evil; and so pain came into the world as a result of man's misuse of God's gift of free will." Later I shall refer again to Dr. Joad, but first it is desirable to go a little more into detail by way of summary of *The Problem of Pain.*

The Problem of Pain

Lewis begins with a substantial statement of the atheistic conviction he once held that, if there were a spirit behind the universe, it was an evil spirit. In a vast and mostly lifeless cosmos, the one world he was able to observe first hand showed the lower forms of life continuously "red in tooth and claw." With man it was worse still, for, unlike animals, he has both consciousness and reason, the first allowing pain to be a ceaseless reality and the second making it a reality to be always anticipated until the time of that last and greatest pain called death.

But one significant question, says he, never arose in his mind: "If the universe is so bad, or even half so bad, how on earth did human beings ever come to attribute it to the activity of a wise and good Creator?" Along with the persistent *fact* of pain we have the equally persistent *fact* of a righteous and loving God. If we had never supposed God to be good, there would of course never arise any problem of pain. The problem is conditional. "If God were good, He would wish to make His creatures perfectly happy, and if God were almighty He would be able to do what He wished. But the creatures are not happy. Therefore God lacks either goodness, or power, or both." This is the issue, and the answer depends upon what is meant by the several implications of the statement.

Take the matter of happiness. Suppose, says Lewis, that in my eagerness to be perfectly happy I persuade God day after day to change all prevailing conditions to my wishes. But if all conditions follow my wishes, it is obvious that they cannot possibly follow your wishes also and you will therefore be deprived of your freedom. Freedom is impossible in a world subject to whim. If two men travel in opposite directions on the same hill, then one must go up and one down. If the hill does not remain stable, meaning itself will soon collapse. Omnipotence itself would not be able to create a world of free souls without simultaneously creating a "relatively independent and 'inexorable' nature." The freedom to play the game of chess depends on the fixed rule about squares and moves. The common experience which makes activity free and meaningful by the same token allows choice to result in pain. Of necessity, rules always precede their violation and make themselves real as they are violated.

Suppose again a universe in which God, by His omnipotence, momentarily corrected the abuse of free will in His creatures so that a club became soft as grass if I attempted to use it against my enemy. No free world is possible under such conditions. Freedom requires my commitment to an order in the universe which can both reward and punish me. The club I wish to use on my enemy must retain its "givenness" when he wishes to use it on me. G. K. Chesterton had suggested that the idea of the lion and the lamb lying down together makes no sense if the lamb is inside the lion. The meaning of the Biblical prophecy is dissipated if either the lamb or the lion is deprived of its essential characteristics.

But the worst thing about a notion of happiness based on God's serving my personal wishes is that it removes God from the center of things. If we keep Him at the center, it is possible to suppose that pain is His method of training us for better things than we understand. If a man really cherishes his dog he will do things to it which from the animal's point of view must at times impugn the goodness of the master. Thus love may punish where indifference would allow the dog its own way. When we ask God to love us, we may be getting more than we bargain for. It is of the nature of love to seek the perfecting of the object loved. God may not be the senile grandfather we glibly assume but rather a father whose love will make us more lovable by the process of correction.

The man who insists upon having God conform to his own notions is usually the one who has never taken a sufficient look at the Biblical account of things, or even at the *Tao* or universal moral sense of mankind. The clear view in both is that man has used his free will to become evil. Lewis believes that the recovery of a sense of sin is much needed today. Though psychoanalysis in particular has left the impression that shame for one's conduct is dangerous and mischievous, Christianity has always taught that shame is a means to ultimate health of mind and soul.[2] While Lewis denies the doctrine of total depravity, he holds that man is a horror before God and that the holier a man is the more fully he realizes this to be a fact. After a chapter devoted to the possible manner in which the ruin of man may have originally come about, and particularly the idea that in our present state the "good" of man must now mean remedial or corrective good, Lewis goes on to discuss the place of pain as the remedy and corrective.

Four-fifths of the world's suffering, says he, grows out of the wickedness of human souls who have misused their freedom of will. An inflamed and swollen self-will does not give itself up easily and in fact when it does the deed may properly be described as a kind of death. Pain is one of God's methods of enabling a man to face his self-will and have it destroyed before self-will destroys the man. "God whispers to us in our pleasures, speaks in our conscience, but shouts in our pains: it is His megaphone to rouse a deaf world." (The *Tao* also reveals the universal human conviction that bad men ought to suffer.) Self-will is so deeply imbedded in the race that there can be no let-up in God's afflictions, that is, in His efforts to bring man to sanity.

In a chapter on hell, Lewis answers five objections to eternal punishment. To the leading objection of retributive punishment

---

[2] *The Crisis in Psychiatry and Religion,* by O. H. Mowrer, Research Professor of Psychology at the University of Illinois, contains a lengthy confirmation of this idea.

itself, he asks what else can be done with a man who has all his life practiced living the hellish, that is, wholly selfish, life. Can God simply condone this evil? To condone it would amount to treating it as if it were good. To that of the apparent disproportion between eternal damnation and transitory sin, Lewis suggests that a man's life is always long enough for God to see its direction. He thinks that if a million chances were likely to do good, God would provide them but that they would make no difference in the evil man's essential choice of self over God. The third objection concerns the frightful intensity of the pains of hell, and here Lewis calls attention to the several words used by Christ to describe hell: punishment, destruction, and privation or exclusion from God. No one of these images should be used to the exclusion of the others, although all of them agree on something "unspeakably horrible."

The fourth objection is that there can be no pleasure in heaven to those who know there is a single soul in hell. If this is true, says Lewis, it means that man is more merciful than God. Furthermore, we must remember that hell is not parallel to heaven any more than Satan is in every way parallel to God. Rather, hell is "the darkness outside" where "being fades away into nonentity," into almost nothing at all. Elsewhere Lewis says that those in hell lose their power to communicate their condition. It is really not a man who is finally cast into hell, only his "remains."

Lastly, to the objection that the ultimate loss of a single soul means the defeat of God, Lewis agrees, but he says this was the chance God took in creating free souls. Of all the feats attributed to God, none is more wonderful or miraculous than that Deity should "make things which are not Itself, and thus . . . become, in a sense, capable of being resisted by its own handiwork." The damned are simply successful rebels. Hell's doors are locked, as Milton indicated, on the inside. Those in hell may vaguely wish to come out but never to the point of actually giving up the selves they have perennially chosen above God. I have already mentioned that even Screwtape felt the pull of heaven. I have heard a story of how certain small monkeys in South Africa put their paw through a small hole to get nuts stored there deliberately for the purpose and how the monkeys are captured and killed because they refuse at all hazards to release the handful of nuts in their grasp. Hell exists because men similarly clutch their private interests at any cost.

If hell is definable as the place where self is eternally fostered, then heaven is the place where self forever renders itself up and in doing so joins that great celestial plan of things in which even Christ took part through the sacrifice of Himself to God. Self is made that it may be abdicated to God, yet the heavenly paradox is that in abdication it becomes more truly self after God's own fashion. All things outside self-giving are Satanic, yet within self-giving we have the ineffable fulfillment of the *Sehnsucht,* the deepest longing of the soul, for the soul, when rendered joyfully and fully back to God, becomes "a hollow which God fills" for all eternity.

In a chapter on animal pain, Lewis concedes the difficulty of accounting for the suffering of animals which, unlike men, have no souls to be brought into conformity with God's purposes. He speculates that animal pain may not be suffering in the strict human sense because animals do not have consciousness in a way identical with man. He thinks that animal pain, such as it is, might possibly be accounted for as the Satanic corruption of beasts even before the corruption of man, and he suggests the possibility of some sort of animal immortality.

Lewis is fully aware that in this book he does not solve all the problems entailed in pain and evil. Yet it is hard to conceive how in so small a volume they could be faced more squarely or treated more honestly or effectively. As I have indicated, Dr. Joad, though regarding *The Problem of Pain* as the most elaborate and careful account known to him on the subject, took exception to some of Lewis's ideas on animal pain, ideas however which Lewis himself carefully indicated to be speculative in nature. Charles Hartshorne, though regarding the book as "vigorous, acute, and honest," found some faults with it and particularly disagreed with Lewis on the idea that the maximum pain in the universe is only that amount which is reached by a single person at a given moment. Hartshorne insisted that the sum of sufferings is itself a suffering.[3] Others also have suggested difficulties, yet always of a minor character.

Lest it be thought that Lewis is callous to animal pain, it should be pointed out that he was actually an animal lover and a strong anti-vivisectionist. In a booklet written for the National Anti-Vivisection Society of London he charges those who justify experiments on animals to prove their claim that animals have no consciousness or "soul." Yet if they should so prove, it would make vivisection even harder to justify, since such animals could not deserve pain, nor profit from the discipline of it, nor be recompensed in another world for suffering in this one.

Lewis believed that a Christian alone may justify vivisection and that on the Scriptural teaching that man is really superior to beast in God's own hierarchical order. Yet even this position, says he, is not without problems. How can we formulate the human privilege to torment animals so that it will not equally imply the angelic privilege of tormenting men? And does not the superiority claimed for man over animals consist partly in not tormenting them? He agrees that there is room for honest difference of opinion on these matters, but he lays down a strict rule: "If on grounds of our real, divinely ordained, superiority a Christian pathologist thinks it right to vivisect, and does so with scrupulous care to avoid the least dram or scruple of unnecessary pain, in a trembling awe at the responsibility which he assumes, and with a vivid sense of the high mode in which human life must be lived if it is to justify the sacrifices made for it, then (whether we agree with him or no) we can respect his point of view."

Lewis was well aware that most vivisectionists are a long way

---

[3] "Philosophy and Orthodoxy," *Ethics*, July, 1944. Lewis's *A Grief Observed* shows that the experience of losing his wife changed and deepened some of his convictions concerning pain. The body, it is said in that book, can suffer twenty times more than the mind, since the mind can always manage to evade. "Thought is never static; pain often is." Yet the mind may add to pain. "I not only live each endless day in grief, but live each day thinking about living each day in grief."

from this background. Most of them are "naturalistic and Darwinian," a fact which presents an alarming possibility, for those who most easily brush aside objections to experiments on animals will likely be the same ones to advocate similar experiments on man. If you deny the Christian idea of a total difference in kind between men and beasts, there is actually no logical ground left to prevent experiments on inferior or captive men. This was precisely the philosophy of Weston and Devine in *Out of the Silent Planet* and of Belbury in *That Hideous Strength*. Of course it was the philosophy of many of the Hitlerites. Lewis is convinced that the victory of vivisectionists in our time marks "a great advance in the triumph of ruthless, non-moral utilitarianism over the old world of ethical law." In *The Abolition of Man* he says that he does not believe history can show one example of men who have stepped outside traditional morality and gained power and have ever used that power benevolently.

Lewis's attitude on this subject will strike many moderns as odd if not ridiculous. Yet it is a conviction which runs deeply in him, as it did in men like Bernard Shaw, C. E. M. Joad, and George Macdonald. Albert Schweitzer has much the same view. He says, "A man is ethical only when life, as such, is sacred to him, that of plants and animals as that of his fellow men."[4] In *That Hideous Strength* Lewis allows the Belbury experimenters to become the bloody victims of their own animals. Uncle Andrew in *The Magician's Nephew,* who talked calmly of his experiments on guinea-pigs and how some of them died and some exploded like little bombs, is made a detestable character. More important, Lewis possesses a deep-seated respect for the selfhood of things. Further in this chapter I shall mention his objection to the need-love which sometimes keeps a pet "permanently infantile" by cutting it off from "all genuine animal well-being." In *The Abolition of Man* he advocates a regenerate science which "would not do even to minerals and vegetables what modern science threatens to do to man himself," that is, a science which would explain without explaining away and which

---

[4] *Out of My Life and Thought,* Mentor Edition, p. 126.

would live inflexibly by Martin Buber's distinction between *It*
and *Thou*. Marjorie E. Wright points out the "important hierarchic
principle of courtesy between species" in Lewis.[5] There may
indeed be a mythic implication in *Prince Caspian* and *The Lion,
the Witch and the Wardrobe* that because men have maltreated
nature, making it a thing simply to be manipulated for their own
ends, nature in its genuine reality, as represented by the talking
animals, has gone off and hidden in secret places and refuses aid or fellowship until a good person, like Caspian, comes
and manifests friendliness. This seems confirmed by Lewis's remark in *The Problem of Pain* that the animals in Eden sporting
before Adam may be more nearly factual than symbolical and that
even today "more animals than you might expect are ready to
adore man if they are given a reasonable opportunity."

Because *The Problem of Pain,* like several other books by
Lewis, has so much to say on hell, it will be good to place
alongside it Lewis's study of love with its special emphasis on
the love of God. That hell and love are two halves of a coin
is indicated by his remark that hell is the only place outside of
heaven "where you can be perfectly safe from all the dangers
. . . . of love."

The Four Loves

Lewis begins by distinguishing different types of love. Need-
love says of a woman, "I cannot live without her." Gift-love
longs to make her perfectly happy. Appreciative love rejoices
silently in her very existence, even when she is not for you.
As to God, need-love cries to Him from our poverty, gift-love
desires to serve Him, and appreciative love thanks Him for
His great glory.

The humblest of the four loves is affection. It is the most
widely diffused also, applying in some measure even to animals.

[5] "The Cosmic Kingdom of Myth: A Study in the Myth-Philosophy
of Charles Williams, C. S. Lewis, and J. R. R. Tolkien," p. 20.

Affection is modest, private, even furtive. It can exist by itself but mostly it colors the other loves and becomes the medium in which they grow and prosper. Affection is not particularly an appreciative love. In its very lack of discrimination it finds its potential to broaden the mind, to give one a "taste" for humanity. It can love the unattractive and reveal goodness that we otherwise should not have seen. It is not a natural love but Love Himself doing His sovereign work in human hearts. Yet affection is ambivalent and may do harm as well as good. Many modern tunes and lyrics express a false affection when they suggest a "ready-made recipe for bliss" or even for goodness.

Affection includes both need-love and gift-love. We greatly desire the affection of other people. King Lear suffered need-love ravenously and paid the price of it with misery. Such people's extreme demands scare others away from them and thereby "seal up the very fountain for which they are thirsty." Affection is an affair of old clothes, yet even old clothes require their own atmosphere of courtesy. The home deserves its own set of good manners and qualifications. True affection, because it is free from all wish to wound, humiliate, or domineer, can say with good grace what would be, without affection, arrogant and spiteful and ruthless. Affection will allow a man to call his wife "Pig" in such a way that she will know it is a term of endearment.

Affection's proximity to the old and familiar leaves it especially subject to jealousy. When two people have shared the same interest for years and then one begins to develop higher interests, the other may become fiercely jealous. It was thus with Orual in *Till We Have Faces*. Sometimes all the members of a non-Christian family will turn on one of their number who becomes a Christian. In the Victorian novel boys broke their mother's heart by falling into drink or gambling, but sometimes it is possible to do the same thing simply by rising above the family ethic.

Affection as a gift-love also has perversions. There is the mother who makes her family completely miserable by "living for" them. The gift-love which "needs to be needed" really chooses domination rather than abdication, chooses making itself ubiquitously apparent rather than superfluous. There is the professor who serves his students so well that they begin to be scholars in their own rights, yet in doing so create in him a mighty jealousy. There is the person who makes his animal pet need him and thus cuts it off from its own world. In spite of these perversions, however, affection provides nearly all of the finest happiness that exists in our natural lives.

The second of the four loves, friendship, is not ordinarily looked upon today as a love at all. Yet the ancients put the highest value upon it, as in such cases as David and Jonathan, Pylades and Orestes, Roland and Oliver, and Amis and Amile. It is perhaps not valued today because not often experienced and not experienced because we are afraid of it. The "togetherness" which is inculcated by schools disparages friendship for the same reason that it disparages solitude. The best sort of friendship consists of a few people absorbed in some common interest. Lovers are properly imagined face to face but friends side by side with their eyes ahead on their common interest. For this reason friendship is the least jealous of the loves. It is also the least biological of them, says Lewis, denying the common homosexual theory.

Companionship is not real friendship but turns into friendship when companions discover some common taste or insight hitherto believed unique to each. Companionship may involve a group of, say, business men but friendship a very few in that group who share something more. Friendship is impossible to anyone who simply wants friends; it is a by-product of wanting something else and discovering another person who shares the same want — "he and you join like rain-drops on a window."

While friendship has a civic value, the value is never direct. In fact, it is usually those small groups of friends who turn their backs on the world that serve it best. Friendship does not inquire into one's personal or professional status or affairs. Modern women who insist upon joining men's circles usually succeed in banishing male friendship without gaining any advantage to themselves. Then there is the militant woman who says, "Never

75

let two men sit together or they'll get to talking about some *subject* and then there'll be no fun." They want cascades of talk but never about a subject. Sensible women do not want to join men's conversational groups but drift off into discussions of their own.

Because every friendship, by bringing together people who differ from the majority, is a sort of rebellion, authorities are likely to frown upon it. Little groups of independents, whether for good or ill, are always dangerous to the top people. The high, even angelic, value of friendship is at once a glory and a danger, for a group starting out simply as friends may come to the point of calling themselves "the Souls" and making exclusiveness the chief mark of their set. The best friendship is that which instead of commending itself on its fine discrimination accepts itself as a gift from God.

The third love, Eros, means "being in love." It is different from sexual desire in that it primarily wants the beloved, not sex itself. While Eros takes the man out of himself into the beloved, sex does not. Lewis believes that though what he calls Venus, that is, the sex act, is connected with the most serious of man's involvements, it should itself be surrounded with an attitude of play and laughter. There is indeed great danger when it takes itself seriously.

Lewis insists that a sinful love may be qualitatively as high as a legitimate one. Eros always speaks like a god. We need to be able to disobey the god's call without denying its god-like quality. Some will be called to total renunciation of Eros, others to marriage. Yet within marriage Eros can never be the final consideration, as popular songs and novels say, but must always be subject to higher principles. If Eros be allowed to have his own unconditional way, he becomes a demon.

Eros bears a parallel to religious conversion. "I will be ever true" is the vow of each, yet in each sooner or later will appear a dangerous "dry" period in which the feeling will be lost. But neither in Eros nor religion does this mean, as many suppose, that the god Eros or God Himself has foisted off a cosmic joke upon us. It means rather that in each one must go forward quietly and confidently under the benediction of humility, charity, and divine grace. When God planted "the garden of our nature and caused the flowering, fruiting loves to grow there, He set our wills to 'dress' them."

The fourth love, charity, transcends all the earthly loves. Because the natural loves are, in fact, rivals to the love of God, keeping right order in them requires dependence upon God's help. All human loves are in one sense dangerous. To love is always to risk a broken heart, yet lovelessness is far more dangerous. The broken heart may be God's way for the Christian's growth. Of course we are not called upon to love any creature less because we love God more; it is a matter of proportioning our love to God above our love to anything else.

God is the perfect example of gift-love, for in Him is no need whatever but "only plenteousness that desires to give." It is essential and not mere scholastic speculation to say that God was under no necessity to create, for otherwise God can easily appear simply as manager of the universe. The best conception of God is that He "loves into existence wholly superfluous creatures in order that He may love and perfect them." God implants in man both gift-loves and need-loves. Man's gift-love even at its highest can never be wholly disinterested like God's, for man's gift-loves, unlike God's, are always directed at objects which in some way are intrinsically lovable.

Man was made for God, and all earthly love is in some respects both a parallel to God's and a symbol of heaven's perfections. Thoughts on these things can awaken in man a supernatural appreciative love in which man reaches the very apex of his existence.

If I confess that this book has not, for me at least, the high merit of some of Lewis's earlier ones, I hope it will not be supposed that it is a second-rate book. Lewis, however, is most at home, and most brilliant, on controversial issues and on those topics which we suppose we have long since settled and which he, like G. K. Chesterton and a few others, is able to bring before us silhouetted within a new perspective. Except for his chapter on friendship, the discussion is pretty much in the traditional vein, and the value I discover is fully as much in the incidental and illustrative remarks as in the theme itself.

We learn once again of Lewis's deep love for good walking and good talking and his antagonism to modern education, the "adjusted" child, and the notion of "togetherness." And we find Lewis taking sides with youth rather than age. He says he has been far more impressed with the bad manners of parents to children than the reverse. He analyzes with great sharpness the perversions of love, yet the reader is surprised to learn that these perversions are not just the ones he might expect. His main point is that all four of the loves are both gifts of God and reflections, when un-perverted, of the very nature of God and of heaven.

IV

MYTH OF DEEP HEAVEN

THE LONDON *Times* POINTS OUT THAT LEWIS WAS WRITING "brilliantly imagined and exciting 'science fiction' long before the term was current, and using it, as he used children's fiction, to convey a deep conviction about God and about living with a subtlety and symbolic power perhaps to be found elsewhere only in the work of his beloved Edmund Spenser." This science fiction, known as the space trilogy, includes *Out of the Silent Planet, Perelandra*, and *That Hideous Strength* and ought to be read in that order. Along with *That Hideous Strength* it is desirable to read Lewis's little volume called *The Abolition of Man*, for he tells us that the novel is an illustration of his point in this expository volume.

The volumes of the space trilogy are among Lewis's most popular books. Gilbert Highet says that he has read them all half a dozen times or more and that they haunt him, representing as they do a world that is "terrifying and beautiful" by means of a mysticism that is at once poetic and religious.[1] Marjorie Hope Nicolson regards *Out of the Silent Planet* as "the most beautiful of all cosmic voyages and in some ways the most moving."[2] The three volumes involve an "attempt to throw over esoteric landscapes the holy light of Joy," says Robert J. Reilly, and Corbin

[1] *People, Places, and Books*, p. 133.
[2] *Voyages to the Moon*, pp. 251-252.

79

Carnell regards them as a great prose poem.[3] Critics are generally agreed that although *That Hideous Strength* contains significant and even powerful elements, it is as a whole less successful than the first two novels.

Before I attempt to outline and discuss these four books, I must make some further explanation of Lewis's belief concerning myth, since I think it is impossible fully to understand these novels, and his fictional work as a whole, apart from this subject. He regards myth-making as one of man's deepest needs and highest accomplishments, and he has written hardly a single book in which he does not, in one way or another, discuss and illustrate this subject.

An Experiment in Criticism, one of Lewis's recent books, contains a chapter devoted to myth. Defining myth, he says it is not merely the miscellany of stories belonging to a people but only a few such stories that are marked by a simple yet inevitable shape which causes them to rise above the others which are often cruel, obscene, and silly. He thinks that myth is written in all periods, even modern ones, and should include stories like Stevenson's *Dr. Jekyll and Mr. Hyde,* Kafka's *The Castle,* and Wells's *The Door in the Wall.* He regards a myth as more nearly a "thing" than a narration and believes it may possess hardly any narrative element. Plato was a maker of great myths. Myth may be told by a variety of writers, even poor ones. George Macdonald, says Lewis, is not a first-rate writer but one of the great myth-makers of the world and a proof that myth is something different from the style in which it happens to be couched.

A great myth contains universal truth. It makes us less interested in the sadness of a given character than in the sadness of all men. Myth also is concerned always with the impossible and preternatural and is always grave. It is also always awe-in-

---

[3] The Reilly item is from an unpublished dissertation called "Romantic Religion in the Work of Owen Barfield, C. S. Lewis, Charles Williams and J. R. R. Tolkien," Michigan State University, and the Carnell item from an unpublished dissertation called "The Dialectic of Desire: C. S. Lewis' Interpretation of *Sehnsucht,*" University of Florida.

spiring and numinous. In lesser literature the reader follows a plot to its logical conclusion and then puts the book aside. In great myth, on the contrary, he is likely to feel a new world of meaning taking permanent root in him.[4]

What is the cause of myth-making? There is a great, sovereign, uncreated, unconditioned Reality at the core of things, and myth is on the one hand a kind of picture-making which helps man to understand this Reality and on the other hand the result of a deep call from that Reality. Myth is a "real though unfocussed gleam of divine truth falling on human imagination" which enables man to express the inexpressible. The glory of the Morning Star is somehow not enough glory for us. We want much more, and it is at this point that poetry and mythology come to our aid. "We do not want merely to *see* beauty. . . . We want something else which can hardly be put into words — to be united with the beauty we see, to pass into it, to receive it into ourselves, to bathe in it, to become part of it. That is why we have peopled air and earth and water with gods and goddesses and nymphs and elves."

There is also eternal *Sehnsucht,* the longing which seems to be coexistent with consciousness itself. Lewis's description of the consciousness of Mr. Bultitude the bear in *That Hideous Strength* is perhaps as good a statement as any, if we transfer it to man, to suggest the cause of myth-making. "There was no prose in his life. The appetencies which a human mind might disdain as cupboard loves were for him quivering and ecstatic aspirations which absorbed his whole being, infinite yearnings, stabbed with the threat of tragedy and shot through with the colours of Paradise. One of our race, if plunged back for a moment in the warm, trembling, iridescent pool of that pre-Adamite consciousness, would have emerged believing that he had grasped the absolute: for the states below reason and the states above it have, by their common contrast to the life we know, a certain super-

---

[4] Some of this material is from Lewis's preface to *George Macdonald: An Anthology.* That which follows is from many different sources in Lewis.

81

ficial resemblance. Sometimes there returns to us from infancy the memory of a nameless delight or terror, unattached to any delightful or dreadful thing, a potent adjective floating in a nounless void, a pure quality. At such moments we have experience of the shallows of that pool. But fathoms deeper than any memory can take us, right down in the central warmth and dimness, the bear lived all its life."

The novels *Out of the Silent Planet* and *Perelandra* are among Lewis's own myths to suggest worlds in which the unity of being so sweetly and desperately longed for are in some measure attained. One of the most significant things Ransom learned on his journeys to Mars and Venus was that "the triple distinction of truth from myth, and of both from fact was purely terrestrial — was part and parcel of that unhappy division between soul and body which resulted from the Fall. Even on earth the sacraments existed as a permanent reminder that the division was neither wholesome nor final. The Incarnation had been the beginning of its disappearance. In Perelandra it would have no meaning at all. Whatever happened here would be of such a nature that earthmen would call it mythological." Myth — the Christian element of myth at least — is therefore something like the Eucharist itself, a symbol of man's relationship to God and of his glorious return to paradisal fellowship with the uncreated, unconditioned Reality Himself.

With this high conception of myth, it is not surprising that Lewis makes much of it. Ransom on Perelandra was allowed to talk with Ares and Aphrodite (Mars and Venus) and to discover that nowhere are the traces of the "celestial commonwealth" wholly lost. Because this commonwealth is in some measure the home of every man, and because goodness is hierarchical rather than merely relative, it is possible for Plato, one of the greatest of all myth-makers, to imagine a completely righteous man who is treated by everybody around him as a monster of wickedness and finally bound, scourged, and crucified. Plato, to be sure, was primarily picturing the fate of genuine goodness in an evil world. It was his quite logical insight into the nature of goodness on the one hand and the nature of the world on the other which led to his imagining the righteous man and his depiction of something resembling the Passion of Christ.[5] In other words, the great myth is a picture of deep and profound truth, and that is the cause of its greatness.

If such a conception be accepted, it is easy to understand Lewis's notion of the effect of myth. He declares that a great myth introduces us to a "permanent object of contemplation" and that it enlarges our being by presenting to us a thing of inexhaustible value. "It arouses in us sensations we have never had before, never anticipated having, as though we had broken out of our normal mode of consciousness and 'possessed joys not promised to our birth'. It gets under our skin, hits us at a level deeper than our thoughts or even our passions, troubles oldest certainties till all questions are re-opened, and in general shocks us more fully awake than we are for most of our lives." It has a quality of inevitability. In the contemplation of a great myth man attains realization.

Discussing a passage from John Gower's *Confessio Amantis,* Lewis indicates the manner in which myth transcends allegory. In Gower, he says, "the symbols, though fashioned to represent mere single concepts, take on new life and represent rather the principles . . . which unite whole classes of concepts. All is shot through with meanings." It really does not matter whether the author was aware of these multiple meanings or not. "An author does not necessarily understand the meaning of his own story better than anyone else," he declared. The more nearly a story rises from allegory and symbol into genuine myth the better it will be.[6]

---

5 In the third edition of *The Pilgrim's Regress* Lewis puts in an explanatory heading which reads, "Even Pagan mythology contained a divine call."

6 See pages 150ff for more on myth from a Christian angle. Marjorie Hope Nicolson believes that Lewis has succeeded in *Out of the Silent Planet* in actually creating myth, "myth woven of desires and aspirations deepseated in some, at least, of the human race," and she says that in reading the book she has Ransom's own "sensation not of following an adventure but of enacting a myth." *Voyages to the Moon,* pp. 254-255.

Out of the Silent Planet

Dr. Elwin Ransom, a philologist of Cambridge University on a walking tour sought shelter in an obscure house and was amazed to discover it occupied by an old but disliked schoolmate named Devine and a large, loud-voiced companion named Weston, the latter a famous physicist. Ransom's appearance defeated their intention to manhandle the dull son of a neighboring farm woman who struggled against entering that "thing" in the back yard. Discovering that Ransom's whereabouts were unknown to his friends and kin, Devine and Weston suddenly got the idea of substituting him for the boy, and they drugged him for that purpose.

Ransom awakened in a room with hot walls and a skylight directly overhead through which he saw a dark sky blazing with brilliant stars. Attempting to arise, he discovered himself almost weightless in a room with walls which seemed to slope outward and quietly vibrated like an object in motion. As he pulled these details together, he was terrified to realize that an object he had seen through his window and supposed to be the moon was actually the earth and that he was in a ship 85,000 miles out in space and on the way to Malacandra (Mars).

He learned that this was actually the second voyage Devine and Weston had made to Malacandra and he was given details of how the ship operated. But his captors steadily refused to say what part he was to have in the excursion. He found that Devine had no use for Weston's scientific idealism and was himself intent on a cargo of gold.

Instead of fearing, Ransom discovered himself mystically responsive to the glories of the sky and the depths of tranquillity and vitality that came upon him. He was delighted to find the sky not a black and cold vacuity but rather an "empyrean ocean of radiance" which inculcated life and deserved to be called not "space" but rather "the heavens." The planets, he became convinced, are islands of pallid and cheerless unreality compared with the glory of the heavens.[7]

[7] It might not be amiss to note that our first men actually traveling into

Out of the ship after a twenty-two-day voyage, Ransom's first impression was of a bright, pale, but beautiful world and a temperature not unlike a winter morning on the earth. In the distance he saw what looked like a heather-covered purple mountain, beyond it even higher shapes of whitish green, and above these a red mass like the top of an exquisitely beautiful and gigantic cauliflower. Everywhere on Malacandra the theme of life was perpendicularity.

Ransom noticed these things while helping unload the space ship and keeping an eye open for a way of escape, for he had earlier overheard a conversation which he interpreted to mean he was intended by his captors as some kind of sacrifice to the Malacandrians. Suddenly, across a body of water near which their ship had landed, there appeared six *sorns*. Three times as tall as a man, they had long, thin legs, top-heavy bodies, and thin faces with long, drooping noses and mouths. The *sorns* moved slowly toward the men and one sent its great horn-like voice across the water. At the same moment from another direction a great shining beast cut through the water straight toward the three men. As Weston emptied his revolver at it, Ransom took advantage of the confusion to make his escape. He ran as fast as he could through the purple shadows of the great vegetables twice as high as English elms.

He traveled as far and fast as he could regardless of direction, crossing blue, hissing streams of warm water and keeping under cover. With night came a flood of self-pity, then exhausted repose in a deep valley beside a warm stream at the foot of a waterfall. Next morning he dared drink the water and found it refreshing. He was sampling the vegetation to find something edible when a herd of great pale furry creatures something like giraffes only much higher came along eating the tops of the

---

space reported experiences quite similar. Scott Carpenter, the second American to circle the earth in space, said, "The colors glowed vigorously alive with light," and he told how he watched the band of sunset narrow "until nothing was left but a rim of blue." He felt that the experience was all but supernatural.

trees. Afterwards he saw another *sorn* and rushed headlong away. He lay down on the shore of a broad river to drink and a gleaming black animal looking like a mixture of otter, seal, and penguin arose nearby. Moments later the creature offered Ransom a drink of water.

Ransom's fear had hardly begun to disappear before the philologist saw his opportunity to try to communicate, and shortly he had learned several Malacandrian words and knew that the creature before him was a *hross* whose name (as he later discovered) was Hyoi. Hyoi now led Ransom to a boat, gave him food, by motions persuaded him to be seated, and carried him through a colorful landscape. Meantime Ransom learned that the *hrossa* lived down in the *handramit* and the *seroni* (plural for *sorn*) lived up on the *harandra*. At dusk Ransom and Hyoi came to the *hrossa* village, Ransom still stunned by the course of events.

Within three weeks he learned to feel at home among the *hrossa*. Hnohra, a venerable *hross*, taught him the language and other things. Ransom had at first estimated Malacandrian culture as about stone-age but was quickly forced to revise this idea when he discovered the *hrossa* understood such things as astronomy and even knew of Thulcandra (Earth), which they mysteriously called the silent planet. When he inquired further about Earth, they referred him to the wiser *seroni*. They told him not only of the *seroni* but also of the *pfifltriggi,* frog-like creatures who are expert in digging gold and fashioning artistic objects from it, and of Oyarsa, who, though neither *hross* nor *sorn,* knew everything and had always lived and always ruled everyone on Malacandra. When Ransom asked if Oyarsa made the world, the *hrossa* amazedly inquired if the people of Thulcandra do not know it was Maleldil the Young who made and still rules the world. Inquiring about Maleldil, Ransom was told that he lived with the Old One and that he was a spirit without body, parts, or passions. He learned also that Oyarsa lived at Meldilorn, ten days' journey to the west.

Continuing his education, Ransom learned that the Malacandrians are naturally continent, naturally monogamous, and without knowledge of war — in short, that their practices closely resembled the unattained ideals of man on Earth. Beginning to be ashamed of Earth, Ransom argued with the *hrossa* that Maleldil has let in the *hnakra,* that vicious animal which had been shot by Weston just after the landing. But that is different, said Hyoi. The *hnakra* was indeed their enemy, yet their beloved also. The days were brighter and life more meaningful because of the danger of the *hnakra.* The *hrossa* actually had images of the *hnakra* in their homes and the children loved to play at being the *hnakra.* A few deaths from the struggle with the creature had little meaning for the *hrossa,* who considered death a good experience because then the *hross* went to Maleldil. The thing which really made *hrossa* miserable is a "bent" creature who blackens the world.

A day came when a great crowd of *hrossa,* taking Ransom along, went out to hunt the *hnakra.* An exciting battle ended with a victory for Hyoi, but at the moment when the *hnakra* lay dead in the water and Ransom was thrilled with a great feeling of brotherhood for the *hrossa,* a shot rang out and Hyoi fell and died. Ransom explained that the bullet had come from the gun of Weston or Devine and, ashamed of his species, told the *hrossa* to take his life and that of the other two Earth men. Ransom was told that only Oyarsa takes life.

A few days earlier Ransom had found a young she-*hross* talking, as he supposed, to herself. When he inquired, she said she had spoken to an *eldil.* But Ransom could see nothing and he concluded she was only pretending. Later Hyoi assured Ransom that *eldila* are a reality, though they are often taken for a sunbeam or the moving of leaves and such. Then on the *hnakra* hunt Ransom had heard, though he could not see, an *eldil* which warned Hyoi that Ransom should not be hunting but rather on his way to Oyarsa. Hyoi's death was perhaps due to failure to obey the voice of the *eldil.* As a consequence Ransom was put quickly on the way to Meldilorn by the shortest way, a mountain road.

Mounting a terrifyingly steep ascent, Ransom on top came face to face with a *sorn* named Augray who gave him oxygen from a container. From Augray, Ransom learned that Oyarsa is the greatest of the *eldila,* creatures placed on Malacandra from the very time it was made and placed there to rule it. He learned that *eldila* can go through walls and rock and wondered if the tradition of bright, elusive beings on Earth might not have an explanation other than the anthropologist's. Before providing Ransom a bed, Augray pointed out Earth to him through a *sorn-*made telescope.

Next morning Augray insisted on taking Ransom upon his shoulders and carrying him to Meldilorn. Gingerly atop Augray, eighteen feet up, Ransom's terror was soon replaced by joy over the bright, celestial light around them and the view far below of pale rose vegetation looking like stone cauliflowers the size of cathedrals. Farther down, they spent the night with a scientist *sorn* whose cave home contained many book rolls. The *seroni* there questioned Ransom about Thulcandra and were astonished at what he was forced to tell them of war, slavery, and prostitution. They concluded that Thulcandra is what it is because it has no Oyarsa, or perhaps because every one there wants to be a little Oyarsa himself.

As they approached Meldilorn, Ransom was ravished at the beauty of *handramit* opening below him. He saw a sapphire lake twelve miles in diameter set within a border of purple forest and in the center of this lake an island surmounted by magnificent trees and a broad avenue of monoliths. A *hross* who ferried him across informed him that the island was full of *eldila,* and walking about Ransom discovered he could barely see them but only from the side of his eyes; the moment he looked directly nothing was visible. Then he discovered the *pfifltriggi* in process of carving their monolithic pictures of history and mythology. Ransom was shocked to find, in a carving of the solar system, that Earth was represented, unlike all the other planets, as a place unoccupied by an Oyarsa.

After a night in the guest-house, he was called early next morning before Oyarsa. He found the avenue of monoliths filled with Malacandrians and earth and sky filled with *eldila.* When Oyarsa came, he astonished Ransom by revealing that he had sent for him from Thulcandra, the silent planet — silent since the Oyarsa of Earth had become "bent" and been forced out of the heavens and bound in the air of Earth because of his intent to spoil other worlds. Oyarsa had sent for Ransom because he wished to hear the outcome of Maleldil's war with the Bent One.

When Ransom began to speak he was interrupted by the appearance of a group of *hrossa* carrying the bodies of three dead *hrossa* and followed by Devine and Weston. Accused of murder, these men evidenced no sense of guilt but rather attempted to bluster their way to freedom from these creatures they supposed to be primitive. Meantime the bodies of the dead *hrossa,* after a ceremony, were made to disappear in a flash of brilliant light.

Weston insisted on making a long speech, translated into Malacandrian by Ransom, saying Oyarsa may kill him and Devine but man is nevertheless destined to occupy all worlds one after another and nothing can stop the ongoing of emergent evolution. Oyarsa was finally forced to conclude that Weston was totally bent like the bent lord of the silent planet and that Devine, the man eaten up with greed, was simply an animal that could talk. Oyarsa did not think it right for him to take the lives of Earth men and his only penalty was that they must return to Earth at once. He would see that the space ship disintegrated exactly at the end of ninety days.

After attempting to answer Oyarsa's many questions about Earth, and particularly its bent condition, Ransom was given the choice of remaining on Malacandra or returning to Earth. It was not an easy choice, but he concluded to return. Next day the space ship left. As Ransom looked back on Malacandra, he realized how very little he had really learned about that land and how little of his experience he could convey to others. After a perilous flight, the space ship landed on Earth barely within the ninety-day limit.

Perhaps we could properly say that the aim of *Out of the Silent Planet* and *Perelandra* is to indicate what might have been and of *That Hideous Strength* to indicate what might yet be. One reading *Out of the Silent Planet* is not impressed that Lewis was dominated by a single idea so much as in *Perelandra* or even in *That Hideous Strength*. Is Mars intended to be a perfect world? Charles Moorman and Edmund Fuller think so.[8] Corbin Carnell says Oyarsa "permits no evil to grow and thus they do not have free will in any moral sense."[9] It seems rather to be a world perfect somewhat more from earth upward than from heaven downward. The *eldila* are everywhere on Malacandra but they are not needed on the perfect Perelandra. What Lewis does clearly say in this novel is that Earth has not done well with its potential. We are reminded at times of the Swiftian method in which the voyage elsewhere becomes the means of satire on conditions back at home. It is the silent planet where the voice of Maleldil is virtually unheard. All the rest of the solar system speaks a uniform language; Earth alone is the exception. Two evil men from Earth invade a distant planet, one wanting gold to satisfy his corrupt longings, the other intent upon sacrificing the Malacandrians and even himself in the interest of the superman of the future. They find there creatures who fear "bentness" (evil) but not death. Actually death is for them a joyful experience. They practice no revenge, always obey their Oyarsa, and cannot understand accounts of slavery, war, prostitution, and the survival of the fittest on Earth. Their hierarchy includes, in order, *hnau* or people generally, the *eldila*, Oyarsa, and Maleldil. Within this hierarchy the Malacandrians have a full, joyful, and completely meaningful existence.

Maleldil represents the Trinity. It is he who gives the Oyeresu or tutelary spirits their power. He still wars with the bent Oyarsa of Earth and its false *eldila*. In *Perelandra* Maleldil walks with and teaches the Green Lady. We learn that Maleldil took human form on earth, and that now no more perfect worlds are possible, i.e., the whole system of things is now changed. Reason itself

[8] *Arthurian Triptych*, p. 108; *Books with Men Behind Them*, p. 145.
[9] "The Dialectic of Desire: C. S. Lewis' Interpretation of *Sehnsucht*," pp. 99-100.

has taken on another form; a corner has been turned and all on this side of it is changed.

Perelandra

Let us now turn to *Perelandra*, which is for me the most interesting of the space trilogy. In this novel Dr. Elwin Ransom takes another voyage into space but not in a space ship. He is transported to Perelandra (Venus) in a specially prepared casket guided by the great Oyarsa of Malacandra on orders from still higher up. He is sent because the Black Oyarsa of Earth is about to attack Perelandra.

Ransom was gone for more than a year, and on his return told his story. The casket had landed in the water of Perelandra and dissolved and Ransom found himself riding great waves in a world of exquisite beauty that filled him with an indefinable joy. He found floating islands of matted vegetation that took on the contour of the waves on which they rested. Eventually he dragged himself onto one of these islands and learned to walk about. The island contained a wooded section filled with fruit more delectable than Earth afforded and odors so delicious that breathing became a sort of ritual.

The first land creature Ransom saw was a small golden-colored dragon with which he was soon friendly. When he was beginning to wonder if he and the dragon were the only inhabitants, he saw in the distance another human being. Later he discovered it to be a woman who looked like a goddess carved out of green stone. She was surrounded by innumerable birds and beasts in a gay, frolicsome mood, and she seemed to possess an unearthly serenity.

Since the Malacandrian language was also hers, Ransom was able to talk to her. He learned that only she and the King inhabited the planet. When he asked about her mother, she could only say she *was* the Mother. Hitherto she had known life only in an unbroken fellowship with Maleldil, but now she began to learn strange additional things from Ransom. First she learned what it meant to choose one thing above another —

91

one good above another, for evil was wholly unknown to her. She had possessed this freedom and practiced it, yet had not known it as such. Now she saw freedom as something wonderful because it was the sign that Maleldil made the world separate from Himself. But now the realization of a self of one's own awakened in the Green Lady the possibility of disobeying as well as obeying Maleldil.

But Ransom was also learning. The Lady told him that she had always lived in deep content under Maleldil and desired nothing other than to obey Him. He was her sovereign just as she herself was the loving sovereign to her sea, earth, and sky creatures whose greatest pleasure was to please her.

When their island drifted toward a shore of fixed land surmounted by huge green crags, the Lady stated her intention to go ashore and seek the King, though she warned Ransom that it was forbidden her and the King to remain there. Together she and Ransom went inland and climbed upward. Near the top they found a beautiful plateau surrounded with great green pillars. Gazing through these at the sea far below, they failed to see the King. What they did see in the water was an unfamiliar round object. Earlier they had seen something streak across the sky and Ransom now saw it to be a space ship and guessing its occupant to be Weston, the man with whom he had gone to Malacandra earlier, was shocked at the Lady's calm proposal to go down and welcome the visitor. Remembering how Weston had killed the *hrossa* on Malacandra, Ransom hurried back to the shore ahead of her.

Prevented by the roughening water from the welcome she had intended, the Lady left on the back of one of her faithful sea beasts, but Ransom was forcibly detained by Weston's pistol. Later Weston launched upon one of his long oratorical harangues. He said that he no longer believed the material interests of man to be supreme, as he had thought when they were on Malacandra, but now held to man's spiritual interests. He insisted that apart from outward theological terms he and Ransom now stood for the same thing. Puzzled, Ransom answered that his own trust in the Holy Ghost was by no means the same as the blind, inarticulate purposiveness which Weston appeared to be describing. When Weston talked of a great inscrutable Force pouring into man and choosing its human instruments, Ransom reminded him that there are both good and evil spirits. But Weston insisted that God and the devil as commonly understood are pictures of the same cosmic Force. Under further questioning, he confessed that because this Force transcends ordinary notions of ethics he would not hesitate to lie, murder, or become a traitor if the Life-Force prompted. When Weston at the height of his declamation called on this Life-Force to take possession of him, he was suddenly convulsed and fell senseless to the ground.

After trying to aid Weston, Ransom left to search for food, and night overtook him. Next day Weston could not be found. Late that afternoon Ransom discovered another of the great fish near shore and was carried on its back to the floating islands. Reaching one of them in the darkness, he fell asleep only to be awakened by voices nearby, those of Weston and the Lady. Weston, now demon possessed, was tempting the Lady much as Eve had been tempted in Eden. Seeing this diabolical purpose beginning to take shape, Ransom became aware of Oyarsa's intention in sending him to Perelandra. It was Ransom against Weston — no, Ransom against Satan himself, and with all the future generations of this Lady and her husband at stake.

There followed many days and many occasions during which Weston with superhuman cleverness persevered in his malevolent undertaking. Though loathing the corpse-like appearance and mechanical mannerisms of Weston, now more properly called the Un-man, Ransom felt obligated for the Lady's sake to remain near him. Sometimes Ransom interrupted the arguments, but he was often made speechless by their cleverness and their approximation to the truth.

The temptation consisted of two main parts. The first questioned the reasonableness of Maleldil's command against remaining on the fixed land. Maleldil, said Weston to the Lady, has obviously sent both him and Ransom to Perelandra to teach her. Has she not already learned through Ransom the wonderful fact that Maleldil has made her separate from Himself with an individuality of her own? Now since Maleldil has never given her and the King anything that was not delightful, he must therefore intend some delight in his one do-not concerning the fixed land. Will not the Lady understand that this do-not is nothing more than a contrivance of Maleldil's, a sort of button to be pushed by her, to prove to Him that she fully understands her separateness. Simply by violating Maleldil's do-not she will *prove* her own freedom — indeed it is the way Maleldil planned for her to walk alone, his carefully planned way of turning her into a "full woman." If she will only learn this, she will be able to inform and assist her husband the King. Also she will be like women on Earth whose minds reach out to know what is good without Maleldil always telling them. And because they have this wisdom, added Weston, they also have beauty and men love them. Has she not learned already from Ransom that on Earth the fixed land is where men dwell? How could Maleldil have one law for Earth and another for Perelandra?

When the Lady remonstrated that Maleldil was himself saying nothing to her, as is his wont, Weston replied that this simply proved what he had been telling her — that Maleldil wanted her wholly apart from his guidance to decide for herself and consciously to disobey him. Ransom interrupted to explain that Weston was misleading her. Is it not better, said he, to suppose that the one do-not is a "contrivance" not oriented toward disobedience but toward loving obedience for its own sake? Maleldil has indeed made her separate from himself and wants her to be an individual but only far-reaching evil can come, said he, from her deliberately disobeying Maleldil.

But Weston renewed his insistence that real, deep life can come about only through becoming truly oneself by disobeying Maleldil, whereupon Ransom described what disobedience did for Adam and Eve on Earth. Weston quickly countered that it was only because of this disobedience that Maleldil was made Man and that other great values accrued to Earth. Weston's persuasiveness was so powerful that even Ransom was shaken.

The second phase of the temptation consisted partly of a

series of narratives told the Lady by Weston, intended to work in her a strong feeling of tragic grandeur with herself as heroine.[10] He overlaid Maleldil's simple command for obedience with a complicated set of images of splendor and sacrifice. He also taught her to clothe herself and to look in a mirror. To her proposal to ask the King concerning these things, Weston answered that she must beneficently risk herself without involving her husband. Then she could go to the King and teach him these amazing things. Thus the Lady, perfect as she was, came slowly to the point of taking on ever so small an appearance of theatricality.

Ransom, believing that the Un-man was moving steadily toward success, questioned in himself why Satan alone should work while heaven remained silent. But in the instant of his questioning he became aware that Maleldil was not absent, had never been absent. He realized that he was himself the miracle, brought from Earth for this experience, and that the fate of Perelandra hinged on the outcome of his struggle. For the first time he saw clearly that the whole world always depends, finally, on individual action and that in his case heaven now stood silent waiting to see what he, Elwin Ransom, would do. The burden at first overwhelmed him, but then he remembered that nothing more was required of him than to oppose the enemy in whatever way appeared necessary at a given moment. Then the Voice said to him, "It is not for nothing that you are named Ransom," and it added, "My name also is Ransom." Overwhelmed by the frightful freedom placed in his hands, he was nevertheless deeply assured that he would do the right thing when the trial came.

Then the day dawned in which Ransom knew that he must destroy his enemy. Searching, he found the Un-man tearing a bird to pieces. He walked up to him and landed on his jaw the hardest blow he could. The Un-man closed in on Ransom and with its long finger nails began to claw strips of skin from his back. Soon both were bloody. After a deep surge of pure

---

[10] Lewis takes some of his imagery here from *Paradise Lost*. See, e.g., his description on p. 68 of his *Preface to Paradise Lost*.

hatred gave Ransom added strength, the Un-man was forced to retreat. He ran to the water and commandeered one of the great fish. Ransom on the back of another such fish followed him in a chase that continued through a long night. Next morning he and the Un-man were alone on the wide sea of Perelandra. Later, only half conscious, Ransom discovered the Un-man beside him and was forced to listen and dispute a long attack on the meaninglessness of the universe. But this ended abruptly when they suddenly discovered themselves in breakers and likely to perish against a rocky shore. The Un-man (or was it Weston — Ransom was often not certain which) screamed and Ransom called on him to pray and repent his sins. The next moment Ransom was being pulled down under the water by his enemy.

When Ransom felt he could hold his breath not a second longer, he found himself again on the surface, the Un-man still clutching his legs. The fight ended on a pebbly beach with Ransom choking his enemy lifeless. There was nothing left for him to do but wait for morning, but after a very long time Ransom found that there would be no morning because the struggle with the Un-man in the water had pulled them downward and up again into a cavern black as night itself. Filled with fear, he stumbled about, discovered finally a place to pull himself upward and precariously moved from ledge to ledge while the sound of the water below grew quieter. He groped his way afterward into a larger cavern overhead lighted by a fiery pit boiling up inside. In addition to the distant sound of the sea he began to hear something closer. It turned out to be the Un-man dragging himself along and followed by a huge fantastic crawling monster.

Then it came to Ransom that the terrible doubts which had beset him of late were Satanic and imparted by the proximity of the Un-man. This time therefore Ransom made very sure of the total destruction by pushing the Un-man's mangled body into the fiery pit. [11] When Ransom turned to do battle with the monster, he discovered it far more harmless than he had first thought and

11 The similarity of this to Frodo's destruction of the evil ring in J. R. R. Tolkien's *The Return of the King* is perhaps not accidental.

watched it slide back into its hole. Almost dead from fatigue, Ransom dropped into a heavy sleep.

Ransom climbed out of the mountain and for many days he passed through a series of visions not knowing for sure whether he slept or waked. Meantime his broken body healed except for a wound in his heel, a wound that he was to carry back to Earth. Though Ransom could not remember when it happened, the wound was clearly that of a bite from the Un-man in one of their fights. Then he traveled through new and exciting landscapes filled with the wild and enormous pleasures of mysterious sights, odors, and music. Afterward he climbed high on a holy mountain and there, in a surpassingly beautiful valley, he found a casket exactly like the one in which he had come to Perelandra. Beside it he discovered two *eldila,* one Malacandra and one Perelandra. "The world is born to-day," said Malacandra to Ransom. Seeking suitable embodiments in which to appear to the King and Queen, the *eldila* decided upon two great shining figures, and when the transformation was made Ransom was astonished to find them the Mars and Venus of human mythology. He discovered that myth is based on solid reality.[12]

Then amid a scene of unparalleled glorious ceremony came "Paradise itself in its two Persons" walking hand in hand, so regal and perfect that even the *eldila* bowed low before them. Ransom, remembering, was overwhelmed with the thought of what Earth lost when Adam and Eve fell. After the ceremony, the new King and Queen offered Ransom their deepest gratitude and said that he had been the instrument of Maleldil to save Perelandra from the Fall.

The Queen (of course the Green Lady) told Ransom that after he had driven the Un-man away she realized clearly the error into which he had been leading her, the error of putting one's own will in opposition to that of Maleldil.

---

[12] All through the novel Ransom is impressed with this idea. It is partly from Charles Williams and, in both Lewis and Williams, may be based on a conception in Hebrews 8:5 that the earthly tabernacle was no more than a "copy and shadow" of the heavenly one.

If the King's absence throughout the story has puzzled the reader, it is now explained. He had been driven away by Maleldil to Lur, there to be taught many things, including good and evil. He had there seen for himself the possibility of Perelandra's fall. He learned that there is really no fixed land but only the Eternal Wave upon which creatures must cast themselves and to which they must forever conform. He learned that what Ransom called the end of things is only the beginning, that Maleldil expects eventually to take the *eldila* of all Deep Heaven and go to war against the Archon, the Black Oyarsa of Earth, and finally how Maleldil himself will make war and establish a glorious new beginning.

After many other glimpses of the glory that has been and will be, Ransom was invited by the *eldila* to take his place in the casket. When he asked that his eyes be covered to protect them from the light of the sun, the blossoms of innumerable rose-red lilies growing nearby were scattered over his face. And that was Ransom's last glimpse of the land that was to remain eternally lovely and good because he, a middle-aged philologist from Cambridge University, had thrown all his strength into resistance against the Black Oyarsa.

The great theme of *Perelandra* is that of an unfallen world into which temptation comes through an earth visitor, a visitor to be sure who allows himself to be demon-possessed, and a world which, through the good offices of another earth visitor, remains unfallen. It is a world of pre-Adamite consciousness, sinless, painless, and where even a small lie told by Ransom made him feel abominable. It is a world of music and ecstasy, of communion between Maleldil and his creatures. It is a world of inexpressible goodness, of laughter and deep joy even among the animals. It is a world of childlikeness, of which the Green Lady herself is the best example. Perhaps the nakedness of creatures on Perelandra is intended to be symbolic, and even Ransom's nakedness might be taken to suggest an ingenuous intent simply to do God's will. It may not be an accident that Weston arrives on Perelandra clothed. Edmund Fuller says that this novel gives the responsive reader not a purgation of pity and terror but rather of exaltation and awe.[13]

The fixed land perhaps symbolizes nothing more than a command of Maleldil to be obeyed simply because He has commanded it. One might, however, speculate on other possible implications as well. Could the floating islands adjusted to the movement of the water be a symbol of the Christian's abandonment to God's daily direction and the fixed land a symbol of merely following the letter of the law? The Green Lady and her husband were not forbidden to go to the fixed land, only to remain there. Later in *Perelandra* I get the impression that the fixed land might signify man's will and the floating islands the Eternal Wave on which men must always cast themselves.

Both in *Perelandra* and *That Hideous Strength* Lewis does not hesitate to depict demons, bent *eldila* from earth, taking possession of and using to their own ends the minds of men. Weston appears to have been partially demon-possessed when he landed on Perelandra, for his face had an unfamiliar look to Ransom and he was not long in propounding his diabolical philosophy that God and the devil are the same. The fact that he made no inquiry as to how Ransom got to Perelandra seems to confirm his monomania. Shortly he was to be so completely under the power of demons that his moments of normalcy were infrequent and filled with excruciating desire for release. His periods of right thinking were as infrequent as those of Prince Rilian in *The Silver Chair*. Rilian recovered, but Weston did not.

In *That Hideous Strength* we eventually learn that the real struggle is between great unseen forces of good and evil. Bent *eldila* — Frost called them macrobes — under the Black Archon or Earth Oyarsa, were the real rulers of the Head at Belbury and through this Head all the others. Ransom explained that these evil forces actually despised those they possessed and, once they were disabled enough to be useless, would destroy them. The apocalyptic demise of Belbury in butchery, fire, and destruction proved that Ransom was correct. On the other hand, the

[13] *Books with Men Behind Them*, p. 157.

presence and power of Maleldil is increasingly apparent as these three novels develop toward their climax.

The best single element of *Perelandra* is the vast amount of detail suggested by Lewis to account, mythically and not allegorically, for the temptation and fall of man. He suggests they were the result of deep-seated and flawlessly logical arguments thrusting at the very nature of mankind. We are led to believe that the fall was no quick and accidental affair but rather the result of a nice balancing of dialectic in which the ego and will of man concluded to reject the notion of their dependence upon God. Yet the book does not attempt to cover all possible theological analogies. It does suggest that self-knowledge is possible apart from evil. It was right for the Green Lady to discover her self-identity, not right for her to misuse the entailed freedom. The Green Lady is carried in the novel to the very brink of the fall, yet persuaded not to make Eve's mistake.

Marjorie Wright points out that in this story Lewis mingles the pattern of temptation and pattern of redemption. One such element is the unhealing wound which the Un-man gives Ransom during their herculean struggle. It is a symbol of the wounds given Christ in His conflict with Satan. Ransom's wound, we learn from *That Hideous Strength,* is not to be healed until his return to Perelandra, that is, until the reconciliation of things, and it splendidly suggests that Christ's wounds for the sins of man will have their final great reconciliation.

It is an interesting question whether Ransom is C. S. Lewis. Even when we are told that Ransom was only Lewis's friend, it is hard to escape the idea that they are one and the same. Like Lewis, Ransom had a bad war wound and was a "sedentary scholar" and philologist. He was a bachelor who found swimming the only sport in which he ever attained any excellence. He was an anti-vivisectionist. And, as might be expected, he was a man who talked very much like Lewis. Dabney A. Hart regards the directness of Lewis's voice as a defect in *Perelandra*.[14] Without denying the literary principle that an author should let

[14] "C. S. Lewis's Defense of Poesie," p. 227.

his characters speak for themselves, we can perhaps say of this novel what Gaëtan Picon said of Albert Camus' *The Plague,* that the author never at any point wished the story to become so obsessive that the moral intention should be forgotten.[15]

The Abolition of Man

Before discussing the last novel of the space trilogy, we need to look at a small book of Lewis's called *The Abolition of Man,* an expository discussion, of which *That Hideous Strength* is the counterpart.

In this study Lewis is concerned with the problem of objective values, whether for instance saying that a waterfall is "sublime" means only that one has the emotion of sublimity while looking at it. If a waterfall is sublime to one person and contemptible to another, does that mean that all values are thereby subjective and even trivial? Or is there a "given," a quality put into things from the outside which demands a certain response whether we happen to make that response or not? It is an odd thing that the debunker of values who insists that the waterfall is merely whatever one's emotions make of it will write a textbook teaching this doctrine to children. If he really believed that values are such, why say anything at all? To write a textbook debunking the notion of objective values is to contradict the very idea assumed by the act of writing, for such an activity proves that the author believed some value was not subjective and trivial, namely, his own. He believed in a "good" but only within himself, and now a good based not on emotion but on reason, a good no longer subject to debunking.

Every man, says Lewis, is ultimately forced to believe either that values reside simply in himself or else that they have objectivity apart from his own feeling about them. There is an infinite difference between the two views. If values are objective and one man may be right and another wrong, then there will be

---

[15] "Notes on *The Plague,*" in *Camus, A Collection of Critical Essays,* ed. by Germaine Brée, p. 146.

an obligation to try to discover the right value and champion it. And then there can be no *ought* in a world where there is no objective value. This ought is built into the essence of things as evidenced in part by the *Tao* or universal idea of good and bad, with one preferred to the other. One cannot reject the *Tao* without, finally, rejecting all value judgment, since no essentially new values are possible. "The human mind has no more power of inventing a new value than of imagining a new primary colour, or, indeed, of creating a new sun and a new sky for it to move in." One can only criticize within the *Tao* or moral order, not outside it.

Now, says Lewis, it is one thing for a good, law-abiding man to hold this subjective position simply by mistake, but it is another and quite terrible thing if a man or group deliberately decides to inculcate such a proposition for ends of its own. Lewis is not so much concerned with vicious political leaders like Hitler or the Communists as with well-meaning philosophers, scientists, sociologists, and educationalists who are unaware that, should they succeed, they will inevitably destroy civilization. Yet he believes that something of this kind is going on today.

Whereas the old objective and moral view involved a kind of propagation to the young of man's place and responsibility in a world of real values, "transmitting manhood to men," the new philosophy tends to "condition" people by propaganda based upon new and continually changing conceptions. In respect to nature, the old science which explained without explaining away is being replaced by a sort of irresistible and omnicompetent scientific technique which will not be satisfied with anything less than a complete conditioning of the whole human race.

The odd thing is that wholly unknown to most of these planners nature has a card up her sleeve. Lewis believes there is good cause to draw the following conclusions about our present situation: 1) Man "conquers" nature by reducing it to smaller and smaller particles of less and less "living" reality. He also "conquers" human nature through psychological study, making it "merely" this or that. 2) As super-scientific planning advances, it tends to fall into the hands of fewer men. 3) Many of these men have abandoned, either deliberately or else unthinkingly, the *Tao* in favor of their private conception of values. 4) Any subjective system, being of necessity in constant change, is irrational and hence its planning for the social "good" is undependable. 5) Thus the conquest of nature actually increases nature's domain and explanation ends in explaining away explanation. You "see through" things but you do not see anything through them. You get a wholly transparent world and it turns out to be an invisible one. "To 'see through' all things is the same as not to see at all."

A portion of Lewis's preface to D. E. Harding's *Hierarchy of Heaven and Earth* is, I think, a good summary of what he attempted to set forth in *The Abolition of Man*. "At the outset," he says, "the universe appears packed with will, intelligence, life and positive qualities; every tree is a nymph and every planet a god. Man himself is akin to the gods. The advance of knowledge gradually empties this rich and genial universe: first of its gods, then of its colours, smells, sounds and tastes, finally of solidity itself as solidity was originally imagined. As these items are taken from the world, they are transferred to the subjective side of the account: classified as our sensations, thoughts, images or emotions. The Subject becomes gorged, inflated, at the expense of the Object. But the matter does not end there. The same method which has emptied the world now proceeds to empty ourselves. The masters of the method soon announce that we were just as mistaken (and mistaken in much the same way) when we attributed 'souls,' or 'selves' or 'minds' to human organisms, as when we attributed Dryads to the trees . . . . We, who have personified all other things, turn out to be ourselves mere personifications . . . . And thus we arrive at a result uncommonly like zero. While we were reducing the world to almost nothing we deceived ourselves with the fancy that all its lost qualities were being kept safe (if in a somewhat humbled condition) as 'things in our own mind.' Apparently we had no mind of the sort required. The Subject is as empty as the Object. Almost nobody has been making linguistic mistakes about almost nothing. By and large, this is the only thing that has ever happened."

Such a background is useful in the understanding of the third novel in the space trilogy.

That Hideous Strength

Lewis calls this a modern fairy-tale for grown-ups and says that it is about "magicians, devils, pantomime animals, and planetary angels." Yet the story begins with the commonplace world of Jane and Mark Studdock, she a discontented housewife and he a newly chosen fellow of Bracton College, and both bright, hard intellectual agnostics whose education has conditioned them against one rag of noble thought. Located in a small midland market town called Edgestow, Bracton College has as its most ancient landmark Bragdon Wood, in the center of which is a well abutted by masonry dating back to the Anglo-Saxon invasion and associated in legend with Merlin.

Bracton College is in the act of selling Bragdon Wood to the National Institute of Co-ordinated Experiments, an organization ostensibly existing for state-planned efficiency, the remedial treatment of criminals, and similar purposes but which has unannounced goals to sterilize the unfit, liquidate backward races, make England a police state, blackmail and murder even its own cohorts when they get in the way, prenatally train toward total social control, turn history into science, and, finally, to conquer death and make man his own God by a process of "sanitation" that would ultimately eliminate organic life in favor of the purely chemical. The N.I.C.E. is under the control of a little pack of men who are convinced that "human" elements such as pity, fear, and religion are irrational, that nature is a crude and shoddy affair which they must remedy, and that positivism is the only value.

The particular interest of N.I.C.E. in coming to Edgestow, kept deeply secret, was simply to obtain Bragdon Wood and recover the comatose body of Merlin, who instead of death had long ago suffered a protracted enchantment, in the expectation of magical assistance from him.

Jane Studdock was a normal "modern" woman in every way but one: her dreams presaged events that came true. Thus Jane

104

was moved willy-nilly into the company of a small group known as St. Anne's, headed by Elwin Ransom of the two former novels and now revealed as the great Pendragon of Logres.

The N.I.C.E. filled little Edgestow with the roar of machinery and the bellow of profanity and deliberately provoked a riot during which Jane was sadistically tortured by the "Fairy," hard-boiled female captain of the Institute police. The two forces — one Christian and one devilish — came to recognize that victory would probably hinge upon the weight of Merlin's supernatural powers. Hence each was eager to recover his body from underneath Bragdon Wood.

Meanwhile Mark Studdock had been slowly and shrewdly drawn into the N.I.C.E. circle and in the course of time met the "Head," literally the guillotined head of a criminal named Alcasan which had been scientifically preserved and intended by the N.I.C.E. as the first experimental step in immortalizing man by removing him from dependence upon nature. To the delight of the particular scientists who were in charge, this Head was caused actually to speak, though a few of the topmost men at Belbury, where N.I.C.E. was located, knew what the scientists in charge did not — that the speaking was more than human and the voice of macrobes, organisms more intelligent than man and unknown to him in earlier and less scientific ages. The truth is that it is no other than the evil *eldila* of Earth who control the Head and the leaders at Belbury, just as Perelandra and the other Oyeresu of Deep Heaven control, albeit with their happy consent, Ransom and the household at St. Anne's.

It was Ransom's belief that Merlin was a fifth-century Christian druid, not the evil man suggested by some of the Arthurian legends, that he lived just at the close of the Atlantean age when magic was relatively natural and harmless rather than during a later period when black arts prevailed and magic had become demonic. But he believed that, as planned by the dark *eldila* for centuries, Merlin might join forces with Belbury if that organization got to him first. Ransom eagerly awaited the instructions of his good *eldila*.

A dream of Jane's was taken to be the signal that Merlin had

105

awakened, and Jane and others went forth on a stormy night to locate the place of his exodus from his ancient underground tomb underneath Bragdon Wood. All that they were able to discover, however, was a tramp's fire in the woodland and evidence that the tramp had only recently disappeared. As they returned disconsolately toward the highway, however, a horse and rider passed them full gallop and they saw them outlined in huge magnificence leaping high over a hedge. Later they learned that Merlin had forced the tramp to give him his clothes and that soon thereafter the Belbury scouts had picked up the naked tramp supposing him to be Merlin.

Merlin rode his horse to St. Anne's, magically put to sleep MacPhee, a skeptic who failed to believe in him, and, after mysterious questions and answers, became convinced that Ransom was the Pendragon and bowed down before him. After many explanations, Ransom revealed that the Oyeresu of Malacandra and Perelandra have been to St. Anne's and communed with him. The dark *eldila* of Earth had banked on a law which said that no inhabitants of Deep Heaven would ever come to Earth until the very end of things. Yet now it was revealed to Ransom that evil men had abrogated that law by building space ships and going out to contaminate unfallen worlds such as Mars and Venus. Thus at the moment when the dark Oyarsa of Earth supposed himself conqueror, the powers from Deep Heaven began to manifest their strength. Merlin learned that the Oyeresu will unmake Earth if they invoke their naked power and that therefore he has been chosen as their instrument. In a scene of terror, yet also of unexampled splendor, the heavenly Masters appeared at St. Anne's and were assumed into Merlin with power.

Knowing that Merlin would be unacquainted with modern English, the people at Belbury had spoken to the tramp only in Latin and other languages wholly foreign to him and he in turn had considered his captors as men speaking tongues other than his own. Baffled from lack of communication, Belbury invited in experts in archaic dialects and Merlin himself went to Belbury in that capacity. Hence it happened that Merlin met the tramp for the second time. He also met Mark, who by now because

106

of disillusionment and insubordination had become a prisoner of the Institute.

Merlin, pretending to speak through the tramp, demanded to be shown all the secrets of the N.I.C.E., including the abominable Head and the extensive section devoted to experiments on men and animals. On the evening of his arrival at Belbury a banquet had been scheduled. Merlin invited himself to it, used his magic to confuse all the speakers, and turned loose upon the assembly the wild animals of the laboratories, who soon left the banquet hall a place of blood and death. After more execrable deeds perpetrated by the few leaders who were left, the last of them locked himself inside the building and indifferently set fire to the building.

That night back at St. Anne's Ransom, now fulfilled as the great Fisher-King, told of his desire to return to Perelandra, the only place where his wounded heel could be cured. He wished to go where King Arthur was. We learn that since the days of Arthur, Britain has never been without its Pendragon and that though none of these things ever gets recorded in the written history of Britain, Logres continues to exist and at times makes itself felt against the dark powers that usually control it. Ransom was carried away from St. Anne's into Deep Heaven by Perelandra.

One consequence of Perelandra's visit was that Earth was temporarily flooded with love and joy. On such a night Jane and Mark Studdock came together again but now ashamed of the shoddy and selfish motives which once governed them and for the first time really in love with each other.

This is the longest of Lewis's religious books, and perhaps he might have done better to turn it into two or more novels. Though it is the least successful of the space trilogy, I think that two things may be said in its favor. The main theme, that of a group of scientific planners zealously intent on taking over the world, is made fearfully clear. Also the very heterogeneity of the characters and ideas shows the richness of Lewis's imaginative resources. It is hard to conceive how so great a variety of ancient and modern, learned and humble, heavenly and earthly, superlatively good and devilishly evil, natural and supernatural could be brought together on any terms and particularly in a volume concerned with "huge cloudy symbols." When Dr. Johnson was asked what he thought of women preachers, he said that their preaching was a little like a dog walking on its hind legs — you are surprised that it can be done at all. So it is with the polychrome of this novel.

I should judge that one's interest in the novel might hinge on whether or not he takes seriously the theme of *The Abolition of Man* and what Chad Walsh calls the "inverted utopias" of our time, such as Aldous Huxley's *Brave New World,* George Orwell's *Nineteen Eighty-Four,* Eugene Zamiatin's *We,* and Bernard Wolfe's *Limbo* and also certain books on the philosophy of science such as Whitehead's *Science and the Modern World,* Bush's *Modern Arms and Free Men,* Standen's *Science Is a Sacred Cow,* and Koestler's *The Sleepwalkers.*

Of the richness of *That Hideous Strength* in conception, consider the involvements growing out of Merlin's question, Why have I been brought back? Ransom explains to him that in the distant past there were neutral "Intelligences" in the earth. They were, however, perhaps hardly conscious, something like mere wills inherent in matter. In Merlin's time these intelligences were neither for nor against man, yet if man used them their normal tendency was to wither him, take something out of him. They laid man's mind open to something "that broadens the environment just a bit too much."

In Merlin's day one could "use" nature. It was alive and one made a truly personal contact with it. One could take an attitude toward it. Even Merlin himself manifested something of this animal quality in his awakened state; he had "the unarguing sagacity of a beast." But since Merlin's day man's attitude toward nature has slowly changed. It has come to mean something dead or a sort of machine to be taken to pieces when it does not work as he wishes it to. Men such as those at Belbury see nature only as something which can increase their own powers by tacking onto it both extra-natural and anti-natural spirits.

Belbury, remembering the tradition that Merlin had not actually died, wanted to dig him up and make use of his magic with nature. Yet the evil men of N.I.C.E. made the big mistake of forgetting that Merlin's use of nature was always within a framework of reverence for it, a use from within nature's own autonomy. (It was actually forbidden Merlin to use an edged tool on a growing thing.) These men despised nature except insofar as they could use it for their own selfish ends.

Because of man's treatment, or else because of a changing condition of things, the soul has now gone out of nature. Not even Merlin can reawaken it much. Evil has moved man farther and farther from an earlier and happier condition, and the Hideous Strength now confronts man. The magical use of nature which Merlin practiced in the fifth century was not then evil, but because of the very character of nature then it was dangerous. Now, says Ransom, it would be utterly unlawful.[16]

Instead, Ransom reveals to Merlin that God has sovereignly planned his awakening just at this time in order that his own soul may be saved, that is, that he may become the agent of God to work a purpose exactly the opposite to that for which Belbury wished to awaken him. He can now serve God directly, not through any "dallying" with nature, by a plan which Ransom is now in process of revealing to him, and thus Merlin can indi-

---

[16] Marjorie E. Wright interprets this difficult section as follows: "The particular history of earth is infected, of course, by the evil of the bent Oyarsa, although since Maleldil's entrance into it he has not been unopposed. But evil develops as does good, and the nature of the world was not at first completely changed. In the earlier days there were some spirits, or creatures of the air, which were neither good nor bad in relation to man. They had their own activities, and man might encounter them without being hurt. He could also investigate the properties of the plant and mineral world with respect to their correspondences to other planes of being, for traces of the celestial correspondences still remained. But these things could not remain in their untouched state. As time goes on, each thing becomes more perfected in its particular function, or if it does not, grows farther away from that function. In the process, good and evil become more sharply defined. This is the reason that Merlin could lawfully perform in Arthur's time magic which cannot now be permitted. The middle ground is being removed in preparation for the final conflict. As a member of the Director's company puts it, 'The universe, and every little bit of the universe, is always hardening and narrowing and coming to a point'." "The Cosmic Kingdom of Myth," pp. 135-136.

cate his true belief in God. Had not some in his own day lied about him by calling him a devil's son? But now he has discovered, to his astonishment, that both he and Ransom call the Oyeresu their Masters. At this moment even greater Powers than the Oyeresu are about to work in the earth.

But how can this be, asks Merlin? Did our Fair Lord himself not establish a law that he would never send down Powers either to mend or mar the earth until the end of all things? Ransom answers that this indeed may be the beginning of the end but that he believes the evil represented by Belbury produced in earth a condition similar to that created by Judas, a new relation between God and man. It came about when men sent space ships into Deep Heaven to spread the contagion of sin on unfallen planets. Now God will act. It is not He who violated His own law not to interfere with man but rather that Weston and Devine, in the evil spirit of Belbury and intent upon the control of the universe through a godless defiance and by means of natural philosophy, have now broken the barrier which God would not Himself break.

Yet in this act, by what these evil men supposed was mere chance, that is, the kidnapping of Ransom and carrying him to Mars, they have touched what is for them, and for all men of like devilish intentions, the fatal button which will be their undoing. They carried a philologist with them and that philologist met and talked face to face with the Oyeresu. Their evil use of nature, that is, their wish to fly to other planets and spread sin, had at the same time allowed an antithetical use of nature, had allowed Ransom to come in contact with Oyeresu and tell them about conditions on earth about which they had until then been unaware.

As a result earth was invaded by *eldila* from Deep Heaven. Indeed, Ransom tells Merlin, they have visited him in this very house and reminded him that he is the bridge between heaven and earth, a kind of intermediary. As in the case of Judas, the evil intention of men like Weston, and even their very method, has brought good to earth.

But it has brought a Power which in its naked strength is devastating. Indeed, asks Merlin, will not the Oyeresu power, or the greater power back of it, unmake all Middle Earth? The naked power would indeed, responds Ransom, but it is their intention to work through a man, through a man whose mind is open to be invaded. (As Weston was possessed by evil powers in *Perelandra,* here good powers take over a man, yet in each case it is as a result of his own desire.) Their purity cannot operate through a black magician, and yet they will not use Ransom himself. They want a man of pure heart yet one who understands the good and evil use of "magic."

Thus a second step of God to create good out of evil becomes apparent. Belbury wanted Merlin because it thought his magic would aid its cause, but now the same gift in him will be used against Belbury. When the far-reaching implications of this divine plan pierces the mind of Merlin, a great Celtic and primitive lamentation bursts from him and he breaks into sobs. Both Ransom and Merlin, in spite of their devotion, are fearful of the oncoming visit from Deep Heaven. To Merlin's plea for earthly help Ransom can only remind him that practically the whole earth is corrupted. "The shadow of one dark wing is over all Tellus."

Merlin has been white and shaken through much of this conversation, but now there comes a gleam into his eye and a happy cunning into his face. He is willing to be the medium of God's work, just as Ransom himself had been that medium in *Perelandra.* He discovers, as Ransom did, that Maleldil's work is to be done by a man wholly committed to him who takes advantage of the circumstances, often mundane and sometimes hideous, and honestly follows instructions.

It is undesirable here to attempt a discussion of all the Arthurian elements in Lewis. That has been done well by Charles Moorman and Marjorie E. Wright. It is obvious that Lewis got many of his ideas about Merlin from Charles Williams. For instance, Williams had suggested that the Pendragon was related to the Plantagenets, which might account for Lewis's saying that this title had been handed down quietly from one to another during the whole history of Britain. The idea of Logres is quite wholly

111

from Williams and perhaps also that of black and white magic. Lewis says that Williams was very learned on magic,[17] and since this is a significant topic all through Lewis, we may suppose he had some of his ideas from Williams.

It is interesting that Lewis makes a comment, through Ransom, on the whereabouts of King Arthur, who, it will be remembered, was finally taken to Avalon to be healed of his wounds. Ransom tells Merlin that Arthur is "in the House of Kings in the cup-shaped land of Abhalljin, beyond the seas of Lur in Perelandra. For Arthur did not die; but Our Lord took him, to be in the body till the end of time and the shattering of Sulva, with Enoch and Elias and Moses and Melchisedec the King. Melchisedec is he in whose hall the steep-stoned ring sparkles on the forefinger of the Pendragon." Ransom himself went to Lur for the healing of his own wound. Marjorie E. Wright points out that Frodo in Tolkien's trilogy has acquired two wounds that do not completely heal until the elves take him to the Far West.[18]

The least successful ingredient of *That Hideous Strength* is the decapitated head of Alcasan. Perhaps Lewis got the idea of it from the much publicized experiments of Dr. Alexis Carrel and Charles A. Lindbergh to keep a human heart alive after it had been removed from the body. The unbearable slobbering of Lewis's monster amid its tubes and pumps is sufficient to make one sick at the stomach, and the Head makes no sense in the story unless it be accepted as the mouthpiece of the evil *eldila* who have usurped the experiments of Filostrato to their own ends. Of course this is the actual use Lewis makes of it, but the gruesomeness of the thing tends to usurp any logical explanation of its place in the novel. In *Perelandra* Lewis had prepared the way for the Head, for there we have Weston during the temptation of the Green Lady gazing with loose, unseeing eyes while some mysterious force caused the mouth to utter thoughts. Chilled with horror, Ransom felt the only proper name for it was the Un-man. The appalling head at Belbury might suggest one

[17] *Arthurian Torso,* p. 160.
[18] "The Cosmic Kingdom of Myth," p. 112.

thing quite apart from the novel itself, that is, how consciousness is essential to any adequate conception of man.

While the satirical element in *That Hideous Strength* is minor, it should not be overlooked. The skill with which Lewis describes the wire-pulling and small politics of the faculty at Bracton College makes it perfectly clear that he has observed such proceedings often. Lewis's antipathy to newspapers and progressive education appears sharply. It is very little trouble for the scoundrels at Belbury by a little manipulating to get into the newspapers their own version of things and to have this version accepted not only by the mass of people but particularly by the educated class. In fact, we learn that the educated are more likely to be hoodwinked by propaganda than others. If one feels that this image of newspapers is prejudiced, he is less inclined to think the same of Lewis's portrait of Mark and Jane Studdock, characterized as moderns who do everything for effect and never for approval of their own consciences. Mark and Jane need to go through an almost complete metamorphosis before they discover they have always been doing things from wrong motives. Radically different circumstances bring about their return to ordinary probity. In Mark's case it is the enormity of the hoax at Belbury while in Jane's it is the selfless peace of the Christians at St. Anne's. Mark feels that his return to normalcy is complete when he can do a simple thing — actually read a children's story — without a feeling of shame.

Finally, the question arises whether Lewis in the four books I have discussed in this chapter is attempting to satirize science. Some are convinced that Lewis is subconsciously afraid of science because it tends to destroy what they call his theological dogmatism. My own reading of Lewis indicates that he stands quite in line with the majority of scientific philosophers of our time who uphold the scientific method but fear the scientism which often follows in its wake. Lewis says, "It is not the greatest of modern scientists who feel most sure that the object, stripped of its qualitative properties and reduced to mere quantity, is wholly real. Little scientists, and little unscientific followers of science, may think so. The great minds know very well that the object, so treated, is an artificial abstraction, that something of its reality has been lost." This I believe is also the position of so great a scientist and philosopher as Alfred North Whitehead.

Professor Chad Walsh says that when he asked Lewis concerning the N.I.C.E. in *That Hideous Strength,* Lewis declared his intent was not to suggest that scientists are launching an attack on humanity but that anyone who is the enemy of humanity would take cover under the prestige of science. Walsh goes on to say that remarkably little actual scientific research went on in the N.I.C.E.[19]

Without pursuing this further, I should like to mention two men who have recently described the potential suggested in Lewis's *The Abolition of Man* and *That Hideous Strength.* The first is Dr. Philip Siekevitz, biochemist at the Rockefeller Institute, who says: "There is a golden age ahead on earth for our species; if only we use to the utmost capacity our heads and our hearts. . . . We are approaching the greatest event in human history, even in the history of life on earth, the deliberate changing by man of many of the biological processes . . . man will be remolding his own being . . . . Events in biological research are happening so rapidly that we will soon have to answer a new question. No longer, What creature is man? But what creature should he become?"[20] Dr. Siekevitz, however, sees quite exactly the danger that Lewis has stated and insists upon the moral use of science. The second scientist describes the problem suggested in *That Hideous Strength.* "The new revolution in science and technology which has so enormously increased man's power over nature, has also reduced enormously the significance of the average individual. With the advent of automation and the utilization of atomic energy, it soon might be possible for a relatively small group of people to satisfy all the country's needs — and fight its wars too — without the aid of the masses. Man's destiny is now being shaped in fantastically complex and expensive laboratories staffed by supermen, and the new frontier has no place for the rejected and unfit.

[19] *C. S. Lewis: Apostle to the Skeptics,* p. 129.
[20] "The Man of the Future," *Nation,* September 13, 1958.

Instead of being the leaven of history and the mainspring of the ascending movement of man, the weak are likely to be cast aside as a waste product. One is justified in fearing that the elimination of the weak as shaping factors may mean the end of history — the reversion to zoology."[21] It has often been remarked that creative minds such as Lewis's get correct intuitions of what is to be, and I should guess that Lewis's theme in *The Abolition of Man* and *That Hideous Strength* may, like Aldous Huxley's *Brave New World* and George Orwell's *Animal Farm,* become more meaningful with the passing of time.

[21] Eric Hoffer, "How Natural is Human Nature?" *Saturday Evening Post,* January 13, 1962.

V

THE KINGDOM OF NARNIA

Lewis rigorously defends the fairy tale against any who claim that it gives a false conception of life. The fact is, says he, that this is the direct opposite of the truth and it is the so-called realistic stories which deceive children. The fairy tale, like the myth, on the one hand arouses longing for more ideal worlds and on the other gives the real world a new dimension of depth. The boy "does not despise real woods because he has read of enchanted woods: the reading makes all real woods a little more enchanted." The child reading the fairy tale is delighted simply in desiring, while the child reading a "realistic" story may establish the success of its hero as a standard for himself and, when he cannot have the same success, may suffer bitter disappointment.

It seems obvious that two purposes guided Lewis in the writing of his Narnia stories. One was to tell a good tale, the other to suggest analogies — I do not think Lewis would wish them called allegories — of the Christian scheme of things. These books have been among Lewis's most widely read. Charles A. Brady thinks that they mark "the greatest addition to the imperishable deposit of children's literature since the *Jungle Books*."[1] Chad Walsh says that he himself felt the fairy-tale atmosphere was curiously cut-and-dried but that two of his daughters, aged six and eight, re-educated him after he had read them the first chapter and they required two chapters a night thereafter, some-

[1] "Finding God in Narnia," *America*, October 27, 1956.

116

times followed by tears when a third chapter was not forth-coming.[2]

The Magician's Nephew

To discover the very beginnings of Narnia one should read *The Magician's Nephew,* actually the sixth book in the series of seven. The book might well be called *The Beginnings of Narnia,* or *How the Wardrobe Gained Its Magic.* Digory Kirke was an old white-haired man when Peter and his friends first discovered that the wardrobe was a doorway into Narnia, yet the story really began when Digory was a boy in London and one morning stuck his head over the garden wall and found Polly Plummer looking up at him. Digory and his invalid mother were living with his uncle and aunt Ketterley while his father was away in India. Before the adventure was over they were to plant in Digory's yard the seeds of an apple brought back from Narnia, and long afterwards the wood from that same tree was to be used in making the magical wardrobe.

The original adventure started when Digory and Polly acci-dentally discovered that Digory's queer and unpleasant uncle was a dabbler in magic. This uncle's godmother, one of the last mortals on earth to possess any fairy blood, just before her death had given him a box containing dust from the lost island of Atlantis. She warned him as she was dying to burn the box. Instead he experimented with its contents and was able to make some little colored rings, yellow and green, with which he caused guinea pigs to disappear. The uncle was too cowardly to become his own subject, but when Polly touched one of the yellow rings she disappeared. Digory, thoroughly disgusted with his uncle, took two of the green rings into his pocket and put a yellow one on his finger. Immediately he was transported to the Wood be-tween the Worlds, where he found Polly. They discovered that

---

[2] Review of *The Lion, the Witch and the Wardrobe,* New York *Times,* November 12, 1950.

by putting on the yellow rings and jumping into one of many small lakes in the Wood they could go into other worlds.

One they went to was called Charn, a world almost dead, and when Digory struck a bell he could not resist, Jadis, a powerful and haughty queen, came to life and told them how by speaking the Deplorable Word she had destroyed her rival sister and all of Charn. When Jadis discovered the children were from a newer world, she coveted it for herself. Scared, the children put their hands on the magic rings to return to London, but they found Queen Jadis in London with them, for she had touched them at the last moment. There Jadis went out in a hansom cab with Uncle Andrew and caused a riot. She had wrenched off an iron guy from a light pole and was flailing policemen with it when Digory and Polly got hold of her and touched their yellow rings.[3] Immediately they were back in the Wood between the Worlds. They quickly jumped into one of the pools of water and went into a midnight world, the world of Nothing. To their consternation, they found they had brought along not only Jadis but the cab driver, Uncle Andrew, and the cabby's horse.

In this world of Nothing they saw Narnia created by a great Lion, Aslan. All, including the horse, were delighted except Uncle Andrew and Jadis. The latter flung her iron guy at the Lion. It stuck in the ground, and because Aslan's great creativity was at work making grass, trees, and all sorts of beings, the iron grew into a lamp post just like the one in London. The whole world seemed filled with right magic as Aslan worked. Jadis ran away and Uncle Andrew hid himself. Aslan created fauns, satyrs, dwarfs, and talking beasts. Even the cabby horse was turned into a talking beast.

Before this new world was five hours old evil had entered into it. Uncle Andrew, refusing to believe that Aslan was anything more than a beast, was unable to hear Aslan's beautiful song as he created things and could not even hear the animals talk and

---

[3] The wild ride of Jadis is modeled on a similar hectic scene toward the end of G. K. Chesterton's *The Man Who Was Thursday*. See page 162 of the Capricorn Edition.

laugh. But Jadis was even a greater evil in Narnia. Digory had brought the evil in, said Aslan to the beasts, but he promised to see that the worst fell upon himself.

Aslan told the cabby — and also his wife Helen, who had been brought to Narnia by Aslan's magic — that they were to be the first king and queen of the land and were to name and rule all the creatures. Also that their children would be kings of Narnia and of Archenland. Then Aslan, that Digory might help to undo the wrong he had done in bringing in evil, sent him far away into the mountains of the Western Wild to a beautiful valley where in a garden on a hilltop grew an apple tree. To carry Digory and Polly to this spot the cabby horse was turned into a great flying Pegasus. Digory was to bring back an apple the seed of which, when planted by Aslan, would produce a tree to protect Narnia from Jadis for many years.

At the end of their aerial journey they found the garden and the tree loaded with beautiful fruit. But Digory also discovered Jadis in the garden, eating an apple. Telling him how delicious it was and otherwise enticing him, she almost persuaded him to eat, yet Digory remembered his instructions and was able to return to Aslan with a perfect apple. From its seed a new tree sprang up quickly, and Aslan gave Digory an apple from it to carry back to heal his sick mother. From the golden leaves of another tree the dwarfs fashioned crowns for the new king and queen of Narnia, and Aslan himself, with all the creatures standing at attention, established King Frank and Queen Helen as the first rulers of Narnia.

After a wonderful farewell and parting advice from Aslan about evils that would come on Narnia, they were transported back to their own world. The apple which Digory had brought along cured his mother. Digory buried the core of it in his back yard, and, to prevent Digory's uncle from further mischief with his magical rings, he and Polly buried them near the apple seeds. This was the tree which Digory much later fashioned into a wardrobe. He did not know that it retained some of its Narnian magic, for that was a discovery to be made a long time afterwards by Peter, Edmund, Susan, and Lucy.

Back in Narnia King Frank and Queen Helen ruled. Their second son became King of Archenland. The boys married nymphs and the girls wood-gods and river-gods. The lamp-post which had grown up in Narnia shone always in the Narnian forest and the place where it stood came to be known as Lantern Waste.

Narnia was quite a different world from ours. This is the manner in which it was created. As Digory and the others stood in the dark and empty land of Nothing, they heard a far-off song that appeared to come from every direction at once, even from the very earth beneath their feet. Though it was hardly a tune at all, it was almost too beautiful to bear. Suddenly the voice of Aslan, for it was he who began it all, was joined by many other voices. At the same time the black sky above was filled with blazing stars which seemed to join their own voices to the swelling music. Then in the east, to the sound of still more glorious music, the sun rose splendidly and revealed fresh and colorful valleys and rivers and mountains. Yet it revealed no trees nor even a blade of grass.

The Lion now sang a new song that was softer and more lilting than before, and as he paced to and fro the ground was covered with grass sprinkled with daisies and buttercups. It was then that Jadis, fearful of the Lion's approach, flung her iron guy from the London light pole straight at him. The object struck Aslan between the eyes and fell into the grass. It began to grow like the other new creations. After this Aslan sang a wilder tune and the land in front of him began to take on queer humps of many different sizes and out of these humps burst all sorts of animals, stags, panthers, dogs, frogs, and elephants. Hundreds of birds came out of the trees, and bees and butterflies soon filled the air and got busy. To Aslan's music were soon added hundreds of other sounds from the teeming land.

Then Aslan touched some pairs of animals and called them aside into a circle. They stood in perfect silence with their eyes upon him, and it was apparent that something marvellous was about to happen. As Aslan stared at them they turned their heads as if to understand. Yet Aslan did not speak, but only breathed out a long, warm breath. Then from far overhead the stars began to sing and there came a blinding flash of light which made the children's bodies tingle. Aslan in a deep, wild voice then sang, "Narnia, Narnia, Narnia, awake. Love. Think. Speak. Be walking trees. Be talking beasts. Be divine waters."

This was the beginning of Narnia. It was all quite perfect, except that the powerful and vengeful Jadis, brought to life by Digory's sinful curiosity, had gone off to the edge of Narnia and would remain. Yet she could not return as long as the apple tree flourished.

Narnia was a small land compared to some of those near it.[4] Rabadash reminded the Tisroc that Narnia was not one-fourth the size of the smallest of his provinces in Calormen, and even Edmund confessed that Narnia might be overcome easily by its more powerful enemies roundabout. It was a land of heather and thyme and of sweet air, of rivers and plashing glens, of mossy caves and great forests filled with the noise of dwarfs' smithies. It was a land of freedom, where maidens were never forced to marry against their will, and where even a mouse like Reepicheep had a great sense of honor and chivalry.

Just to the south of Narnia, and connected with it by a pass through high mountains, lay Archenland, a country ruled over by King Lune from his castle at Anvard and later by his son Ram the Great, the most famous of all Archenland kings. Farther south, across a great desert, was the large and cruel country of Calormen. Its dark-skinned and proud people always dreamed of capturing both Narnia and Archenland. The capital of Calor-

---

[4] Marjorie E. Wright says that the name Narnia is that of a small Italian town mentioned by Livy. She also notes the source and variety of creatures Lewis caused to inhabit Narnia. The fauns, dryads, and centaurs are from classical myth and the red and black dwarfs and the wolf Fenris from Norse myth. There are also scatterings of Persian and medieval flavors, also such creatures as the lamb from Christian symbolism. She thinks the marsh-wiggles are Lewis's own invention whose fame might become equal to that of Tolkien's hobbits. "The Cosmic Kingdom of Myth," p. 153.

men was the great city of Tashbaan, and the country had many provinces.

To the west of Narnia lay a wild land of big mountains covered with dark forests or else with snow and glaciers. It was called the Western Wild. A river rushing down from it created a vast and thundering waterfall, underneath which was Caldron Pool, and out of this flowed the River of Narnia which ran all the way across to the sea. On the east side of the Western Wild was Lantern Waste, where the children first entered Narnia and where Jadis, the White Witch, had her kingdom.

The capital of Narnia was Cair Paravel, located in a beautiful spot on the east coast near the River of Narnia, and this was where Aslan established Peter, Edmund, Susan, and Lucy as kings and queens of Narnia and where they reigned for many years. A little to the north of Cair Paravel lived the marsh-wiggles, and above them one crossed the River Shribble and came to a desolate moorland called Ettinsmore which led, finally, to mountainous country and the giants' stronghold of Harfang. Nearby were the ruins of a great city underneath which once lay the kingdom of the Green Witch and her unwilling vassals. Here also in a deep cave had slept Father Time until Aslan awakened him to sound his final horn over Narnia.

On the east of Narnia lay the ocean, over which, if one were courageous enough, he could sail to Galma, Terebinthia, the Seven Islands, the Lone Islands, Dragon Island, Deathwater Island, Darkness Island, and World's End Island to the Silver Sea and the very end of the world, and there he could look beyond the sun itself into the high mountains of Aslan's own country.

In olden times there were many chinks or chasms between the world and Narnia, but they had grown rarer. One of the last was a magical cave on an island in the South Sea, upon which a few men and women had once accidentally blundered and discovered the Land of Telmar, which was then unpeopled. They lived there for generations and became a proud, fierce nation. Finally Telmar suffered a great famine and its people, led by King Caspian the First, went a long distance to the Western Mountains of Narnia, crossed them, and conquered Narnia which was then in some disorder. It was not then a land of men at all but of talking beasts, walking trees, fauns, dwarfs, and giants. Actually it was the Telmarines who silenced the beasts and trees and fountains and killed and drove away dwarfs and fauns, and even tried to cover up the very memory of such things.

These are the places in which the events of the Narnian stories take place.

The Lion, The Witch and the Wardrobe

The first of the adventures, after the creation of Narnia by Aslan, began about sixty years later when the four Pevensie children, Peter, Edmund, Susan, and Lucy, left London because of air-raids during the war and went to stay with old Professor Kirke in his great country mansion. One day Lucy, while playing in an old wardrobe, accidentally discovered it was a doorway — one never reached Narnia twice in the same way — to Narnia and eventually all four of the children got in. Just inside was the lamp-post of Jadis the White Witch. She was now queen of Narnia, having slain most of its inhabitants and turned its weather to perpetual winter yet with never any Christmas.

Jadis had overcome most of Narnia and had as her henchmen a vast number of giants, werewolves, ghouls, wraiths, horrors, efreets, sprites, vultures, giant bats, orknies, wooses, ettins, spectres, boggles, ogres, minotaurs, crucls, hags, people of the toadstools, wolves, bull-headed men, evil dwarfs, and spirits of evil trees and poisonous plants. Even though Jadis magically turned all her enemies to stone, there were many loyal Narnian talking beasts hidden away and eager for her downfall. One of these was Tumnus the Faun, whose friendship with Lucy brought on Jadis's wrath and lined up the forces of good and evil. Mr. and Mrs. Beaver led the children southwards toward the Stone Table. They were followed by the furious Jadis, who had learned of Aslan's return to Narnia.

In the south, where once again spring had returned, Aslan took Peter to a high hill and showed him in the distance on a peninsula jutting into the sea the castle of Cair Paravel where he and the other children were to reign. Aslan also predicted the death of Jadis. Meanwhile she and her cohorts arrived at the Stone Table and she was about to kill Edmund, now her prisoner, with her stone knife when Aslan volunteered to die in his place and thus appease the Deep Magic involved. That night Lucy and Susan met Aslan near the Stone Table, wept bitterly at the sadness in his countenance, and later horrifiedly saw Aslan bound by his enemies, spit upon, jeered at, and finally slain by the White Witch. At sunrise the Stone Table itself split into two great pieces. Later Lucy and Susan returned sorrowfully to the dead body of their leader.

Yet with the coming of daylight Lucy and Susan were overjoyed to hear a great voice behind their backs and turning saw Aslan shining in the early sunrise. He was larger and more glorious then ever. When they inquired how he could be alive again, he told them it was by a very Deep Magic. After a happy romp, Aslan took the two girls upon his back and traveled like the wind to the White Witch's castle in the West. There he brought all the stone animals back to life and laid her castle waste. Hurrying back eastward, they found Peter and his friends in deadly combat with the White Witch and her followers. The result was a complete victory, Aslan himself joining the battle and slaying the White Witch herself.

Then Aslan and all the loyal inhabitants of Narnia took the children to Cair Paravel and crowned them, and they grew up to be as dignified kings and queens as one could imagine. Long afterwards while one day in the west hunting the White Stag, who could give you wishes if you caught him, they came upon the lamp-post in Lantern Waste. At first they did not recognize it. Later they became convinced that if they passed the post they would either find strange new adventures or else some great change in their fortunes. They passed through the thicket in which the post was located and the next moment were children again among the clothes hung in the wardrobe of the old professor's mansion. To their amazement they found that though they had been in Narnia a great many years no earth time at all had elapsed. Old Professor Kirke comforted them by saying, "Once a King in Narnia, always a King in Narnia" and assuring them that sooner or later they would again discover an entrance to that marvellous country.

Prince Caspian

A year later the children did indeed return to Narnia, called back by magic from a railway station in which they were waiting while on their way back to boarding school. Whisked away by an irresistible pull, they landed on a densely forested island in the center of which they came upon a ruined castle and eventually found it to be Cair Paravel. They could understand the ruins only when they remembered that time in Narnia is always different from time on earth. In the ancient treasure room below the castle they located their own armor and Lucy discovered also her diamond flask of magic cordial which Father Christmas had given her long before.

The next day a boat came from the nearby mainland intent on drowning one of its passengers. Susan's well-aimed arrows drove the men off and the passenger, a dwarf, was rescued. Asked for his story, he told them a long tale about Prince Caspian, whose uncle King Miraz and aunt Queen Prunaprismia had usurped Caspian's throne. Prince Caspian, instructed by a nurse and later by Doctor Cornelius, had learned the ancient history of Narnia and, when Queen Prunaprismia bore a son, was warned to save his life by escaping. The young prince traveled southward toward Archenland, got lost in the mountains, and was knocked unconscious by a limb when a storm scared his horse and caused him to dash through the trees. Awakening in the presence of a talking badger named Trufflehunter and two dwarfs, Nikabrik and Trumpkin, the prince realized that he had discovered the Old Narnia which had long survived under cover in the deep woods. After a while, and not without opposition, the hidden Narnians decided to make Caspian their king and with him as leader make war on Miraz.

But Miraz did not need to be sought out, for he had trailed

Caspian and with his army was near at hand. Caspian and his new friends took refuge in Aslan's How, a much tunneled hill, and were surrounded by Miraz' army. When the situation looked very desperate for Caspian, he remembered to blow Susan's magic horn, which had been given to him by Doctor Cornelius, and it was the blast of this horn which had rushed the four children back into Narnia from the railway station. Trumpkin had meantime volunteered to go to Cair Paravel island to seek help but on his way had been captured and sentenced to drowning. It was he of course who had been saved by Susan's arrows.

Realizing why they had been summoned to Narnia, the children made immediate plans to aid Caspian. Attempting to go up to Aslan's How by an untraveled road, they got lost in the mountains. In their uncertainty about the right path, Lucy caught a glimpse of Aslan and urged them to follow him, but they went another way, found it rougher and rougher, and finally returned and accepted Lucy's direction. That night Lucy, unable to sleep, walked out among the trees and found them stirring with conscious life. She awakened her companions, who grumbled at the idea of traveling at night and also at Lucy's notion that Aslan would lead them, yet they slowly made the discovery that Aslan was indeed ahead of them and showing the way. By daybreak they had arrived at the How.

There they found the dwarf Nikabrik quarreling with King Caspian and insisting that they must call upon the White Witch and a hag and werewolf to save them from Miraz' army. Nikabrik had no faith in the existence either of Aslan or of Peter and his friends, though the latter stood just outside the room in which the quarrel was under way. In that room a desperate fight came on in which Nikabrik and his evil friends were slain.

After the fashion of ancient knighthood, Peter sent a challenge to Miraz to meet him in single combat which would decide the issue between them. Their long and difficult combat was watched by a great crowd of friends and enemies, the latter consisting of an army of Telmarine soldiers and the former of Giant Wimbleweather, the Bulgy Bears, the Centaur Glenstorm, the brave mouse Reepicheep, the badger Trufflehunter, and a vast array of other talking animals, backed up by thousands of dryads, hamadryads, and silvans. When finally Peter slew Miraz, the wicked king's followers rushed in to attack, but at the moment when things looked very desperate for Caspian's forces the walking trees were seen approaching and all enemies were taken prisoner. Aslan later gave these the privilege of returning to Telmar. By Aslan's magic the children were returned to the railway station from which their adventure had started.

The Voyage of the Dawn Treader

The third adventure occurred one earth year (three Narnian years) later and began in Cambridge when Edmund and Lucy Pevensie (Peter was studying for an exam and Susan had gone on a visit to America) were at the home of their cousin Eustace Clarence Scrubb, a snob whose parents had him read economics instead of fairy tales. It began when a framed picture of a ship crashing through great blue waves became real and turned out to be King Caspian on his way to the unknown eastern seas to discover what became of the seven lords sent away by King Miraz. The gallant mouse Reepicheep had another reason for going, for he wished to find the edge of the world and Aslan's country.

It was a happy company except for Eustace, who found fault with everything and promised to repay injuries which he judged the others were bringing upon him. Stopping at the Lone Islands, some of their number were captured by a slave trader and escaped only when King Caspian's true identity became known. Next they ran into a great storm and with their ship in ruins landed at Dragon Island. Here Eustace ran away, got lost, and turned into a dragon yet with his human mind, a condition which taught him how wickedly he had acted. He was transformed when Aslan tore off his dragon skin, which Eustace himself could not possibly remove, and threw him into a well of water.

Their ship repaired, they sailed on eastward — always eastward — and encountered a sea serpent which coiled round their ship and almost crushed it. Next they stopped at Deathwater Island, where they discovered a lake which turned everything in it into gold. One of the seven lords they found lying, solid gold, at the bottom. Next they reached an island where everybody was invisible and all the Dufflepuds had only one large foot apiece. Lucy proved herself a heroine by braving the upstairs of the great magician's house and discovering in his book of magic the spell to release the people from their invisibility. Next they sailed to the Island of Darkness and were almost lost, and afterwards they came to a land where three men had sat at a sumptuous table — it was really Aslan's — for years without eating anything because they were fast asleep. They turned out to be among the seven lords King Caspian sought.

After this they sailed into quiet and clear seas where they were able to see people and castles below them in the water. As they went along the light kept increasing and the sun became many times its normal size. They discovered the water through which they sailed had become fresh. They were all filled with joy and peace, and the light itself seemed to be such that they could drink it. Older sailors on board began to grow young again. Sailing through the glorious Silver Sea, they found the water alive with white lilies.

Because the water finally became quite shallow, the children left the *Dawn Treader* and took Reepicheep a little farther and saw him off in his own little boat bravely sailing for Aslan's own country. They found a shore where they saw a lamb who gave them fish to eat that he had cooked and then turned into Aslan. When they asked Aslan how to get into his country, he told them there were entrances from all worlds, also that he was the great Bridge Builder. He told Lucy and Edmund that they were now too old to return to Narnia, yet that they should meet him in their own world. With Aslan's mane and his kiss upon the children's foreheads, they found themselves back in their aunt's house at Cambridge and the picture once more only a picture above their bed. The *Dawn Treader* returned safely to Narnia, but only after Caspian had married a beautiful maiden he had met on one of the islands he visited. She was the daughter of Ramandu, a great man who had once long ago been a star in the sky, and she became a splendid queen and the mother and grandmother of many kings.

The Silver Chair

The fourth adventure involved two cousins of the Pevensies, Eustace Scrubb and Jill Pole, two unhappy youngsters just beginning a term in horrid Experimental School, and carried them to the heart of Narnia and the castle of Cair Paravel, and afterwards, on instructions from Aslan, to the home of the marshwiggle Puddleglum and onward into a vivid adventure across the desolate moorland plain of Ettinsmore to Harfang and the City Ruinous. Eustace and Jill entered their experiences by way of a door in the school wall and were afterwards gently blown by Aslan into Narnia from a high cliff. Far below they landed unharmed and found King Caspian the Tenth, now an old man, ready to depart for a visit to one of his island provinces.

They learned from Glimfeather the owl how a large green snake had killed the queen and how Prince Rilian, going northward to slay the snake, had met a beautiful woman with a green dress who had apparently persuaded him to remain with her. Many had gone to search for the prince but none had ever returned. Aslan, the great lion, had commissioned Eustace and Jill to find the prince and had given them careful instructions for doing so.

Glimfeather and another owl carried the children to Puddleglum and the three pursued their way northwards over the River Shribble and past the stupid giants of Ettinsmore to the cold mountains of the north. At a bridge they met two on horseback, one a beautiful woman in a green dress and the other a knight who did not speak or raise the visor of his armor. The woman encouraged them to make their journey to Harfang and be entertained by the giants living there. Struggling through the snow and icy wind, they finally reached Harfang and were bathed, fed, and entertained in magnificent comfort. Yet Puddleglum's pessimism was soon justified when they discovered they were meant to be served up as giant food.

Escaping through the kitchen door of the castle while the leading giants were away on a hunting trip, the three were discovered and forced to squeeze themselves into a little crevice as a means of eluding their enemies. In the black darkness they slid down a long underground gravel bank and discovered themselves surrounded by a hundred odd-looking soldiers who led them captives through many passages and finally on a lengthy boat trip to a silent but busy city and into a castle. There they discovered a fair-haired young man who turned out to be Prince Rilian. He had no recollection of his past and all his interests centered in the beautiful woman he adored, who had promised him a great kingdom that she would soon establish inside Narnia.

The prince explained to them that for a short period each night he became abnormal and would turn into a serpent unless he suffered himself to be tied to a silver chair. When the fit came upon him, however, the children discovered that this was rather the only time he was normal, for then he insisted that the beautiful woman was actually a wicked witch who had kept him in her control for years. Puddleglum and the children were uncertain what to do until Prince Rilian asked them in the name of Aslan to cut his cords. Remembering that Aslan had told them such a request would be made of them, they released the prince and broke the spell. The powerful magic of the queen was shortly brought to bear upon the prince and his new friends and they were at the point of succumbing when the common sense of Puddleglum enabled him to destroy the source of her spells. Whereupon she turned into a great green serpent and did all she could to destroy them but lost her own head.

Thereafter the prince and his friends freed the underworld of the slavery which the queen had long imposed. After experiencing an underground volcano and a great tidal wave, and after a dangerous journey they discovered an opening above them which led into the heart of Narnia and the glorious upperworld of trees and stars. They went to Cair Paravel, where the people welcomed their long lost prince and where, their work done, Aslan blew the children back to the top of the great cliff and to their school labors, yet only after he allowed them to see him resurrect King Caspian to new life and a youthful, joyous existence.

The Horse and His Boy

This fifth adventure actually happened earlier in the history of Narnia a few years after Peter, Edmund, Lucy, and Susan became kings and queens there. Though they have some part in the story, it is mainly about two children named Shasta and Aravis and all that happened to them on their way from Calormen to Archenland.

Far to the south of Calormen lived Arsheesh, a poor fisherman who had a helper, supposedly but not actually his own son, a boy named Shasta. One day there came by a Tarkaan or great lord who demanded hospitality and also the purchase of Shasta as a slave. At the same time that he discovered this plan Shasta also discovered that Bree, the Tarkaan's horse, was a Narnian talking animal, and they agreed to slip away together in the night.

They traveled northwards toward the wonder city of Tashbaan where the great Tisroc had his court. On the way they met Hwin, another talking horse, carrying a girl, Aravis, northward, and though she and Shasta quarreled a good deal, they went along together. Aravis confessed that she was a Tarkheena and the only daughter of Kidrash Tarkaan and a descendant from the god Tash. She left home when her step-mother persuaded Kidrash to promise her to Ahoshta Tarkaan, an ugly but important old man.

In the course of time they came to Tashbaan, knowing that if they could get through this city unnoticed they would be in no further danger on their travels northward. But in Tashbaan they had many unexpected troubles. It happened that Queen Susan was held there as virtual prisoner until she should marry Prince Rabadash, whom she detested. Mistaken, as it turned out, for his twin brother, Shasta was picked up and welcomed into the Narnian company in a great palace. Tumnus the Faun figured a way for the Narnians to escape Tashbaan by feigning plans for a big announcement banquet for Rabadash on board their ship; instead the Narnians sailed away during the night.

Shasta and his friends had agreed that if they got separated they would meet in the tombs north of the city. Escaping over the city wall, Shasta made his way there and spent a whole night alone except for a cat which appeared and kept him warm. In the night when jackals howled and came close, Shasta missed the cat and heard a lion's roar that drove the animals away. The cat then returned.

Meantime Aravis had discovered in Tashbaan an old friend of hers, Tarkeena Lasaraleen, who was silly and loved clothes and finery. She persuaded Lasaraleen to help her escape by a small city-wall door near the palace, and they were on the way to it when they accidentally overheard Rabadash planning to invade Narnia because Susan had escaped him.

Aravis and Shasta, with Bree and Hwin, finally met at the tombs and hurried across the great desert to warn Archenland, the country south of Narnia, which had to be overcome before one could go into Narnia by the land route. On their way to warn that Radabash and his army were coming, they were almost exhausted when a great lion showed up behind and scared the horses into headlong flight. The lion tore Aravis' shoulder with ten light scratches. They came to a hermit's hideaway and Shasta alone was sent forward to warn Archenland. He was very tired but went willingly.

Shasta discovered King Lune, who was out on a hunting trip, and the king mistook Shasta for his own son Corin. Warned, King Lune and his men rushed back to the castle, but Shasta's horse moved so slowly that Rabadash's men passed him on their way to attack. He went instead over another road unknown to him and was kept from danger by the lion. In southern Narnia he discovered King Edmund, Queen Lucy, Lord Peridan, and others on their way to aid King Lune. (King Peter was away in the north battling the giants there.) Among the company was Corin, King Lune's son for whom Shasta had been mistaken. Shasta and Corin were required, against their will because they wished to be in the battle, to trail the war procession into Archenland.

The Narnian party reached Archenland just as Rabadash's men were battering the castle door with a tree trunk. A hot fight ensued, watched over at the hermit's house through a magical spring that reflected the struggle. Rabadash's forces were completely overcome, and Shasta was discovered to be the twin brother of Corin — Shasta's name was really Cor.

Meantime Bree, the skeptic, back at the hermit's was proving how Aslan could not be a real lion when Aslan himself quietly jumped over the wall and rubbed himself against Bree and proved himself a "true Beast." Bree confessed himself a fool for disbelieving.

Cor's long wandering was explained as a result of a prophecy that he would some day save the kingdom when it was in great danger. He had done so and all could end happily.

When Rabadash, now captive, acted foolishly and no one could put down his bragging about how brave and strong he was, Aslan appeared and turned him into a donkey. When Rabadash went back to Tashbaan he was to become a man again but he must never go more than ten miles from Tashbaan or else he would again become a donkey and remain one.

Aravis and Shasta, who loved each other in spite of their disagreements, finally were married and after the death of King Lune became king and queen of that land. They had a son called Ram the Great, afterwards the most famous of all kings of Archenland. Bree and Hwin were happy to be back in wonderful Narnia.

The Last Battle

I have already explained that *The Magician's Nephew,* the sixth book in the Narnian series, is actually the account of the beginnings of Narnia, so we have now only to look at the events of *The Last Battle,* perhaps in one respect the most unusual children's book ever written, for in it we have the death of the principal characters.

The story begins with Shift, an ape living in the west of Narnia, persuading an ignorant donkey named Puzzle to wear a lion skin which they found in the river. The ape then made all the talking animals believe Puzzle to be Aslan, even though none of them really thought he talked or acted like the great lion. When King Tirian, last of the rulers of Narnia, heard that the talking trees were being cut for the Calormenes far to the south, he and Jewel the unicorn killed two Calormenes, then were sorry and gave themselves up. While they were captives, Tirian prayed to Aslan and asked that the children be sent. Because the Pevensies were now too old to return to Narnia, only Eustace Scrubb and Jill Pole were allowed to go. These two landed in Narnia just beside King Tirian, rescued him and Jewel, discovered the ape's evil plan, and even managed to get possession of Puzzle.

Farsight the Eagle came and reported that Cair Paravel had been overcome by Calormenes. Sadly, Tirian and the children decided to fight to the death. They returned to the scene of Shift's activities, a small stable on a hill where he had kept the donkey and, to make the Narnians think him the real Aslan, had displayed him for a few minutes nightly in the flickering light of a bonfire. The ape told the Narnians monstrous lies, yet with such cleverness that his firelight audience believed them. Then he invited anybody who wished to go into the stable and see Aslan face to face. By a prearranged plan Ginger, a cat favorable to Shift, went proud and confident through the stable door, yet came out completely terrified. The cat had unexpectedly come face to face not with Aslan but with Tash, an evil bird-headed god with four arms.

Now King Tirian and his friends rushed out and called upon all the Narnians to join them in battle against Shift. Some came over, especially the talking dogs, but the dwarfs, now refusing to believe either in Aslan or Shift, decided to trust only in themselves and fought both sides. Then the last battle began in earnest. Spears and arrows flew and swords flashed. Jewel the Unicorn killed many with his sharp horn. A Calormene dragged poor Jill away by the hair. The main object of the struggle was to force one's enemy through the stable door. Finally Tirian found himself fighting the chief Calormene leader and was able to wrestle him through the door. This man, whose name was Rishda Tarkaan, was promptly confronted by the terrible god Tash. "Thou hast called me into Narnia, Rishda Tarkaan," said Tash. "Here I am. What hast thou to say?" Rishda, terrified, failed to reply and was picked up and carried away by Tash, yet not before another voice, strong and calm, was heard, saying, "Begone, Monster, and take your lawful prey to your own place." It was the wonderful voice of Aslan himself.

When the hideous Tash had vanished, Tirian turned to see who had spoken and was thrilled as never before in his whole life to discover seven kings and queens before him with crowns on their heads and all dressed in glittering clothes. He was suddenly ashamed of his own dusty and sweaty garments, but when he looked at himself he found he was in fresh, clean clothing. The kings and queens turned out to be Peter, Edmund, Lucy, Digory, Polly, Eustace, and Jill.

Thereafter the children, gazing through the open doorway of the stable, saw with utter amazement the end of Narnia. Aslan called down the stars themselves, and he called all men and talking beasts and even the inhabitants of Archenland and Calormen. All those who on looking Aslan straight in the face hated and feared him turned aside from the door to disappear in a great black shadow, but the others who loved him came joyfully through the door. Among them were Jewel the Unicorn and others thought to be dead. Then the children learned that they had actually been in a great train wreck back in England and realized that they also were alive again after death.

Aslan called the children to go with him "further up and further in" and as they went along their joys increased as they saw the delectable land. They discovered that it was really still Narnia, yet more colorful, beautiful, and meaningful. Finally, they were allowed to look away westward and see many familiar views of England and even the railway accident which had marked the end of their lives on earth. Lucy and the others looked sad for a while for fear Aslan might send them away as he had done

135

before. Their hearts leaped up with ecstasy when Aslan told them they should never part from him again, that for them it was the morning and that all their adventures in Narnia had only been like the title page and that "now at last they were beginning Chapter One of the Great Story, which no one on earth has read: which goes on for ever: in which every chapter is better than the one before."

Concerning Lewis's Christian purpose in these stories there can be no possible doubt. They are the chronicles of Aslan as of Narnia. Yet there is seldom the sense of contrived situations for didactic purposes. Lewis's deep theological conviction that Aslan is not a tame lion is at the same time an aid to his fiction. Sometimes Aslan sports with the children and allows them to hide their faces in his golden mane, yet they never become merely familiar with him. There are no easy and slick explanations of Aslan's conduct. For instance, in *The Last Battle* we are never told why Aslan was not present to help the children and King Tirian when they were about to suffer defeat at the hand of their evil enemies. To a friend of mine who was deeply moved by Aslan's symbolism and wondered precisely why, Lewis wrote: "The reason why the Passion of Aslan sometimes moves people more than the real story in the Gospels is, I think, that it takes them off their guard. In reading the real story the fatal knowledge that one *ought* to feel in a certain way often inhibits the feeling."[5] To take people off their guard was of course Lewis's hope, not only in the children's stories but in all his Christian writing.

The first and last books of the series make most of the character of Aslan as Christ. In *The Lion, the Witch and the Wardrobe* the struggle is between Aslan and the evil witch Jadis who has brought everlasting winter upon Narnia. It is climaxed when Aslan, to fulfill a magic deeper than that known to the witch, allowed her and her abominable followers to slay him at

[5] Letter to Thomas Howard, who also tells me that Lewis's friend J. R. R. Tolkien thinks the Narnia books far too allegorical.

136

the Stone Table as recompense for the life of Edmund, a traitor. Jadis was unaware of a magic going back before the birth of time which declared that when a willing and perfect victim was slain in a traitor's stead, the Stone Table would crack in two and "Death itself would start working backwards." In *The Last Battle* it is Aslan who receives the children after their death, feeds them upon the most delicious fruit they have ever tasted, and leads them on to everlastingly more delightful adventures.

Other books in the series have also their Christian implications. In *The Silver Chair* Aslan lies between Jill and the sparkling water for which she thirsts. She asks him if he will promise not to do anything to her provided she comes toward him. Aslan says he will make no promise. When she replies that she is afraid to come, he tells her that she will else die of thirst. When she proposes to seek water elsewhere, he says there is no other. In the same story the underground episode is perhaps intended to indicate that though evil succeeds it is never quite able to take over completely. Though Prince Rilian was, by normal standards, insane twenty-three hours of the day, he was himself one hour. The suggestion is that a very little bit of genuine reality, with Aslan's help, is capable of clearing the air of the unreality which fools man most of the time. Even the wish of Eustace and Jill to play hooky from school coincides with Aslan's purpose for them as rescuers of the prince. "You would not have called to me unless I had been calling to you," he told them after they had "prayed" to visit Narnia.

In *The Magician's Nephew* Aslan sends Digory and Polly to an allegorical Garden of Eden where Jadis appears and proposes many good reasons why Digory should eat one of the delicious apples. It is interesting that in this instance Lewis allows Polly to remain outside the garden! Almost concomitant with the creation of Narnia by Aslan came evil in the form of Jadis who, it will be recalled, was brought into Narnia, even though unintentionally, by Digory and Polly. Various fine points of theology might be pressed for and against Lewis's teaching here, but I am sure he intended mainly to imply simply that evil is both very ancient and very real.

Within limitations, it is not hard to suppose that Peter's shield with the great red lion on it is the Christian armor, that Aslan's breath which brings greatness is like Christ's breath imparting the Holy Spirit, that Susan's magic horn is a symbol of prayer, and that the Noble Order of the Table is intended to suggest the Eucharist. The implication of the men who sit half alive at Aslan's sumptuously furnished table in *The Voyage of the Dawn Treader* is that there is plenty for those who will but eat.

Obedience to God is made very clear in *The Silver Chair*. Eustace and Jill were told by Aslan to follow to the letter his instructions unless they wished to fail. These instructions were to be repeated morning and evening and even if one awakened in the middle of the night. There is an old Christian saying that one should never forget in the darkness what has been taught him in the light, and Aslan so instructs Jill. "Here on the mountian I have spoken to you clearly: I will not often do so down in Narnia. Here on the mountain, the air is clear and your mind is clear; as you drop down into Narnia, the air will thicken. Take great care that it does not confuse your mind . . . . Remember the signs and believe the signs. Nothing else matters." Later on, when Eustace and Jill were in the very confusion against which Aslan had warned, it was Puddleglum who had to remind them, "There *are* no accidents. Our guide is Aslan."

And again it was Puddleglum who saved the day for them against the enchantment of the witch when by music, incense, and persuasive words she had brought them to think that their notion of reality was only a dream. A very great deal of Lewis's overall conviction about the nature of reality resides in Puddleglum's defiant speech to the witch: "Suppose we *have* only dreamed, or made up, all those things — trees and grass and sun and moon and stars and Aslan himself. Suppose we have. Then all I can say is that, in that case, the made-up things seem a good deal more important than the real ones. Suppose this black pit of a kingdom of yours *is* the only world. Well, it strikes me as a pretty poor one. And that's a funny thing, when you come to think of it. We're just babies making up a game, if you're right. But four babies playing a game can make a play-world which licks your real world hollow. That's why I'm going to stand by the play world. I'm on Aslan's side even if there isn't any Aslan to lead it. I'm going to live as like a Narnian as I can even if there isn't any Narnia."[6] The "myth" of Narnia, even if myth be taken simply as glorious falsehood, is in Puddleglum's opinion better than all of the witch's unreal real world. I hope I have made it clear, however, that Lewis does not at all look upon myth as falsehood.

Even *The Horse and His Boy,* which perhaps has the fewest Christian inferences of any book in the Narnia series, depicts Aslan often behind the scenes to bring about certain ends. I have mentioned also that in this book we find Aslan confronting the skeptic Bree at the very moment Bree insists there can be no Aslan and suggesting that Bree handle him and see that he is indeed a "true Beast." Like St. Thomas on a similar occasion, Bree confesses the foolishness of his former attitude.

There are some satiric and other implications beyond the Christian in the Narnia books. There is just a hint at the beginning of *The Last Battle* that Shift, the ape, hopes to set up a socialistic state in Narnia. Uncle Andrew's experimentation on guinea pigs is satirized in *The Magician's Nephew* and progressive education in *The Silver Chair.* There are psychological as well as Christian implications in the fact that dragonish thoughts turn Eustace into a dragon in *The Voyage of the Dawn Treader,* and there are Platonic overtones in the idea that earth was nothing more than a shadow-land to the glorious new Narnia.

Lewis manifests his usual realism even in these children's stories. There are numerous quarrels and backbitings among the characters, both human and animal, and not even conversion turns anybody into a goody-goody. There are indeed genuine doubters among those who have seen Narnia with their own eyes, such as Eustace at the beginning of *The Silver Chair,* and even though Eustace and Jill have been directly called by Aslan,

---

[6] Lewis's own last testimony was surprisingly similar to Puddleglum's. Toward the end of *Letters to Malcolm: Chiefly on Prayer* he says that even if the impossible supposition that God is dead were true, he would still wish to die on God's side.

they are so negligent of his instructions that they muff the first three of four signs he gave them for rescuing Prince Rilian. In *Prince Caspian* when the children are lost in the mountains and Lucy sees Aslan beckoning them in the right direction, she finds all of them, including Peter himself, of the opinion that Aslan is nowhere around. The battles of Narnia are often fierce, and the children help in slaying their enemies. Perhaps the most realistic touch in all the stories is Susan's failure to get into the new Narnia at the close of *The Last Battle*. When King Tirian discovered the seven glittering kings and queens inside the happy land, he asked about Susan. Peter answered shortly and gravely, "My sister Susan is no longer a friend of Narnia."

Each Narnian story has its own set of individualized characters, yet the reader will inevitably come upon a few favorites. For me the mouse Reepicheep is one, standing straight with his long crimson feather attached above his ear and his paw always resting on the hilt of his long sword, with his grave and courtly manners and his deep conviction that danger is something to meet head-on valiantly. Another is the marsh-wiggle Puddleglum, a tall and angular creature something like a man and something like a spider or frog. Not much to look at, and as completely pessimistic, on the surface at least, as Milne's Eeyore, he nevertheless proves a shrewd and faithful guide to Eustace and Jill. There is Jewel the creamy white Unicorn who, like Aslan himself, possesses grace, delicacy, and gentleness yet could be fierce and terrible in battle. There is the long-suffering and delightful donkey Puzzle who loved Aslan devotedly and who looked so splendid in the new Narnia that Lucy rushed forward to throw her arms around his neck and kiss his nose. There is the giant Rumblebuffin, courteous but, like most giants, not very clever; there are Trufflehunter the badger, old and kind, and his rash and sometimes bloodthirsty dwarfs Nikabrik and Trumpkin; there is Fenris Ulf, the fierce grey wolf who served as killer for the White Witch. There is Prince Rabadash, the impetuous Calormene who made himself so ridiculous that he became a by-word for stupidity.

One senses the pleasure Lewis must have had in his invention of creature and place names. Few can approach the vast accomplishment of Lewis's friend J. R. R. Tolkien in this regard, but Lewis has no mean array of them himself. In both Lewis's and Tolkien's naming of things we find a singular combination of philological astuteness and creative imagination, and, in Lewis in particular, a love of nature which gives him insight into good onomatopoeic names also. Hence we are never quite out of hearing of such an array of characters and places as Glimfeather the owl, Moonwood the hare, Mr. Tumnus the faun, Sallowpad the raven, Pattertwig the squirrel, Rogin and Poggin the dwarfs, Lord Octesian and Queen Prunaprismia, the Tisroc and Terebinthia and Anvard and Ramandu and Glenstorm and Puddleglum.

Narnia is indeed a world in itself — again not so deep and profound a cosmos as that created by Tolkien, yet with few exceptions whole and consistent. In one respect Lewis's Narnia may be more properly called a cosmos, for he more than Tolkien takes account of our world, the world of Narnia, and the heavens themselves. Tolkien's is a neater world, more consistent and logical, but Lewis's contains paradox and in that sense is firmer. As one might expect, Lewis's Narnia is essentially original. Perhaps inevitably there are parallels in it reminding one of other writers, such as the Alice-like opening of *The Lion, the Witch and the Wardrobe,* the Kafka touch in Eustace's experience as a dragon, or the Pooh-like bears. The unseen hands of the Duffers serving food are like similar hands in *Gulliver's Travels,* and the voyage made by the *Dawn Treader* is a little like the voyage of Odysseus. In *The Magician's Nephew* the scene in which swelling humps of earth sprouted living animals is much like similar happenings in Macdonald's *Lilith.* Lewis's Christian theme is ancient, fixed, and orthodox. His events, on the other hand, are created from the rich world of fantasy. It is no small accomplishment to merge these two effectively.

Narnia is less a place divided into good and bad-acting creatures than those with a "germ" of goodness or badness developing towards fulfillment. Jadis the White Witch had so far committed herself to evil that she dared not come within a hundred miles of the tree planted in Narnia because, as Aslan told the Narnians, "its smell, which is joy and life and health to you, is death and horror and despair to her." Indeed, Jadis had so long regarded people simply as pawns for her own evil ends that she grew pale and powerless in a quiet place. She could comprehend nothing apart from her own selfishness.

The most striking illustration of this law of growth toward values basically precious is Emeth the Calormene who was admitted to the new Narnia even though he had always been a worshipper of Tash and hated the name of Aslan. Yet all his life Emeth had also hated hypocrisy and evil. He was so intent upon knowing the reality of Tash that he determined to go into the stable and face him even though Tash should slay him for the attempt. Once inside, he saw the glory of the place and later came upon Aslan, before whom he fell down in fear and a new obedience and confession that all his days he had worshipped Tash. Aslan said to him, "All the service thou hast done to Tash, I account as service done to me . . . . I take to me the services which thou hast done to him, for I and he are of such different kinds that no service which is vile can be done to me, and none which is not vile can be done to him. Therefore if any man swear by Tash and keep his oath for the oath's sake, it is by me that he has truly sworn, though he know it not, and it is I who reward him. And if any man do a cruelty in my name, then, though he says the name Aslan, it is Tash whom he serves and by Tash his deed is accepted . . . unless thy desire had been for me thou wouldst not have sought so long and so truly. For all find what they truly seek."[7] After this Aslan breathed upon Emeth and took away his trembling, and also told him to go farther in and higher up.

[7] In *That Hideous Strength* when Jane answered Ransom that she knew nothing of Maleldil but was willing to place herself in obedience to Ransom, he told her, "It is enough for the present. This is the courtesy of Deep Heaven: that when you mean well, He always takes you to have meant better than you know."

This account of Emeth is told to illustrate Lewis's deep-seated conviction of a great basic right and wrong in the cosmos rather than that there are many roads leading to Christ. Two possible explanations may be made of Emeth's experience. One is that he was a pagan living fully up to the only truth he knew and all his life eagerly searching for the Good. Lewis himself reminds us elsewhere that the word Emeth means "truth," "intrinsic validity, rock-bottom reality," something rooted in God's own nature. He cites the instance of the Pharaoh Amenhotep IV, who out of a seemingly clear sky "nearly tore Egypt into shreds" in his conviction that, contrary to all previous Egyptian belief, there was a single God who ought to be worshipped. "His Monotheism appears to have been of an extremely pure and conceptual kind." Lewis obviously intended Emeth in the Narnian story to be this sort of individual, the kind who "shall come from the east and the west and sit down in the kingdom." In *Surprised by Joy* Lewis says, "You must not do, you must not even try to do, the will of the Father unless you are prepared to 'know of the doctrine.'" To reconcile the account of Emeth with Lewis's customary teaching that Christ is the only way to salvation it might be pointed out that the doorway in *The Last Battle* is not altogether the symbol of salvation. Indeed an unbelieving pagan and many cynical dwarfs managed to get on the other side of it, as did Tash himself. Perhaps the door is to be looked upon as similar to the purlieus of heaven in *The Great Divorce,* where a great many people caught glimpses of the glory within and yet refused to enter. The moment Emeth saw Aslan he fell down before him for blessing.

Emeth contrasts with Rishda Tarkaan who had called upon Tash and tried selfishly to use him even though he did not believe in him. Beside Emeth, Rishda was a genuine unbeliever, as also were the dwarfs who, even inside the door, had so completely made a prison of their own minds that they mistook Aslan's glorious feast for hay and turnips and leaves of cabbage and Aslan's wine in golden goblets for dirty water out of a stable trough. Emeth was a believer in a hierarchy with Absolute Goodness at its pinnacle; Rishda and the dwarfs were real "unbelievers."

As everywhere else in Lewis, the Narnian stories contain the motif of joy and longing, both joy-in-longing and the greater joy-in-possessing. There is a good deal of romping and joking both among the people and animals, yet there is a deeper happiness and wonder which is "too good to waste on jokes." The latter is far the more prominent sort of joy depicted. Always there is incipiently the far look toward Aslan's land and at times that land comes into view, as in the end of *The Voyage of the Dawn Treader* when Reepicheep quivers with happiness before his final departure for its celestial mountains. The Unicorn summed up the feelings of the others beyond the stable door in *The Last Battle* when he stamped his right fore-hoof on the ground, neighed, and cried out: "I have come home at last! This is my real country! I belong here. This is the land I have been looking for all my life, though I never knew it till now. The reason why we loved the old Narnia is that it sometimes looked a little like this." Yet Aslan assured them there were better things ahead, higher up and farther in where everything gets bigger and the inside is larger than the outside. Corbin S. Carnell reminds us of the abundance of sensuous pleasures depicted by Lewis, in contrast with what he describes as the "tortured misgivings and inability to enjoy" in T. S. Eliot's work.[8] Kathleen Nott castigates Lewis for his failure to stress the joys of salvation.[9] Such a preposterous claim leaves open no possibility but that Miss Nott has failed to read Lewis.

A dominant idea in these stories is that of an earlier time when things were more a harmony and unity. The coming of the White Witch to Narnia separated it into two elements and forced the good element into hiding in the deep woods. By the time of King Miraz only a few people knew of its existence at all, and Prince Caspian was shocked when he accidentally came upon talking animals, since it was supposed they no longer existed. Always there is the notion of an older and better world, and

[8] "The Dialectic of Desire: C. S. Lewis' Interpretation of *Sehnsucht*," a doctoral dissertation at the University of Florida, p. 158.
[9] *The Emperor's Clothes*, p. 297.

very often that world in Lewis is simply the Garden of Eden. On the other hand, there is not only the Eden that was but also the Eden to come, the new Narnia of *The Last Battle*.

Lewis suggests the idea that one of the functions of the natural world may be to furnish symbols for the spiritual experience of man. It is of course out of the natural world that the substance, though not necessarily the meaning, of myth arises. Talking trees in mythology are possible because there are real trees. Giants are possible because we know some men to be very large. Space is a symbol of God in its hugeness and matter is like God in having energy. But Lewis makes it very clear that the symbol is less than the reality symbolized.

Excellent as are the Narnian stories, I feel that they are not entirely without defects. There are minor errors, as when Digory's last name is spelled both Kirk and Kirke, Calormen is spelled Kalormen, and Ettinsmore called Ettinsmuir. More serious are some lapses in structural unity such as the unmotivated appearance of the underwater people toward the end of *The Voyage of the Dawn Treader* and the uncharacteristic conversation of the Tarkeena Lasaraleen in *The Horse and His Boy*. One wonders where Lasaraleen learned to say, "My dear, how perfectly thrilling. I'm dying to hear all about it. Darling, you're sitting on my dress" in a court where others speak like Rabadash, "I desire and propose, O my father, that you immediately call out your invincible armies and invade the thrice-accursed land of Narnia and waste it with fire and sword and add it to your illimitable empire." Even though one conversation is private and the other court, Lasaraleen's giddy language strikes a pretty incongruous note in the class-conscious society of Tashbaan. I should adversely criticize the appearance of Father Christmas in *The Lion, the Witch and the Wardrobe* as being also incongruous. Likewise it seems to be a lapse in good judgment for Lewis to make Aslan the trickster who in *The Horse and His Boy* changes Rabadash into an ass.

Yet the defects are as nothing compared to the excellencies. My own judgment is that *The Lion, the Witch and the Wardrobe*

145

is the best of the stories and I should put *The Magician's Nephew* perhaps next in order. I like *The Last Battle* greatly for its meaning, particularly the last six chapters, though I feel that as story it has some defects. The involvements of Tash and the Calormene soldier inside the stable door seem especially difficult for a children's book. I think I should put *The Horse and His Boy* at the bottom of my list so far as any organic Christian implication is concerned. Yet I have read and re-read all of the Narnian series with increasing pleasure and much profit.

VI

PSALMS, MIRACLES, AND ORTHODOXY

IN THIS CHAPTER I SHOULD LIKE TO OUTLINE SOME OF C. S. Lewis's theological beliefs, particularly as they are expressed in *Reflections on the Psalms, Miracles, Mere Christianity,* and *Letters to Malcolm: Chiefly on Prayer.* It is not correct to say that Lewis has a "theology" if by that term is meant a systematic, all-embracing complex like that of John Calvin or Karl Barth. He repeatedly declared that he was not a theologian. Perhaps his chief aim in attempting to retain amateur status is that he may be "a man talking to men." Yet any man who writes a score or more of books on Christian topics inevitably will possess, in some sense, a theology. Perhaps the big difference between him and the "professional" theologian is less abstraction and more particular instance and creativity. I am especially interested in this chapter in Lewis's view of the Scripture itself as the source of theological truth.

One of the important ideas in *Reflections on the Psalms* is that the Bible itself has a creative rather than an abstractive quality. The Psalms are poems rather than doctrinal treatises or even sermons. The Bible is literature. Of course one must not read it merely as literature, else he will miss the very thing it is about. On the other hand, unless such parts as the Psalms are read as poetry "we shall miss what is in them and think we see what is not." The Psalms, he continues, are great poetry — some, such as Psalms 18 and 19, perfect poetry. At the same time the Bible is made up of a great variety of elements some

147

of which may seem inconsequential, crabbed, practical, or rhapsodic.

Lewis starts with those elements in the Psalms which trouble him. The first is the cry on the part of the Hebrews for judgment, a thing quite different from the Christian's fear of judgment. In the first case the Jew sees himself as the plaintiff while in the second the Christian is the defendant. Lewis is confident that the Christian's cry for mercy is more profound, since the Christian sees infinite purity as the standard against which he will be judged. The Jews failed properly to distinguish the difference between the belief that one is in the right and the belief that one is righteous. Because no man is righteous, this second conviction is always a delusion.

The self-righteous Psalms, however, are not nearly so troublesome for a modern reader, says Lewis, as the vindictive or cursing Psalms. Occasionally indeed we come upon a verse that is nothing short of devilish, as where the Psalmist asks the Lord to slay his enemies or that extreme instance in which a blessing is offered to anyone who will crush a Babylonian baby against the pavement. Such maledictions, declares Lewis, are sinful and when seen as such rather than minimized in any way, will suggest to the Christian reader similar sins in his own life, even if such sins are more cleverly disguised. They cannot be excused, the Jews, since they had plenty of Scripture against vengeance and grudges, in fact plenty of teaching very similar to that of Christ's. The truth is that Christ's teaching was anticipated by all teachers of truth, even some outside Judaism. This, Lewis insists, is exactly what should be expected as a result of that Light which has lighted every man from the beginning. All truth is from God.

The Hebrews seem to have been even more vitriolic than their Pagan neighbors. Lewis thinks this might be based on the principle of "the higher the more in danger," that is, a man with greatness of soul and an abiding conception of right and wrong is more likely to show fanaticism than a smaller man who is not so much above temptation as below it. Under some circumstances the absence of indignation may be a worse sign than indignation itself. The very elevation of religion is bound to make a religious bad man the worst sort of bad man. Satan himself was once an angel in heaven. Shocking as the cursing Psalms may be, it is clear that their composers were men neither morally indifferent nor willing, like some men today, to reduce wickedness to a neurosis.

Lewis next turns to the strange lack of much Old Testament discussion about a future life, made even odder by the fact that neighboring nations to the Jews were often overwhelmingly taken up with it. God may have needed to teach the Jews that secondary things ought never to replace primary ones, that He and not mere safety of heaven is paramount. The hope of heaven apart from one's love of God is always mischievous. On the other hand, it may have been God's plan to postpone until later in Israel's history the full revelation of truth about the future life. Lewis cites his own experience as something of a possible parallel; he had been a Christian for a whole year before any belief in a future life was given him.

With these difficulties out of the way, Lewis turns to the great positives of the Psalms. First is the Jew's robust, virile, spontaneous, and mirthful delight in God, something quite different from the routine of worship most people now experience. The Jews often felt a genuine longing for the mere presence of God that shames Christians. They had an "appetite" for God and did not let a false sense of good manners preclude their enjoyment of Him. They were ravished by their love of God's law, which they believed to be firmly rooted in His nature and as real as trees and clouds.

Lewis reminds us that the ancient Jews were not merchants and financiers at all but farmers and shepherds. Though their poetry says little about landscape, it does give us weather "enjoyed almost as a vegetable might be supposed to enjoy it": "Thou art good to the earth . . . thou waterest her furrows . . . thou makest it soft with the drops of rain . . . the little hills shall rejoice on every side . . . the valleys shall stand so thick with corn that they shall laugh and sing." The Jews understood better than their neighbors, and perhaps we also, a pristine doctrine of God as creator of nature, one that at once empties nature of anything like a

149

Pantheistic divinity and at the same time makes her a symbol or manifestation of the Divine.

Lewis confesses that when he first became a Christian he was disturbed by the continuous command in the Psalms to praise God. It sounded as if God were saying, "What I most want is to be told that I am good and great." Even the very quantity of the praise seemed important to the Psalmists. Then he discovered the principle that praise is simply the sign of healthy understanding. To ascribe praise to whatever is truly praiseworthy reflects the character of both the thing praised and the one who praises. Praise likewise completes enjoyment, whether of God or a sunset or one's friend.

Lewis completes his reflections by three chapters devoted to what he calls "second meanings," that is, prophetic or allegorical meanings, and the doctrine of Scriptural inspiration. Since both these topics are in Lewis's view related to myth, I should like to give special attention to them.

As to prophecy or allegory, he cites the famous passage from Virgil which describes a virgin, a golden age beginning, and a child sent down from heaven, also Plato's discussion of the fate of a perfect man in a wicked world, and says that a Christian reading either of these two non-Christian accounts will be struck by their similarity to the Biblical accounts. Now Lewis holds that the similarity in Virgil was doubtless accidental but in Plato only partially so. Plato perhaps had in mind the recent death of his teacher Socrates, a great man who died at the hands of people who feared and despised justice. It was not mere luck but rather great wisdom which enabled Plato to extrapolate from the experience of Socrates the vision of the perfect man who dies as a sacrifice to evil, even though Plato probably had no intuition that such an instance would ever become history.

Mythology is replete with the dying god, with death and rebirth, and the idea that man must undergo death if he would truly live. The resemblance between such myths and Christian truth has the same relation as the sun and its reflection in a pond. It is not the same thing but neither is it a wholly different thing. The kernel of wheat is indeed, as Christ said, "re-

150

born" after "death." Because God made wheat thus, it should occasion no total surprise if a Pagan sees there a symbol and puts it into the form of a myth. Because, like all men, the Pagans suffered longing for Joy, even when they were unable to identify its source, they incorporated their unsteady conceptions into myths and, because no myth was ever quite equivalent to the longing, created more and more myths. Myth arises from "gleams of celestial strength and beauty falling on a jungle of filth and imbecility." A "pressure from God" lay upon the Pagan myth-makers. Yet they would have been as surprised, as anyone else if they had learned that they were talking a better thing than they ever dreamed.

If Pagan sources did so well, what of Sacred ones? We have two excellent reasons, says Lewis, for accepting the truth of the Biblical second meanings. One is that they are holy and inspired, the other that our Lord Himself taught it and indeed claimed to *be* the second meaning of many Old Testament passages such as Isaiah 53, the Sufferer in Psalm 22, the King in Psalms 2 and 72, and the Incarnation in Psalm 45. Lewis confesses that though he once believed the interpretation of the Bridegroom as Christ in the Song of Songs was "frigid and far-fetched," he later began to discover that even in this instance there might be second meanings that are not arbitrary and meanings indeed that spring from depths one would not suspect.

As to the inspiration of the Bible, he does not consider the Old Testament as "the Word of God" if by that we mean that each passage, in itself, gives us impeccable science or history. Rather, the Old Testament "carries" the Word of God, and we should use it not as "an encyclopedia or an encyclical" but "by steeping ourselves in its tone or temper and so learning its overall message." He cites St. Jerome's remark that Moses described the creation "after the manner of a popular poet" and Calvin's doubt whether Job were actual history as his own views also. The fact that miracles are recorded in the Old Testament has nothing to do with his view on inspiration. Belief in God includes belief in His supernatural powers.

151

Lewis is even willing to accept the Genesis account of creation as derived from, though a great improvement upon, earlier Semitic stories which were Pagan and mythical — provided "derived from" is interpreted to mean that the re-tellers were themselves guided by God. And so with the whole of the Old Testament. It consists of the same kind of material, says Lewis, as any other literature, yet "taken into the service of God's word." God of course does not condone the sin revealed in the cursing Psalms but causes His word to go forth even through the written account of sin and the sinner who wrote it. We must even suppose that the canonizing and the work of redactors and editors is under some kind of "Divine pressure."

One might be at first inclined, says Lewis, to think that God made a mistake in giving us such a Bible rather than a rigorously systematic statement of His truth in a form as unrefracted as that of the multiplication table. But even the teaching of Christ, "in which there is no imperfection," does not come to us in that manner and is not a thing for the intellect alone but rather something for the whole man. Understanding the true meaning of Christ is not learning a "subject" but rather "steeping ourselves in a Personality, acquiring a new outlook and temper, breathing a new atmosphere, suffering Him, in His own way, to rebuild in us the defaced image of Himself."

The seeming imperfection in the way the Bible is composed may be an illusion. "It may repel one use in order that we may be forced to use it in another way — to find the Word in it, not without repeated and leisurely reading nor without discriminations made by our conscience and our critical faculties, to re-live, while we read, the whole Jewish experience of God's gradual and graded self-revelation, to feel the very contentions between the Word and the human material through which it works. . . . Certainly it seems to me that from having had to reach what is really the Voice of God in the cursing Psalms through all the horrible distortions of the human medium, I have gained something I might not have gained from a flawless, ethical exposition." Even the "nihilism" of Ecclesiastes with its "clear, cold picture of man's life without God" is a part of God's Word.

In view of the importance of Scriptural inspiration to many Christians, I take the liberty of submitting here an additional comment which Professor Lewis was kind enough to send me. "I enclose what, at such short notice, I feel able to say on this question. If it is at all likely to upset anyone, throw it in the waste paper basket. Remember too that it is pretty tentative, much less an attempt to establish a view than a statement of the issue on which, whether rightly or wrongly, I have come to work. To me the curious thing is that neither in my own Bible-reading nor in my religious life as a whole does the question *in fact* ever assume that importance which it always gets in theological controversy. The difference between reading the story of Ruth and that of Antigone — both first class as literature — is to me unmistakable and even overwhelming. But the question 'Is Ruth historical?' (I've no reason to suppose it is *not*) doesn't really seem to arise till afterwards. It can still act on me as the Word of God if it weren't, so far as I can see. All Holy Scripture is written for our learning. But learning *of what?* I should have thought the value of some things (e.g., the Resurrection) depended on whether they really happened, but the value of others (e.g., the fate of Lot's wife) hardly at all. And the ones whose historicity matters are, as God's will, those where it is plain."

The notes enclosed with this letter are as follows: "Whatever view we hold on the divine authority of Scripture must make room for the following facts: 1. The distinction which St. Paul makes in I Corinthians 7, verses 10 and 12. 2. The apparent inconsistencies between the genealogies in Matthew 1 and Luke 3; between the accounts of the death of Judas in Matthew 27:5 and Acts 1:18-19. 3. St. Luke's own account of how he obtained his matter (1:1-4). 4. The universally admitted unhistoricity (I do not say, of course, falsity) of at least some narratives in Scripture (the parables), which may well extend also to Jonah and Job. 5. If every good and perfect gift comes from the Father of Lights then all true and edifying writings, whether in Scripture or not, must be *in some sense* inspired. 6. John 11:

153

49-52. Inspiration may operate in a wicked man without his knowing it, and he can then utter the untruth he intends (propriety of making an innocent man a political scapegoat) *as well as* the truth he does not intend (the divine sacrifice). It seems to me that 2 and 4 rule out the view that every statement in Scripture must be *historical* truth. And 1, 3, 5, and 6 rule out the view that inspiration is a single thing in the sense that, if present at all, it is always present in the same mode and the same degree; therefore, I think, rules out the view that any one passage taken in isolation can be assumed to be inerrant in exactly the same sense as any other: e.g., that the numbers of Old Testament armies (which in view of the size of the country, if true, involves continuous miracle) are statistically correct because the story of the resurrection is historically correct. That the over-all operation of Scripture is to convey God's Word to the reader (he also needs His inspiration) who reads it in the right spirit, I fully believe. That it *also* gives true answers to all the questions (often religiously irrelevant) which he might ask, I don't. The very *kind* of truth we are often demanding was, in my opinion, never even envisaged by the ancients."[1]

To Lewis the story of creation in Genesis is mythical, but that does not mean it is untrue. It means rather that it is truer than history itself. The account of Adam and Eve, God and an apple symbolizes clearly a time long ago when catastrophe fell upon mankind. "For all I can see," says Lewis, "it might have concerned the literal eating of a fruit, but the question is of no consequence." Indeed, one might ask whether man and history are not actually as mysterious as myth. The great historians are quite agreed that to state the *facts* of history may be to leave out its essence, since history is made up both of objective, overt actions and also of the joys, agonies, and deep motives of the human soul. Christianity is the Christian creed, but it is also the glorious experience of God in the heart of a believer. We must not think we have a greater thing when we accept the "hypostatised abstract nouns" of a creed as more real than the

[1] Letter dated May 7, 1959.

myth which incorporates them and Reality itself. Melville once remarked that the true places are never down on any map. A myth is indeed to be defined by its very power to convey essence rather than outward fact, reality rather than semblance, the genuine rather than the accidental. It is the difference between the factual announcement of a wedding and the ineluctable joys actually incorporated in the event. Corbin S. Carnell says that for Lewis "the great myths of the Bible as well as of pagan literature refer not to the non-historical but rather to the non-describable. The historical correlative for something like the Genesis account of the creation and fall of man may be disputed. But the theological validity of the myth rests on its uniqueness as an account of real creation (out of nothing), on its psychological insight into the rebellious will of man, and on its clear statement that man has a special dignity by virtue of his being made in God's 'image.' "[2] The historical correlative is less significant than the thing it signifies. All facts are misleading in proportion to their divergence from Eternal Fact.

Perhaps Marjorie E. Wright has stated it correctly when she says that for Lewis and certain other writers Christianity itself is the great central historical embodiment of myth. "It is the archetypal myth of which all others are more or less distorted images."[3] Christ is the great Reality which makes every other reality a jarring note and cracked vessel. The trouble is, says Lewis, that we are so inveterately given to factualizing Christian truth it is practically impossible for us to hear God when He says that one day he will give us the Morning Star and cause us to put on the splendor of the sun. It is when we begin to assent to such Scripture that "we may surmise that both the ancient myths and the modern poetry, so false as history, may be very near the truth as prophecy. At present we are on the outside of the world, the wrong side of the door. We discern the freshness

2 "The Dialectic of Desire: C. S. Lewis' Interpretation of *Sehnsucht*," p. 124.

3 "The Cosmic Kingdom of Myth," p.141.

and purity of morning, but they do not make us fresh and pure. We cannot mingle with the splendours we see. But all the leaves of the New Testament are rustling with the rumour that it will not always be so. Some day, God willing, we shall get *in*." In *The Pilgrim's Regress* John was troubled about Wisdom's remark that because no man could really come where he had come, his adventures were only figurative, but at that moment a Voice spoke to John saying: "Child, if you will, it *is* mythology. It is but truth, not fact: an image, not the very real. But then it is My mythology. The words of Wisdom are also myth and metaphor: but since they do not know themselves for what they are, in them the hidden myth is master, where it should be servant: and it is but of man's inventing. But this is My inventing, this is the veil under which I have chosen to appear even from the first until now. For this end I made your senses and for this end your imagination, that you might see my face and live." Thus it is clear that for Lewis myth, so far from being falsehood, is the best means of embodying those ultimates that transcend fact.

Only once did myth ever become fact and that was when the Word became flesh, when God became man. "This is not 'a religion', nor 'a philosophy'. It is the summing up and actuality of them all."

It would be a bad mistake to infer from what has been said in the last few pages that Lewis regarded the Bible as simply another good book. He repeatedly calls it "Holy Scripture," assures us that it bears the authority of God, sharply distinguishes even between the canon and the apocrypha, presses the historical reliability of the New Testament in particular, and often assures us that we must "go back to our Bibles," even to the very words. The Biblical account, says he, often turns out to be more accurate than our lengthy theological interpretations of it. It is all right to leave the words of the Bible for a moment to make some point clear. "But you must always go back. Naturally God knows how to describe Himself much better than we know how to describe Him."[4]

Doctrinally, Lewis accepted the Nicene, Athanasian, and Apostles' creeds. He was never failing in his opposition to theological "modernism." Some of his most acerose satire is employed against it in both his fiction and expository works. It is as ridiculous, he declares, to believe that the earth is flat as to believe in the watered-down popular theology of modern England. In *The Screwtape Letters* a major employment of hell itself is in encouraging theologians to create a new "historical Jesus" in each generation. He repeatedly insists that, contrary to the opinion of many modern theologians, it was less St. Paul than Christ who taught the terrors of hell and other "fierce" doctrines rather than sweetness and vapid love.[5] Lewis hated the depiction of Christ in feminine modes. I have pointed out that in the Narnian stories Aslan is always pictured as more than a tame lion. God is not someone to be bargained with but obeyed. Christ is Deity Himself, the Creator, coexistent with the Father, yet also His only-begotten Son, the Penalty of the Law, Prince of the universe, the "Eternal Fact, Father of all facthood," the Everlasting and Supreme Reality, perfect God and perfect Man, the best of all moral teachers but not merely such, the forgiver of sins and the only Savior who gave His life for man's ransom and eternal health.[6]

Though Lewis denied the doctrine of total depravity on the grounds that if man were totally depraved he should not know it and because man has the idea of good, the denial is more nearly theoretical than actual in his works. Everywhere we find him representing man as a horror to God and a "miserable offender."

[4] Does this sentence contradict Lewis's charges against some of the vengeful Psalmists?

[5] It occurs to me that, following the same analogy, Lewis might well have controverted the idea of a vengeful deity in the Old Testament by showing how often the Psalms speak of His mercy.

[6] "Most of my books are evangelistic," he says. "Rejoinder to Dr. Pittenger," *Christian Century*, November 26, 1958.

In "Religion and Rocketry"[7] he says that non-Christians often suppose that the Incarnation implies some special merit in humanity but that it implies "just the reverse: a particular demerit and depravity" because "no creature that deserved Redemption would need to be redeemed . . . . Christ died for men precisely because men are *not* worth dying for." In this essay Lewis contemplates space travel as a possible major catastrophe for mankind and urges men to go on record now against planned exploitation of other worlds and even the unhappy "gun and gospel" aspect of some missionary work.

The most vivid picture of what it means to be saved — and Lewis does not hesitate to use this word — is the transformation of Eustace from a dragon back into a person in *The Voyage of the Dawn Treader.* Eustace tells how he remembered that a dragon might be able to cast its skin like a snake and began to work on himself. At first the scales alone came off but as he went deeper he found his whole skin starting to peel off and finally was able to step right out of it altogether. This is the point at which a less orthodox writer might stop, but not Lewis. Eustace started to wash himself but when he put his foot into the water he saw that it was as hard and rough and scaly as it had been before. So he began again to scratch and finally peeled off another entire dragon skin. But once again he found under it another. At this point Aslan said, "You will have to let me undress you." Though Eustace was deathly afraid of Aslan's claws, he lay down before him. His fears were justified, for the very first tear made by Aslan was so deep he felt it had gone clear down to his heart. When the skin was at last off, Eustace discovered it "ever so much thicker, and darker, and more knobbly looking than the others had been." Afterwards Aslan bathed him and dressed him in new clothes, the symbolism of which is clear enough.

In respect to the Church, Lewis teaches that it has no beauty except that given it by Christ and that its primary purpose is to draw men to Him, "the true Cure." The Christian's vocation,

[7] In *The World's Last Night.*

however, is not mainly to spread Christianity but rather to love Christ. The Christian is not so much to follow rules as to possess a Person and to wait upon the Holy Spirit for guidance. The Christian is not called to religion or even good works but to holiness before God. Christianity is not a "safe" vocation, for Christ is to be followed at all hazards.

Lewis believed that prayer must include confession and penitence, adoration, and fellowship with God as well as petition. "Prayer," he says, "is either a sheer illusion or a personal contact between embryonic, incomplete persons (ourselves) and the utterly concrete Person." He believed that where Christianity and other religions differ, Christianity is correct. He held that conversion is necessary and that heaven and hell are final.

If in some of his beliefs Lewis stands somewhat to the left of orthodoxy, there are others in which he moves toward the right, at least as orthodoxy is normally practiced by most Christians. For instance, the speaking in tongues at Pentecost is not only accepted by Lewis but explained in an ingenious manner that is worth describing. The holy phenomenon of talking in tongues bears the same relationship to the gibberish sometimes taken for it as a miraculous event to a natural one. Looking from below, one will always suppose a thing to be "nothing but" or "merely" this or that. The natural to which one is accustomed will so fill the eye that the supernatural does not appear. One sees clearly the facts but not their meaning. But from above one can see both the fact and the meaning, the supernatural and the natural. The supernatural must be transposed if sinful man is to have any notion of it, yet the transposition is bound to be like that of a man required to translate from a language of twenty-two vowels into one of only five vowels — he must give each character more than one value. Hence St. Paul's admonition that spiritual things must be discerned not naturally but spiritually.

Again, Lewis believes firmly in prayer for the sick. I think he is talking about Mrs. Lewis when he tells of a woman suffering from incurable cancer who was apparently healed by the laying on of hands and prayer. Lewis defends the proposition that the devil is alive and active, and he goes further than most of us in his belief concerning the reality and work of angels. He believes one enters heaven immediately at death. He thinks the Bible teaches clearly the Second Coming of Christ, and he thinks this may be the next great event in history. Generally Lewis stands with St. Paul in upholding the man as head of the wife, though he does not forget the rest of St. Paul's analogy. Despite his conception that the early part of Genesis is mythical (in the sense I have described), Lewis's frequent discussions of the Garden of Eden make it apparent that it means a hundred times more to him as myth than it does to most Christians as history. And we can say also that Lewis's God is *alive,* not static and not in the least hazy and far away. Lewis is set apart from most Christians, says Chad Walsh, by the "vividness of the gold in his religious imagination."[8]

Also Lewis's theological world staunchly admits the possibility of miracles.

Miracles

Different from the meditative and devotional nature of *Reflections on the Psalms,* the book called *Miracles* is closely reasoned. It consists of three parts plus an epilogue and two very interesting appendices. The first seven chapters, preliminary to the main theme, describe two basic types of thought about the universe. One is that of the Naturalist, the man who believes that nature is "the whole show" and that nothing else exists. He thinks of nature as being like a pond of an infinite depth with nothing but water. The other is the Supernaturalist, who believes that one Thing exists outside time and space and has produced nature. He believes that the pond is not merely water forever but has a bottom — mud, earth, rock, and finally the whole bulk of earth itself.

The Naturalist believes that nothing exists beyond some great process or "becoming," while the Supernaturalist believes nature may be only one "system" or choice among possibilities chosen

8 *C. S. Lewis: Apostle to the Skeptics,* p. 107.

by some Primary Thing. If Naturalism is true, then miracles are impossible, yet if Supernaturalism is true, it is still possible to inquire whether God does in fact perform miracles. But Naturalism contains a great self-contradition; it assumes that the mind itself is also "nature" and hence irrational. It is nonsense when one uses the human mind to prove the irrationality of the human mind. "All arguments about the validity of thought make a tacit, and illegitimate, exception in favor of the bit of thought you are doing at that moment." Lewis insists that reason exists on its own and that nature is powerless to produce it. Nature can only "keep on keeping on."

Naturalism is also faced with an insurmountable problem in the "oughtness" of things. If nature is all, then man's conscience is also a product of nature and there is no logical place for the notion that a man ought to die for his country or practice any other moral action. Contrariwise, Lewis holds that the practices of conscience are a product of man's reason derived from a greater Moral Wisdom which exists absolutely and could not possibly arise out of a theory which supposes blind nature as the basis of life and thought. In fact, human rationality is itself a miracle.

Lewis then proceeds to his main theme and begins with an instance of what he calls chronological snobbery, that is, the idea that people in older times could believe in miracles because they were unacquainted with the laws of nature. Joseph, he points out, was fully as wise as any modern gynaecologist on the main point of Mary's situation — that a virgin birth is contrary to nature. In finally accepting the situation as a miracle, Joseph was affirming not only the miracle but, equally, the law of nature itself as it applies to childbirth. Joseph is by no means an example of a naive or primitive ignoramus but rather of a realist whose head was as hard as anybody's so far as the regularity of nature is concerned. He saw the exception in Mary's case only because he had a pristine conviction about the rule. Believing in miracles does not at all mean any hazy notion about the regular operation of the laws of nature but rather the opposite.

The Naturalist makes the mistake of taking a partial system, that is, nature, for the whole. He is without a sense of what D. E. Harding calls "elsewhereness."[9] The Supernaturalist simply has a larger system in which a supernatural Cause brings about a result that interlocks with natural law originating from the same Cause.[10] A child supernaturally conceived is born in nine months like any other baby, and for the Christian the supernatural and natural are bound into a single harmony. In the very act of "violating" nature miracles assert a deeper and greater unity than that of nature by itself.

Lewis says that at one time he despised the notion of nature as something that God had "made." He wanted nature to exist on its own rather than as a backdrop to the play or as a moral symbol. But he eventually discovered that this autonomy led to opposite attitudes toward nature — one man could call it cruel and another benevolent and thus eventuate in reducing the meaning of nature to an inner attitude. He concluded also that to believe God had created nature meant to give nature a greater reality still, to see nature not as an absolute but one of God's "creatures" with her good and bad points like those of the dishonest grocer who is kind to his wife. You get the same "flavor" both in nature's excellences and her corruptions. Nature, like the groceryman, needs redemption, though of course not in the same manner.

Next Lewis tackles what he regards as the modern fallacy that the articles of the Christian creed are unacceptable because they are primitive in their imagery, for instance, the statement that God "came down from Heaven" rather than, as we prefer today, "entered the universe" and the notion that since hell "fire" is a metaphor it means nothing more serious than remorse. He insists that such metaphorical conceptions reveal just as supernatural a

[9] *Hierarchy of Heaven and Earth,* p. 209.
[10] Lewis strongly recommends the *De Incarnatione* of Athanasius as the complete answer to people who regard miracles as arbitrary violations of the laws of nature. This treatise shows rather that miracles are, in Lewis's words, "the re-telling in capital letters of the same message which Nature writes in her crabbed cursive hand." See Preface to Athanasius' *The Incarnation of the Word of God,* Geoffrey Bles, London, 1944.

cosmos as modern abstractions and, what is more significant to his purpose, that both the so-called primitive and the modern and supposedly unmetaphorical imagery are equally figurative. To call God a "spiritual force" or "the indwelling principle of beauty, truth, and goodness" is to make one or both of two mistakes — to suppose one has escaped metaphor into some more realistic imagery, or actually to hide from reality in a verbal smoke screen.

Lewis declares that because most accounts of miracles are probably false, a standard of probability is needed. How can we distinguish a real from a spurious claim of miracle? One way is by the "fitness of things," a method actually deep in the best of science, a conviction which is as real to man as the color of his hair. It was this conviction which earlier led to the very possibility of science. Men expected law in nature because they believed in a Legislator. A modern agnostic science will yet discover how the omission of God inevitably leads to improbabilities in the uniformity of nature. It is a dangerous thing to make nature absolute, because claiming too much you are likely to end up with too little. "Theology offers you a working arrangement, which leaves the scientist free to continue his experiments and the Christian free to continue his prayers."

This fitness of things tells us that the miracle of the Resurrection is on a different level from someone using her patron saint to find her second best thimble. The Resurrection is a part of an immutable and eternal plan, not a last minute "expedient to save the Hero from a situation which had got out of the Author's control." The whole story is actually about Death and Resurrection. The grand miracle is that of the Incarnation, a part of an eternal plan. Christ is indeed the corn-king of mythology but not for the reason ascribed by the anthropologists. The death and re-birth pattern is in nature because it was first in this eternal plan, a plan going back of both nature and nature-religions. There is re-birth in nature myths, but the Resurrection of Christ is described in the Bible as a completely unique event. The whole of creation shadowed, "mythologized," in a thousand ways the event which was to change all of history.

Lewis's epilogue suggests further study to those interested and warns against certain modern scholars who are likely to expound naturalistic assumptions and also against "that soft, tidal return" of the falsely scientific outlook habitual to our time. In the second of his appendices, Lewis discusses how God's creative act is "timeless and timelessly adapted to the 'free' elements within it," and hence how a Christian's prayer spoken today was "present" to God at the creation of all things and will be present to Him a million years from now.[11]

Miracles, which Lewis sub-titles *A Preliminary Study,* is directed not at the subtleties of theological parlance but at people who really want to ask the question of whether miracles are possible. It is addressed to people of naturalistic and pantheistic minds, groups which Lewis believes to include the great mass of people today. He holds that "an immoral, naive and sentimental pantheism" is the chief obstacle against Christian conversion in our time. Most people in effect regard God as incapable not only of miracle but of anything else. They have some place heard the usual anthropological accounts and hazily suppose that because these are modern they are more enlightened than the Christian revelation. Pantheism, says Lewis, is not new but very ancient and in fact the natural tendency of the human mind. Only the Greeks were able to rise above it and then only in their greatest men. Today it is manifest in theosophy, the elevation of a life-force, and the race worship of the Germans under Hitler. The tragedy is that people suppose "each new relapse into this immemorial 'religion'" to be the last word in truth and fact.

God is not diffused in all things, as Pantheism teaches, and neither are we contained in Him as "parts," but God is the great Concrete who feeds a torrent of "opaque actualities" into the world. God is not a principle, a generality, an "ideal," or a "value" but "an utterly concrete fact." On the contrary, today our minds are congenial to "Everythingism," that is, that the whole show is merely self-existent and inclusive. The Pantheist thinks that "everything is in the long run 'merely' a precursor or a development or a relic or an instance or a disguise, of everything

11 See p. 167 for further discussion of this subject.

else." Lewis is completely opposed to such a philosophy. He contrasts the Pantheistic conception of God as someone who animates the universe much as you animate your body with the Christian idea of God as the inventor and maker of the universe, the artist who can stand away from his own picture and examine it.

Letters to Malcolm: Chiefly on Prayer

The rich conception of God as creative artist continues in the posthumous volume *Letters to Malcolm: Chiefly on Prayer.* In this book Lewis describes creation as a "delegation through and through" and argues that "there are no words not derived from the Word." Life is, or ought to be, a continuous theophany. Every bush is a Burning Bush and the world is "crowded with God." Because sin defies not merely God's law but His whole creative purpose, it is more than disobedience — it is sacrilege. No physiological or psychological explanation of man goes deep enough. Neither the "I" nor the object is ultimate reality and we are deceived when we take them as such. One great value of prayer is that it forces us to leave the continually impinging secularism of life and awaken to "the smell of Deity" which hangs over it. In prayer, as in the Lord's Supper, we take and eat. Understanding, desirable as it may be, is for the time replaced by a contact with ultimacy.

Our pleasures are "shafts of the glory as it strikes our sensibility." What we call bad pleasures are actually those obtained by unlawful acts. "It is the stealing of the apple that is bad, not its sweetness. The sweetness is still a beam from the glory." Lewis says that ever since he learned this long ago he has tried to make each pleasure of his life into a channel not simply of gratitude to God but of adoration. He thinks the difference is significant. "Gratitude exclaims, very properly, 'How good of God to give me this.' Adoration says, 'What must be the quality of that Being whose far-off and momentary coruscations are like this!' One's mind runs back up the sunbeam to the sun."

Lewis calls this book more nearly autobiography than theology and says that he has often simply "festooned" theological ideas with his reflections. Some years ago he wrote me that he had done a book on prayer but was not satisfied with it. That he still felt the tentative nature of some of his conclusions may be evident in the fact that he has put the book in the form of off-hand letters to an old college friend.

Had we not known before, this volume would leave little doubt that *A Grief Observed,* the book which appeared under the name N. W. Clerk, is by Lewis, for here we find numerous poignant allusions to the "great blow," i.e., the death of his wife, and the deep love he had for her. It also gives us the best glimpse anywhere into the practical aspect of Lewis's prayer life. He had a lengthy list of people for some of whom he had prayed over a long span of years and some of whom he knew simply as "that old man at Crewe" or "the waitress" or even "that man."

It is a book which seems particularly appropriate as a sort of final reiteration of many of Lewis's convictions. Here we find repeated his respect for the ordinary and commonly overlooked values in the world and his great sensitivity to the loveliness of the creation. Let us bless matter, he says, and remember that the human senses are a gift above that of angels. We find again Lewis's antagonism to liberal theology and to religion as a substitute for Christianity. Speaking of the desire of some liberal theologians to scrap the "outgrown" from the Bible, he says, "If we are free to delete all inconvenient data we shall certainly have no theological difficulties; but for the same reason no solutions and no progress." He repeats his opposition to Reinhold Niebuhr and to all efforts to "demythologize" the Scriptures. There is the same clear assertion that modern intellectuals, however sincere, who substitute abstractions for the older anthropomorphic imagery are getting no nearer the truth about God and are often disastrous in their teaching. There is the usual warning against the dangers of an undue faith in science and the practice of handling God's unique creation in terms of averages and measurement. Lewis believed that among the many things which would be excluded by a deterministic universe is prayer. On the contrary, he upholds a universe shot through and through with the glowing vibrancy of a personal God, a creation "made for the sake of all it does and is, down to the curve of every wave and the flight of every insect."

In this book Lewis repeats the idea discussed in an appendix to *Miracles* that our prayers are granted, or not, before the beginning of time. In the initial act of creation God dovetailed all "future" spiritual and physical occurrences. Our difficulty in understanding this is that we experience in time the things which to God are outside time. The acts of men, whether prayer or sin, are not "predetermined," for there is no "pre" with God. Because man cannot, like God, experience life in an "endless present," it does not at all mean that he is not, living or dead, eternal in God's eyes. Of a good act we may say with equal validity, "God did it" and "I did it."

Lewis's remark that he believes in Purgatory can best be understood in terms of his conviction that God continues His beatitudes in the soul after death, that there is a "farther in and a higher up" and that all eternity perhaps involves a growth. Like Dr. Johnson, Lewis thinks that the closer one comes to the purity of heaven the more he will wish for some preparation, some hallowing of the soul, before it takes up its new citizenship. Purgatory is for him a place not of retributive punishment but rather of purification in which the saved soul "at the very foot of the throne, begs to be taken away and cleansed."

Then there is in this book the same profound sense of the reality of heaven that has permeated all of Lewis's mature thinking. As usual, and with particular meaning in this his last book before his death, Lewis closes with a discussion of the resurrection and the joy of heaven. He repeats that he came to believe in God before he believed in heaven and adds that even if the "impossible supposition" that there is no resurrection were true, he would still take his stand on the side of Christianity. After his speculations concerning the nature of the resurrected body, he concludes that if he is incorrect something even better than he has imagined will be the Christian's happy discovery at death.

167

Mere Christianity

This book consists of what were published originally as three small volumes called *The Case for Christianity* (in England called *Broadcast Talks*), *Christian Behaviour,* and *Beyond Personality.* It is a lucid, brilliant, and witty book of which no summary can be adequate, and I shall confine myself to a brief outline.

Lewis begins with two facts which he calls "the foundation of all clear thinking." One is that people everywhere have the curious idea they ought to behave in a certain way, the other that they do not in fact so behave. The notion of right and wrong is not local and cultural but lodged deeply in the moral wisdom of mankind. We can call this "constant" in the world the Law of Human Nature, or the Moral Law, or the Rule of Decent Behavior. This law is not the "herd instinct" but rather directs the instincts. It is not a social convention inculcated by education but rather a Real Morality which measures conventions and systems. There is a big difference between the Law of Nature and the Law of Human Nature. The former includes such laws as that of gravity and tells you, for instance, what a stone actually does if you drop it. But the Law of Human Nature tells you what people ought to do and fail in doing.

The materialist view of the universe is that it simply happened and that our earth and man are what they are by strange or lucky accidents. The other view is the religious one that the universe came into being as the result of a conscious Person. If the second view is true, we must assume that such a Person is the creator of the facts as we observe them, not something to be discovered inside the facts. There is a third in-between view called Creative Evolution or Emergent Evolution or the Life-Force View which produces a kind of tame God. Lewis wonders if this view is not the world's greatest illustration of the folly of wishful thinking. The moral law, on the contrary, is as hard as nails and suggests that the universe is governed by an absolute goodness.

Now among people who think there is a God, one class sees Him as more or less animating the universe and such that if the universe expired He would expire with it. Another sees Him as very separate from the universe and opposed to the bad things in it. But this second view leads to the important question of how a benevolent God should create a world in which badness could enter. People who get to thinking about the justice of God often conclude that the world is simply senseless. But, strangely, their conclusion proves that one part of the world is not senseless, namely, their own idea of justice.

Atheism is too simple, and so is the Christianity-and-water view that God's in His heaven and all's right with the world, a view which omits sin, hell, and redemption. Christianity is complicated and "odd," yet with the density of reality itself, not something you would have guessed. Take the matter of free will. Why should God give men free will if He knew they would misuse it? Because although free will makes evil possible, it is the only thing that makes joy and love and goodness possible. Without free will men are toys on a string. With free will they have vast possibilities for good as well as evil. If men choose evil, God's law will withhold from them the happiness they thirst for. This is the key to all history.

Although Satan tries to destroy all good in the world, God woos people back to Him through conscience, good dreams or myths, the Scriptural depiction of His dealings with the Jews, and, by far the greatest, His own Son and Redeemer. This Son was either all He claimed to be or else a lunatic or worse, and He claimed to put us right with God not through following His teaching but through baptism, belief, and Holy Communion. The mystery of Christianity has unfathomable depths but its reality is genuine. The Christian has Christ actually operating in him.

From the next section of *Mere Christianity,* which deals with Christian behavior, I shall mention only a few of Lewis's exceptions to common viewpoints. He says that Moses, Aristotle, and the great Christian teachers of the Middle Ages all agreed against the lending of money at interest, one of the main things on which our present economy is based. As to Christian giving, the only safe rule is to give more than we can spare. Like Christianity, psychoanalysis claims to put the human machine right. The philosophy of Freud is in direct contradiction to Christianity but psychoanalysis itself is not when it tries to remove abnormal feelings connected with moral choices. Christianity is concerned primarily with the choices. A man's choices through a period of many years slowly turn him into a heavenly or hellish creature. This is why when a man is getting worse he understands his own badness less and less.

The sexual instinct seems to have gone desperately wrong somewhere. We are less hostile to illicit and perverted sexual relationships than since pagan times. The boast that if we were only franker about sex it would tend to disappear has been proved horribly wrong. Yet neither the sin of unchastity nor any other sin of the flesh is as bad as spiritual sins such as hatred, self-righteousness, and the like.

Marriage, despite modern views to the contrary, is for life. Novels and movies have misled us to believe that "being in love" should be a normal lifetime expectation, whereas it is properly no more than the explosion that starts the engine of a quieter and different sort of love. Forgiveness is much unpracticed as a Christian virtue. To love one's neighbor does not at all mean making out that he is a nice fellow when he is not; we are only asked to love our neighbors as we love ourselves, and what is very lovable in any of us? The great vice loathed by all when observed in another person yet common to man is pride, "the complete anti-God state of mind." It can subtly reside like a spiritual cancer at the very center of even a religious man. In the Christian sense, love is not a condition of the feelings but of the will. You are not to be always weighing whether or not you "love" your neighbor but proceed as if you did and then you will come to love him. The hope of heaven is not escapism. The failure of Christians to think effectively of another world is a cause of their ineffectiveness in this world. In the attempt to satisfy a deep longing which haunts him, a man may try ocean voyages, a succession of women, hobbies, and other things. Yet the longing is from God and only God can satisfy it. "If I find in myself a desire which no experience in this world can satisfy, the most probable explanation is that I was made for another world." Dependence on one's moods will allow a man to be neither a good atheist nor a good Christian. Faith consists in holding on to things your reason has accepted despite moods that may overtake you and the recognition that one's own efforts are to be swallowed up in Christ's indwelling power.

Then, on the ground that people today are quite ignorant of Christian doctrine, Lewis moves to theology itself. He says that Christianity purports to show what a Being who is "beyond personality" may be like. The Trinity meets a man on his knees and a community of Christians gathered in worship. With God there is no such thing as time in the sense of moments following each other; hence He is already in tomorrow and the actions of tomorrow are known to Him. Christianity is different from all other religions in having at its center not something static but a dynamic, even dramatic, Power, "a great fountain of energy and beauty" that makes man a new creation. Christ was the first "real man" and He made it possible for us to be real if we only will. Yet the proper development of the Christian requires that every morning when one awakens and all through the day he shove back his own wishes and hopes and let the voice of God take over and let His "larger, stronger, quieter life come flowing in" and guide toward His own perfection. God has no intention of bringing people barely within the gates of heaven; He intends their absolute perfection and here and hereafter will direct toward that end. There is a principle running through both natural and spiritual life that giving up is finding, death is life. This, in the highest possible manner, is that toward which God calls.

I do not believe that either *Miracles* or *Mere Christianity* needs special discussion. Both books are intended as simple presentations of orthodox views. One section of the latter volume Lewis submitted in manuscript to an Anglican, a Methodist, a Presbyterian, and a Roman Catholic for their criticism and discovered

171

only minor differences from his own view. The difference between these books and most others, particularly theological, on the same subjects is resident in Lewis's ability to select the basic issues from the *corpus* of their vast theological history and to present them in apt analogies, homely illustrations, clear insight, and classically simple diction. His method is proof that a sanctified imagination is a legitimate tool for any Christian apologist.

One theologian who objected to *Miracles* did so partly on the ground that Lewis was, as he said, crude in visualizing the Trinity as like a cube of six squares while remaining one cube. But was not this the very method employed by our Lord who seemed invariably to turn to things close at hand as illustrations of holy things — vines, and fig trees, and lamps, and bushel baskets, and even vultures. It was likewise St. Paul's method when he spoke of sounding brass and tinkling cymbals or the resurrection of Christ as the first-fruits. Indeed it was St. Augustine's method in *De Trinitate* and has been the method of great writers ever. Lewis points out that Plato, one of the great creators of metaphor, is "therefore among the masters of meaning." He holds that the attempt to speak unfiguratively about high abstractions is likely to result in "mere syntax masquerading as meaning" and indeed that metaphor, while not primarily the organ of truth, is the great organ for the depiction of essential meaning either in this world or others.

VII

THEMES IN LEWIS

PERHAPS IT IS INEVITABLE THAT A STUDY OF ANY WRITER'S works will reveal certain basic assumptions and themes. It is so in Lewis, and in this chapter I want to identify some of them. I shall devote the first half of the chapter to his conception of the modern world and the second half to briefer accounts of some additional themes. Since I have already discussed his theology, I shall not repeat the broad foundations upon which he builds, and I shall also leave out, for fear of not encompassing it adequately, his innumerable remarks on the meaning of the self and its relation to God. I have of course not omitted this subject from all those places where it naturally falls throughout this book. Because I have treated the theme of myth quite thoroughly in Chapters IV and VI, I shall also omit that topic here.

The Modern World

I think that Lewis would plead altogether guilty to the adverse charge made by Kathleen Nott that he wished to "make theology paramount again,"[1] that in fact hers is an accurate phrase to describe a large portion of his activities for the last thirty years of his life. He might point out that the word "again" seems, on the contrary, Miss Nott's tacit confession of her own belief that what was once "the chief end of man" has shifted from God to a

---

[1] *The Emperor's Clothes*, p. 254.

secondary, and possibly insignificant, place in the world. Obviously a good deal is at stake.

In his inaugural lecture at Cambridge in 1954,[2] Lewis made the proposal that the largest shift in human culture was not, as usually claimed, the shift from Medieval to Renaissance but rather that which occurred early in the nineteenth century and introduced the post-Christian era. He expressed the surprising idea that Christians and ancient pagans had much more in common than either has with the post-Christian culture of today, and he enumerated four main areas in which the change could be observed: politics, the arts, religion, and "the birth of the machines."

In political life the change manifested itself as a shift from government seeking the quiet ongoing of life to government devoted to "the organisation of mass excitement." From "rulers" who, for the most part, sought justice, diligence, and clemency, the shift was to "leaders" marked by dash, "magnetism," and "personality." In the arts the change brought about bewildering new schools and for the first time a poetry so different from poetry of the past that seven literary scholars discussing a short poem by T. S. Eliot showed not the slightest agreement as to its meaning. In religion man, with certain notable exceptions, is so completely cut off from the Christian past that it is a misnomer to call him even a pagan.

But the greatest shift of all is the alteration of man's place in nature by the domination of the machine — not the machine as such but a new archetypal image it has created that because old machines are inevitably superseded by new and better ones a parallel is to be expected with ideas and beliefs. Elsewhere Lewis calls this chronological snobbery, with its deadly assumption that because in machines the old is primitive and clumsy the same must be true of everything. Today trust in technical advances is, to use Miss Nott's word, paramount. Along with contempt for the past we now assume that everything will shortly be superseded by something better. The automobile

---

[2] Available in *They Asked for a Paper*, Geoffrey Bles, London, 1962.

graveyard shows us those odd-looking things we thought wonderful a few years ago, and in ten years the sleek-looking models we now enjoy will be as seedy and out of date. And so with ideas. The emergence of this conception Lewis describes as the greatest change in the history of Western man.

Such a conception, says Lewis, developed with the nineteenth-century belief in spontaneous progress, which in turn owes something to Darwin's theory of evolution and perhaps to the "myth of universal evolutionism" which is different from Darwin and also pre-dates him. Lewis's opinion about the Darwinian hypothesis seems to be unsettled, except that he always makes a clear distinction between men and animals, but he is very sure about the meaning of universal evolutionism, which he defines as "the belief that the very formula of universal process is from imperfect to perfect, from small beginnings to great endings, from the rudimentary to the elaborate: the belief which makes people find it natural to think that morality springs from savage taboos, adult sentiment from infantile sexual maladjustments, thought from instinct, mind from matter, organic from inorganic, cosmos from chaos." Though he believes this to be the very image of contemporary thought, he regards it as "immensely unplausible, because it makes the general course of nature so very unlike those parts of nature we can observe." We would do better, he says, to emphasize less that an adult human being came from an embryo than that the embryo was produced by two adult human beings.

I have already mentioned the accusation that Lewis despises science and that what he actually dislikes is "scientism" or the popular unthinking assumption that there is no truth other than truth revealed by the scientific method. In his essay "On Obstinacy in Belief,"[3] he distinguishes between scientific and Christian thought. Scientists, he says, are less concerned with "believing" things than simply finding things out. When you find something out, you do not any longer say you believe it, any more than you would say you believe the multiplication table.

---

[3] In *The World's Last Night.*

The scientist in the laboratory is endeavoring to escape from unbelief or belief into knowledge. Lewis defines belief as "assent to a proposition which we think so overwhelmingly probable that there is a psychological exclusion of doubt, though not a logical exclusion of dispute." The scientist himself holds "beliefs" of this sort concerning his wife and friends, beliefs which though not wholly subject to laboratory demonstration assume a large measure of evidence.

It is a mistake, Lewis goes on, to think that the obstinacy of Christians in their belief is like that of a poor scientist doggedly attempting to preserve a hypothesis although the evidence is against him. Their obstinacy is more like that of the confidence of a child who is told by its mother that to ease the pain from a thorn in its finger it must undergo the additional pain of removal. That confidence rests not in a scientific demonstration concerning the mother but in confidence, even emotional confidence, in her as a person. If the child acts on its "unbelief" and refuses to let its mother touch the finger, then no "mighty work" can be done. Yet if it acts on its confidence the thorn will be got rid of and an increasing confidence in the mother will be established. Christian doctrine requires us to put confidence in God who, being infinitely superior to us, will sometimes appear unreasonable to us, but in whom, as with the child and its mother, confidence yields the results promised. God commands us to love Him, and all love involves trusting beyond and perhaps even in spite of the laboratory evidence. The confidence of friends, something hardly related to "evidence" of any sort, is always praised. When you become a Christian, you are "no longer faced with an argument which demands your assent, but with a Person who demands your confidence." Trust is the opposite of demonstrative certainty, for the demonstration would eliminate the trust by turning it into mere knowledge.

The atheist or agnostic may object to a Christian's initial assent to God, but he has no right to demand afterward that the Christian proportion his belief to fluctuations in the apparent evidence. He is the child with the thorn in his finger standing before One he trusts as a friend, yea loves as the Omniscient and Perfect.

176

A great scientist who is also a Christian is here on the same ground with any other Christian.

Later in *The World's Last Night* Lewis discusses travel into space and makes a few additional remarks on the relationship of Christianity and science. When he was young, he says, he was taught that the universe was so hostile to life that only a millionth chance resulted in life on our earth, and this idea was submitted to show there was no Creator who could possibly be interested in humanity. Later the cosmologists decided that the universe was perhaps inhabited very widely, but strangely this antithetical idea was likewise put forward to suggest the absurdity of man's importance to God. The notion, he says, that some new scientific discovery will make a big difference either in the unbelief of non-Christians or in the belief of Christians is unlikely. Real belief transcends this sort of thing.

For the most part the essays in *The World's Last Night* have to do with Lewis's concern over degenerating civilization, democratic conformism, sterilized education, and culture as a thing in itself. Whether education is responsible for such conditions or whether these conditions have brought about our low level of education, Lewis believes that an appalling situation exists. "Lilies That Fester" attempts to show the difference between culture as a general term for worthy activities and the unendurable notion of culture hypostatized into a faith, of people who read poetry or listen to music to improve their minds rather than go to such things spontaneously and compulsively and let culture, if and as it will, show up as a by-product.

All sorts of activities which erect themselves into systems and then assert their autonomous rights are dangerous, even Theocracy. We are in far less danger today of a Theocracy, however, than what Lewis calls a Charientocracy, a combination of apostles of an hypostatized culture and of the Managerial Class. Influenced by Charientocracy, education now proposes to do more to the pupil than ever before. By usurping the whole life of the pupil it allows him no time to dwell with his own mind, to examine himself and his life. Furthermore, education imposes "appreciation" and culturally correct responses for admission to the Managerial System. It teaches the hypocrisy of "getting along in the world" at the expense of real virtues. Lewis is afraid that democracy does not really want great men and he thinks that schools are becoming increasingly successful in crushing individuality and creating a passive response to environment. Genius becomes less and less possible as students are forced to "adjust" or else be kicked out of school. He wants more individuality, more rebellion, less "togetherness," and some place where the "utterly private" can exist.

In his essay "Good Work and Good Works" Lewis suggests that we are victims rather than enjoyers of our vast productive system. Money, not the satisfaction of doing a job, is too often the main motive for labor. Of course many are still doing worthy things — the teacher, the doctor, the artist, etc., yet the majority serve more or less mechanically for money's sake. Production has so occupied us that snobbery, sex, and the like in advertising have become necessary so that useless and even pernicious luxuries may keep the wheels rolling. Even international relations are often dominated by the search for customers.

Although seventeen years elapsed between *The Screwtape Letters* and "Screwtape Proposes a Toast," Lewis shows in the latter the same or even a greater satirical vigor. Indeed, one cannot help comparing the view of man there with Swift's Yahoos in the fourth book of *Gulliver's Travels*. Screwtape, now a respected elder in the Lowerarchy, reminisces before the Disgraces, Thorns, Shadies, and Gentle-devils of the Tempters' Training College. It is their annual dinner and they have been feasting on human souls, which in spite of the cook's best efforts are quite tasteless. Screwtape longs for older times when a Farinata, a Henry VIII, or even a Hitler gave you something really to enjoy. Yet hell, says he, is to be congratulated that though the quality has declined the quantity has greatly increased. Snaring souls for hell, however, is no less a problem than earlier, since now souls have become so flabby and passive that the task of hell is lifting them to the point where they know enough to commit a mortal sin.

Thanks to the mass production method by which dictators, demagogues, film-stars, and other popular idols draw tens of thousands after them, the work of individual temptation is rapidly diminishing. The schools likewise are a great asset to hell with their efforts to disguise individual differences and inculcate a false culture and the I'm-as-good-as-you doctrine, while teacher-nurses are too busy reassuring dunces to accomplish any real teaching.

The philological arm of hell continues its excellent job of substituting jargon for thought and the Yahoos — the name comes very naturally — are well taught to dismiss any rule of conduct which they do not like by calling it "conventional" or "puritan" or "bourgeois morality" rather than inquiring whether it is really true or false. Nowhere has a better job been done than with the incantatory use of the word "democracy," by which the Yahoos mean pulling everything down to the level of the inferior — what Jung would perhaps call depotentiation — and regarding anybody a crank or a prig who refuses to be integrated with the large mindless group. It is a system calculated to eliminate great men and produce a world of cocksure subliterates resentful of any criticism and a state of mind which naturally excludes humility, charity, true contentment, and the pleasures of gratitude and admiration.

Lewis is no less severe with certain other aspects of contemporary life. In aesthetics he thinks the artist has tended to isolate himself from mankind. Instead of feeling any duty to man, the artist often haughtily calls for "recognition." By token of his leadership, the artist should be a doer of Good Work, yet too often substitutes for it the "significant," "important," "contemporary," and "daring."

Everywhere Lewis, as might be expected, shows his antagonism to theological "modernism." He says in *The Pilgrim's Regress* that Mr. Broad's notions are "little more than a kindlier version of common sense and its fair-weather optimism," and he makes John ask this same preacher, "Do you mean that I must cross the canyon or that I must not," i.e., be converted to Christ, after Broad has talked vaguely about the need to re-interpret the truth

179

in each generation. The view of the modernist preacher in *The Great Divorce* and *That Hideous Strength* is even more sarcastic. In *The Screwtape Letters* Father Spike proudly constructed his sermons so as to shock and humiliate people of orthodox religious belief. In *Mere Christianity* Lewis declares that many of the supposedly new theological ideas are ones rejected centuries ago.

Yet I shall be sorry if what I have said thus far in this chapter leaves the impression that Lewis was a calamity howler, for I do not believe that to have been the state of his mind or to be the effect of his books. He was simply not the type for that. His innate sense of humor prevented the Swiftian moroseness even when Lewis's trituration was no less vigorous than Swift's. If his view of contemporary man is low, it is because his estimate of man's eternal potential is high. Lewis was an Old Western Man who wanted to make theology paramount again and restore to humanity some of the ancient graces as well.

His overstatement of some detail of his case against modern culture should not be allowed to obscure the sanity of his total view, a view concording with that of many other great minds in our generation. In addition, Lewis was deeply convinced that man is not made to live seventy years but forever. Thus man is more important than any of his institutions, for they will die while he lives on. And for Lewis the stakes were the loftiest possible. He was convinced that the "climate of opinion" in our day is neither a pebble on the beach nor even a dangerous boulder on the mountainside but rather the eternal "stone of stumbling" that will send men to hell.

Now I turn to a briefer discussion of several other themes in Lewis's books.

Additional Themes

One of the most prominent of these is that every living being is destined for everlasting life and that every moment of life is a preparation for that condition. There are thousands of roads in the world but not a single road which fails to lead either to heaven or hell. There will be surprises as to those who reach either place but only for onlookers, not those people themselves, for they will have been so long getting ready that heaven or hell will appear, in a sense, quite natural. The onlookers have not seen the inner, choosing man, but in heaven or hell only that part of him will appear. Even the devil himself will snicker at that time when the man's nakedness reveals that it was not goodness at all which made him act with chastity or bravery or self-control but rather that cancerous sin called pride.

Every choice a man makes changes him, perhaps in a very small way, yet the total is massive enough slowly to turn him into something heavenly or else hellish.[4] If the latter, he comes to wish that black was a little blacker. Eventually he sees gray and finally white as simply black, until ultimately the inner man is fixed in a universe of blackness. The Belbury crowd in *That Hideous Strength* were once good men but had become altogether devilish. It is the pure in heart who may properly tell each other that they shall see God, for it is only they who want to.

Yet it is not man alone who works out his salvation but God who works in him. It is He who if a man allows will lead him to Himself and thenceforward. Even a meagre desire for God, if truly recognized, is enough to start God's operation. "No soul that seriously and constantly desires joy will ever miss it." God, in fact, gives the desire in the first place, allowing it to remain in the man's life like the Narnian sap in the magical tree in Digory's back yard and the breeze from Narnia which caused the tree sometimes to bend when no breeze was blowing on earth.

After a man is saved, God will continue His training efforts. "Putting on Christ" and Christ "being formed in us" and having "the mind of Christ" certainly do not mean simply reading what Christ said and attempting to put it into practice. Rather they mean that a real Person, not something remote and abstruse, comes

---

[4] "Our character is the result of a choice that is continually being renewed," said Henri Bergson.

to you day after day and "interfering with your very self" shapes you into a being with a life similar to God's own. The command to the Christian to be perfect is no hyperbole but precisely what Christ meant. He begins on earth a process that will be consummated in heaven, but it is a *process* and will not allow you successfully to play the hypocrite with your naked self. God will not allow you to take the attitude, "I never expected to be a saint, I only wanted to be a decent ordinary Chap." His plan is indeed to make you into a heavenly being. This may account for the rough time Christians go through, for He is turning every one of his children into "a little Christ." He is not like a trainer who teaches a horse to jump better; He is in the business of turning horses into winged creatures.

Even our natural loves will live forever in heaven but only after they have died and risen again. We shall be more human in heaven than we ever succeeded in being on earth. The Christian's true personality lies ahead, and he will be a real person only when he has occupied God's own designated place for him in the entire cosmos. God called Himself the "I Am." Christians also shall have being, is-ness, real identity in heaven. At the close of *Till We Have Faces* Orual found Psyche a thousand times more beautiful than she had been earlier. "I had never seen a real woman before," said Orual. In *The Great Divorce* the one visitant who decided to enter heaven was immediately filled with an immense richness and energy. This is what it means to choose God.

Self-choice, however, is the key to hell. Without it there would indeed be no hell. The Green Lady in the unfallen world of *Perelandra* could not understand what was meant by self-choice. Hell is inhabited by those who through thousands of little daily acts have elevated self above God. Self has turned all experiences into its own province until there is little "other" left and the capacity for good is simply quenched. The grumbler has turned into a grumble, that is, lost the ability to discern anything other than self. There is nothing left but self, and this is nothing more nor less than hell. When Eustace slept on the dragon's hoard and filled his mind with greedy, dragonish thoughts, he turned into a dragon, but it was a great shock to him to be told what had happened, for he was not fully aware that he had become a dragon. Lewis says that the deeper a sin the less the victim suspects its existence. On the other hand, a mind given to good tends to become opaque to evil powers.

Like Albert Camus, Lewis believes death to be the most significant fact in the interpretation of man's life, yet, unlike Camus, he is convinced that man is primarily made for eternity. With Socrates, he holds that true wisdom is the practice of death. He is confident that the myths are heavy with the teaching, from nature and perhaps revelation, that death and resurrection are paramount. Christians of the past taught this doctrine, and the Bible itself makes extremely clear that the whole universe was created for no other purpose than a positively spiritual one. Man, however, is both spirit and body, and there are legitimate human functions that may occupy him provided they are always kept in the right perspective. Speaking at Oxford during the trying days of World War II, Lewis raised the question whether in such times the study of literature, art, mathematics, and biology could be justified and the parallel question whether in the continuing war with Satan any cultural activities on the part of the Christian could be justified. His answer was that there has never been any such thing as "normal" life and that if the search for knowledge and beauty must be postponed until man is altogether secure, those things will never be enjoyed. On the Christian side, he argued that Christianity does not mean the replacement of the natural life with a totally different one but rather the exploitation of natural materials to supernatural ends. Even the intellectual life often becomes the appointed road to Christ. Indeed, this was Lewis's own experience. Hence, though man is created for eternity, there are perfectly legitimate activities in which he may enthusiastically take part.

Another close corollary which Lewis obviously likes to emphasize is that God is the creator, transformer, and ultimate possessor of common things. Lewis thinks that Christianity, more than any other religion, approves the body and teaches that matter is good. God invented matter. He invented sex. He invented eating and drinking, and He sustains both natural and supernatural life by such material things as bread and wine. A gourd-like fruit which Ransom found on Perelandra was so delicious that he felt only an oratorio or a mystical meditation would be adequate to express its quality. Though Lewis has no use for the I'm-as-good-as-you aspect of democracy, he holds that a bootblack or a scavenger is as intrinsically pleasing to God as a scholar or a scientist. It is demonically proud Screwtape who despises the notion that a Christian "thing of earth and slime" comes before God. Not only does Lewis like to depict people coming into the presence of God but he prefers those who had no earthly fame. We have around us daily potential gods and goddesses, and the least interesting person we know "may one day be a creature which, if you saw it now, you would be strongly tempted to worship." Sarah Smith from Golders Green possessed a glorious beauty in heaven, and Mother Dimble, who had nothing more to recommend her socially than grey hair, a double chin, and service as the provincial housewife of an obscure scholar, was a holy and mighty priestess in the service of God. The first rulers of Narnia were King Frank and Queen Helen, a London cabdriver and his wife. Lewis believes that if Paradisal man appeared among us now we should first look upon him as an utter savage and only a few of the holiest people of earth would afterwards fall at his feet. Perhaps Lewis meant to suggest something like this in his depiction of Merlin in *That Hideous Strength* and to imply that more recent people have acquired with their culture a false sense of delicacy and station.

Still another corollary of Lewis's high estimate of man and life is that Christians must wait for God's leading and then obey Him explicitly. Screwtape makes it very clear that one of the great strategies of hell is to induce postponement of known duties and that the cause of hell is greatly in danger when a Christian, in

a period of dryness when God seems to have disappeared from
the universe, gets on his knees to pray or in some other way
objectively manifests his faith. Concerning Abraham's intention to sacrifice Isaac, Lewis cites St. Augustine's opinion that,
whatever God knew, Abraham himself could not know whether
or not his obedience would endure God's command except as
the event taught him, so that the reality of Abraham's obedience
resided in the willingness to act. Thus objective acts of obedience
are desirable as the manifestation of faith. One may sit through
endless years remembering that he ought to love God but discovering in himself no feeling of love for Him. If this occurs,
the solution is not to try to manufacture feelings but to ask oneself,
"If I were sure that I loved God, what would I do?" and, having
decided upon an answer, to go at once and do it. Lewis cites the
epigram which defines religion as "what a man does with his
solitude" and denies that this is the teaching of Christianity,
which forbids its adherents to neglect the act of assembling
themselves together. The Christian life must be lived dutifully
from one moment to another. Either to worry about the future or
to postpone to the future what ought to be done now is sin.
"It is only our *daily* bread that we are encouraged to ask for.
The present is the only time in which any duty can be done
or any grace received." This was what Ransom learned in his
struggle with the Un-man in *Perelandra*. In *That Hideous Strength*
we note that despite the radical emergency to act, the Pendragon
is quietly waiting for orders. Jill and Scrubb, in *The Silver Chair*,
finally concluded, after muffing most of Aslan's directions, that
death itself should not interfere in carrying out the last one. Their
reward was an immediate sign of Aslan's power. The Bible
was given us, says Lewis, not to satisfy our speculative curiosity
but as a book of instructions and encouragement. It is to be
constantly consulted and its commands carried out exactly and
enthusiastically.

Lewis's charities may be cited as one example of his own attempt to practice a direct Biblical obedience. It was rumored that

in his big house at Oxford, which he loved so much that he still considered it home even while teaching at Cambridge, he supported the mother of one of his World War I comrades, together with various other dependents. "He was prodigally generous with his money," said the London *Times* shortly after his death. Yet his liberality was accompanied by so thorough a secrecy that his closest friends were never fully aware of its extent.

Like other thoughtful Christians, Lewis believed that a study of the Garden of Eden and the Fall of Man can yield valuable hints to the Christian, and this subject is recurrent in his works. I have indicated that most of *Perelandra* is given to this topic, and that Mother Kirk repeats it briefly to John in *The Pilgrim's Regress*. A full chapter in *The Problem of Pain* is given to the practical implications of the Fall. Screwtape explains that Satan's ejection from heaven was a falsehood and insists that Satan removed himself because of what he considered God's cock-and-bull story about His disinterested love of man. Speaking of the man supposed to be Merlin, Frost, in *That Hideous Strength,* described him as a fifth-century survival of something far more remote — "something that comes down from long before the Great Disaster, even from before primitive Druidism; something that takes us back to Numinor, to pre-glacial periods." Although Marjorie E. Wright suggests that Numinor might be equated with Atlantis, it seems to me proper to equate it also with Eden. I have mentioned the creation of Narnia by Aslan and how Digory suffered the Edenic temptation. The White Witch in *The Lion, the Witch and the Wardrobe* is half Jinn, half giantess, and a descendant of Lilith, first wife of Adam. Lewis also has a fine poem called "Adam at Night," in which he tells of the joys of Adam and Eve before the Fall.[5] Lewis sees man not only as fallen from his Edenic glory and happiness but also penetrated by a deep longing to return.

[5] Published in *Punch* under the initials N.W., where many other of his poems also appeared. In the collected *Poems* (ed. by W. Hooper, 1964) it is called "The Adam at Night."

This longing or *Sehnsucht* permeates all of Lewis's writing. Perhaps the best single account of it is in "The Weight of Glory," the first essay in the book by that title. He calls it the inconsolable secret which inhabits the soul of every man, a desire which no natural happiness can ever satisfy, the lifelong pointer toward heaven, a nostalgia to cross empty spaces and be joined to the true reality from which we now feel cut off, the "faint, far-off results of those energies which God's creative rapture implanted in matter" and which give us such delight and yet are the meagre signs of the true rapture He has in heaven for redeemed souls. As the whole vegetable system of the country described in *The Pilgrim's Regress* was infected with the taste of wild apples, so longing is the God-like infection implanted in earthly joys like a drop of nectar in a glass of water which is sufficient to give it a new taste. The culmination of *Sehnsucht* in the rhapsodic joy of heaven is, for me at least, the strongest single element in Lewis. In one way or another it hovers over nearly every one of his books and suggests to me that Lewis's apocalyptic vision is perhaps more real than that of anyone since St. John on Patmos. I suspect that for most Christians the idea of attaining heaven means little more than coming within the golden gates, but for Lewis that stage is merely the start of a journey. "Farther in and higher up" was Aslan's call to the children in *The Last Battle,* and the very words he spoke set them to tingling all over.

Another theme which so far as I know is unique to Lewis is the danger, or perhaps evil, of repeating a pleasure for its own sake. In *Perelandra* Ransom was several times restrained by an inner and mysterious compulsion from a second taste, once his body was no longer hungry or thirsty, of the unimaginably delicious fruits he found there. He remembered that on earth he had often repeated pleasures not from desire but actually in the teeth of desire, but he felt a different principle in operation on Perelandra. Ransom came to wonder if this "itch to have things over again, as if life were a film that could be unrolled

187

twice or even made to work backwards" was not perhaps the root of all evil. Later the Green Lady explained that clinging to the old good simply for its own sake would turn it into an evil, that in her world every joy was beyond all others.

Lewis may be suggesting something of the Platonic doctrine that a pleasure is to be judged in terms of its peculiar and legitimate object. Screwtape said that God created the pleasures and hell's strategy was to cause men to take them at times, or in ways, or in degrees that God forbade. Sexual pleasure, for instance, is as legitimate as the pleasure of eating, yet in adultery one isolates a certain kind of union, that is, the sexual, from all other kinds of union that should go along with it. You must not attempt to get a pleasure from any act which is illegitimate to it as a whole. The legitimate end of tasting is swallowing, and the legitimate end of food is satisfying hunger rather than indulging in gluttony. The legitimate use of sexual intercourse is a function of the whole life of a man and woman joined together in marriage. A lover embracing his beloved may very innocently and legitimately get a sexual thrill. The trouble begins the moment the second embrace seeks that thrill for its own sake, for that means the *I-Thou* relation is shifting to an *I-It* relation and the beloved becoming a thing, a machine usable for the purpose of sex. "Thus the bloom of innocence, the element of obedience and the readiness to take what comes is rubbed off every activity." Macdonald, in *The Great Divorce,* when asked if many people were not lost through sensuality, said that the sensualist is a man who begins with a pleasure that grows smaller and smaller while at the same time his craving grows fiercer and fiercer and who comes so to prefer lust for its own sake that he would die to keep it. "He'd like well to be able to scratch: but even when he can scratch no more he'd rather itch than not." But even an illegitimate craving, like that for the brown girls in *The Pilgrim's Regress,* if a man faithfully lives through "the dialectic of its successive births and deaths," can be used of God.

Perhaps Lewis sees the "farther in and higher up" principle as legitimate for earth as well as heaven. If the Christian believes, as indeed he ought, that God is living in him and that his experience from hour to hour is that which, apart from sin, God vouchsafes, then the routine of life is transformed into experiences edged with joy. The Green Lady said, "Every joy is beyond all others. The fruit we are eating is always the best fruit of all." This is an ideal for fallen as well as unfallen worlds.

In his last book, *Letters to Malcolm: Chiefly on Prayer,* Lewis returns to this subject and says he believes that Christians often reject present blessings from God simply because they have filled their minds with the image of some past splendid experience with God, and thus leave no room for Him to give them a newer and perhaps even richer experience. "God shows us a new facet of the glory, and we refuse to look at it because we're still looking for the old one." In such a process we seldom get the old experience again, and the process itself precludes new blessing. Furthermore, to expect a mere repetition from an infinite God — a God to whom "all space and time are too little for Him to utter Himself *once*" — is to frustrate God's plan for the maturation of Christian experience.

Another of Lewis's themes is that right things are right not because God commanded them but that He commanded them because they are right. Between *The Problem of Pain* and *Reflections on the Psalms* Lewis's opinion on this subject appears to have increased in certainty. In the former he said that he took his stand with Hooker and against Dr. Johnson on this conception, but by the latter he had concluded that some "terrible theologians" of the eighteenth century held that things are right because God commanded them, a view which Lewis insists would make God an arbitrary tyrant and elevate atheism to an ethical standard above faith itself. "God's will," says Lewis, "is determined by His wisdom which always perceives, and His goodness which always embraces, the intrinsically good." To a critic who charged Lewis with denying, in *The Abolition of Man,* that God made the *Tao,* Lewis answered, "If I had any hesitation in saying that God 'made' the *Tao,* it would only be

189

because that might suggest that it was an arbitrary creation (*sic volo sic jubeo*), whereas I believe it to be the necessary expression, in terms of temporal existence, of what God by His own righteous nature necessarily is. One could indeed say of it *genitum, non factum*, for is not the *Tao* the Word Himself, considered from a particular point of view?"[6] The Lord Himself is righteous, not simply His commands, and his laws possess "rock-bottom reality" because they are grounded in His own nature. They have the same solidity that His creation has. God is not even the "inventor" of religion; rather religion consists of God's statement to us of "certain quite unalterable facts about His own nature." In *That Hideous Strength* Merlin was astonished that Ransom said the ancient pass-word without knowing it specifically, and Ransom replied, "I said it because it was true." The whole notion indeed of Deep Heaven and the *eldila* inhabitants is that the cosmos is one world with the law of righteousness built deeply within its core.

I believe Lewis means to say that we do not have a world *plus* God but that, so to speak, God has built the moral principle into the very atoms. Sin violates not simply the commands of God but the very principle of life. "Be sure your sins will find you out" is not an edict from outside or the capricious decree of God but rather a law at the center of creation. The world is so constructed that this world as well as the next pays off for ill conduct.

[6] In a letter to me dated January 11, 1961.

APPENDIX

INSTEAD OF A STANDARD BIBLIOGRAPHY I HAVE CHOSEN TO GIVE below brief descriptions of five doctoral dissertations and six books devoted either wholly or in part to Lewis. The best overall bibliography on Lewis is contained in Dabney A. Hart's dissertation. Corbin S. Carnell's dissertation has a bibliography containing some items, especially those dealing with Christian works, not in Hart. Marjorie E. Wright's dissertation contains no bibliography, owing to the fact that she was killed in an automobile accident just before completing her study.

None of the five dissertations have been published, and they are therefore available only on library loan from the institutions at which they were written. I list the studies in the chronological order of their appearance.

THE THEOLOGY OF C. S. LEWIS.

This dissertation was submitted by Edgar W. Boss for the Th. D. degree at Northern Baptist Theological Seminary in Chicago in May, 1948. The writer endeavors to survey Lewis's writings in order to evaluate them in terms of their adherence to or deviation from orthodox doctrines. He regards Lewis as unorthodox in respect to Sacramentalism and the belief in Purgatory. He also interprets Lewis as an organic evolutionist, an occasional friend to liberal higher criticism, and a believer in the "Example Theory" of the Atonement Though Lewis is said not to accept the plenary verbal inspiration of Scripture, he nevertheless takes for granted that it was given by God and assumes that if something is said in the Bible it ought to be ac-

191

cepted. Lewis is declared to hold that man is fallen and needs transformation.

Dr. Boss sets forth what he believes to be Lewis's theological position on such topics as the origin of the idea of God, the corroborative evidence of His existence, the attributes of God, the Trinity, the works of God, miracles, angels, Heaven, Hell, and Purgatory, and the Second Coming. On the last, he thinks that Lewis believes Christ is literally, personally coming again.

He says that Lewis is often repetitive from book to book but he thinks this more a virtue than a fault. He sees Lewis as the champion of supernaturalism who by his cleverness as a writer gets a hearing.

Despite Dr. Boss's sincere effort to evaluate Lewis's theology, his study in my opinion neglects to consider the subtlety of some of Lewis's ideas.

C. S. LEWIS: APOSTLE TO THE SKEPTICS

Professor Chad Walsh's study, published by the Macmillan Company in 1949, has only one serious shortcoming: that some of Lewis's most significant books have appeared since its publication. It is based on a careful examination of Lewis's works to 1949 and also some talks and a good deal of correspondence with Lewis.

It begins with a brief biography, including a good description of what Lewis was like personally, with the usual contrast between the dead-pan picture of him on the dust jackets of his early books and his vital and charming reality in the flesh. It describes his rooms at Oxford and his friends.

There are brief but meaty summaries of Lewis's books. Though his treatment of Lewis is sympathetic, he does not hesitate to cite adverse opinions. Professor Walsh is especially antagonistic to *The Pilgrim's Regress,* which he finds heavy and wooden in style and characterization and on the whole mediocre as a work of literature. He thinks the space trilogy among the works of Lewis which are most likely to survive. Walsh regards Lewis's poetry as unimportant except for a great but almost unused gift for nonsense verse.

Professor Walsh likes the keen psychology of *The Screwtape Letters* but feels that *The Great Divorce* lacks the wit and variety of the former. He finds Lewis's expository books clear, lively, and well-mannered but less likely to survive than his creative works. No one seriously questions that Lewis is a great scholar and literary critic, says Professor Walsh.

He attempts to distinguish between Lewis's "Classical Christianity" and Fundamentalism. By the latter Dr. Walsh seems to mean snake handlers. Yet he thinks that a Fundamentalist would go along with Lewis most of the time. He believes also that of great Christian teachers perhaps St. Paul would feel most at home with Lewis. He points out some of Lewis's unpopular doctrines, especially that of hell, and the fact that a good many things not denied but rather "embalmed" by orthodox theology are brought to life by Lewis. One is the doctrine of Christ's return, which Professor Walsh thinks has grown more urgent in Lewis's works. Another is Lewis's antagonism to the "spiritualizers" who look upon Christ's Resurrection as proof of a bodiless immortality in a mystical heaven.

Professor Walsh discusses Lewis's theory of myth and his strong appeal to reason. He points out that Lewis is no enemy to science, and he regards Lewis's psychology, particularly on religious topics, as splendid. He describes the influence of Macdonald, Williams, and others on Lewis.

I would take exception to Professor Walsh's illustration to prove that Lewis has the great advantage of "not being a puritan." He says that in *The Pilgrim's Regress* when John left Puritania he left it for good. The fact is that Lewis brings John back to Puritania and John dies there. While it seems to me that Lewis bears the same sympathetic attitude toward the term "puritan" that he does to the other orthodox ideas described by Professor Walsh, I would agree with him that "God's approval of sensible pleasures runs through Lewis's thinking about morality."

This study contains a bibliography of books and prefaces to 1949, though not of pamphlets or poems and essays in periodicals. It lists a few "sustained studies" of Lewis.

THE EMPEROR'S CLOTHES

This book by Kathleen Nott was first published by William Heinemann, London, in 1953, and was issued in a paperback by the University of Indiana Press in 1958. It is an attack on T. S. Eliot, T. E. Hulme, Basil Willey, Graham Greene, Dorothy Sayers, C. S. Lewis, and others considered by her as neo-scholastics who in their fear of the ongoing strength of science wish to re-establish a dogmatic theology. She treats Lewis and Dorothy Sayers together, calling them bold, emotional "fundamentalists," popularizers of "glaringly fallacious thinking," and smug know-it-alls whose nature demands authority and hence cannot stomach open-minded inquiry.

Her objection to Lewis is centered almost exclusively on his *Miracles.* She attempts to show that he hypostatizes reason and projects this embodiment of it into the scientist whom he subconsciously hates, that he sees nature as "the mute slave" attendant upon the rational will of God, that he erects "an impassable Cartesian barrier" between reason and nature and thus destroys the whole thesis of his book. She believes that Lewis and many of the others become irrational because they are taken with a "passionate wish to discern hierarchy in the universe." She declares that Lewis fails to understand the Heisenberg Uncertainty Principle and that he understands only popular and superficial accounts of both the Marxian and Freudian theories. She believes that in *Miracles* he habitually misuses language — this in the face of his expertness as a philologist. Lewis's belief in the devil she characterizes as partly owing to his "sado-masochistic imagination." Her own belief is that the methods of science and theology can never converge and that "scientific method can treat mystical experience only as a department of psychological experience."

Miss Nott, a poet and novelist, writes with much skill. Yet, as John W. Simons said in his review of her book, she is "passionately involved in a vindication of the scientific method" until it becomes "her own 'dogmatic orthodoxy' and thereby renders ineffectual her attacks on the dogmatic orthodoxies of her opponents . . . her book is strewn with the sophistries she would foist upon others." It is also, he said, filled with semantical blunders.[1]

C. S. LEWIS'S DEFENSE OF POESIE.

This doctoral dissertation by Dabney A. Hart was submitted to the University of Wisconsin in 1959, and is the outgrowth of Hart's residence at the University of London as a Fulbright scholar and of acquaintance with Lewis and many of his friends. It is a definitive study of Lewis's theory of literature and of the extent to which his imaginative writings measure up to that theory. It recognizes but does not attempt to evaluate Lewis's Christian orthodoxy.

This study contains an extended and excellent account of Lewis's conception of the meaning of myth and allegory. Dr. Hart says that Lewis considers myth "the embodiment of universal truth" and "affirms, with regret, that the old mythical imagination, which he would consider the birthright of humanity, has been lost by the increasing emphasis on the mathematical methodology of science." Allegorical thought, via the imagination, is in Lewis's opinion "the natural way of human thought," and men's deepest and truest instincts are always the best guide to what is "truly significant."

Dr. Hart believes that Lewis's hope as a critical theorist was to decrease the gap between literary specialists and the ordinary reader. She believes that writing exists not for itself or the writer but for the delight of intelligent and responsible readers. Though Lewis's judgments as critic are intensely personal, they are not capricious but fit into his conviction that myth is fundamental in man's make-up. He has succeeded by a provocative *tour de force* and great originality in reassessing all literature after his own mythopoeic viewpoint. He holds, for instance, that ex-

[1] *Commonweal,* April 22, 1955.

cellence of style is not in itself a sign of greatness and may in fact be a defect. All great literature he believes finds the source of its imaginative power and beauty in ultimate Truth and should be regarded as derivative rather than original.

The main body of Dr. Hart's thesis is given to an evaluation of Lewis's imaginative works in terms of his critical theory. She believes that Lewis frequently fails to measure up, owing sometimes to his weighting his story with more of his own ideas than it can sustain, sometimes to the complexity of his basic myth which requires "more filling in than the author can provide," and sometimes to style itself. As to the latter, Dr. Hart says that Lewis "often seems to attempt the scope of Bunyan with the resources of Swift or Pope." She agrees with other critics that Lewis is most at home in satire and she thinks this gift militates against him in the writing of sublime fantasy. She believes that Lewis's novels and children's stories lose spontaneity by concentrating too much on myth simply as myth.

She devotes an entire chapter to Lewis's conception of metaphor, noting especially the influence of Owen Barfield and of Rudolph Steiner through Barfield. Lewis, says Dr. Hart, believes that reason is the organ of truth and imagination the organ of meaning and that hence valid criticism requires both.

She believes that Lewis steers a middle course, though never a dull or mediocre one, between sociological or psychoanalytical criticism on the one hand and diagrammatic or textual criticism on the other. His is a criticism based on confidence in the enlightened human imagination to judge correctly.

The concluding chapter of this dissertation cites at some length opinions, pro and con, on Lewis's works, both scholarly and imaginative, and suggests some evaluation of Lewis's place in the future.

Dr. Hart spent many months in the compilation of a bibliography of Lewis's critical and imaginative works and of criticisms in secondary sources. No one who wishes to study Lewis seriously can afford to ignore this bibliography.

ARTHURIAN TRIPTYCH

Charles Moorman's study was published in 1960 by the University of Califorina Press. He wishes to show how the effective use of myth gives an added dimension to any writer. Myth comes ready-to-hand, full of its own allusive potentiality and ordered experience to aid the writer in the assembling and presentation of his meaning. In fact, he says, it is only through metaphorical eyes that any person can see his times in a genuinely true perspective. The language of myth, he concludes, is noted for its fusion of metaphorical and logical terms, for employing language symbolizing archetypal reality and also identifying everyday reality. It is an "objective correlative."

The particular writers chosen by Dr. Moorman as illustrations are Charles Williams, C. S. Lewis, and T. S. Eliot. It was, for instance, an evidence of Lewis's genius as a writer that in *That Hideous Strength* he placed the world of Jane and Mark Studdock and the struggle between Bracton College and Belbury against the "backdrop" of Merlin and the Arthurian myth. In this way grandeur and magnitude were added and all the archetypal and symbolic strength of the myth given to otherwise rather ordinary events.

Though Williams, Lewis, and Eliot all use the order, coherence, and meaning contained in the Arthurian myth to pattern and control their vision of life today, their actual methods differ. With Williams the whole Arthurian myth is involved, with Lewis only selected images abstracted as symbols to suggest larger meaning — images such as the Fisher King, Merlin, and Logres-Britain. Eliot, on the other hand, selects an aspect of the myth, that is, the sterility theme of the Fisher King, as correlative of the futile secularism today.

Dr. Moorman points out that though there are "no crap games, 'fixed' elections, or sleeping bags" in these authors, they are all modern writers in the truest sense. "Our contemporary dilemmas and frustrations are seen by these men in relation to the universal issues of morality and religion of which they are parts, and they are presented in terms that are meaningful to all men at all times.

And by means of this sort of aesthetic distance, these writers achieve not less, but more relevance to their own age." He believes that for this reason the stature of these writers will increase with time. In Lewis he believes that *Till We Have Faces* and *That Hideous Strength* will, because of their greater inherent mythic power, outlive *Out of the Silent Planet* and *Perelandra*.

Dr. Moorman thinks that the outlook and aim of these three writers is very similar. They all believe that materialism is steadily displacing the religious perspective of former times and they all desire a return to the spiritual values symbolized by the quest of the Grail. They have all clearly sensed the alienation of modern man from certainties, and each points a means of escape from the wasteland in which we wander.

THE COSMIC KINGDOM OF MYTH: A STUDY IN THE MYTH-PHILOSOPHY OF CHARLES WILLIAMS, C. S. LEWIS, AND J. R. R. TOLKIEN.

This is a doctoral dissertation presented by Marjorie E. Wright at the University of Illinois in 1960. It first attempts to show Williams, Lewis, and Tolkien in relation to their times. They are, says Dr. Wright, deliberately and "unabashedly" romantic in a period of realism; they write "fantasy" yet with a deep conviction of the reality of their subject. All are concerned with theology, metaphysics, and the structure of the universe, and all hold theories of myth differing considerably from those ordinarily expressed by scholars. In a time increasingly disillusioned by man's vision of reality, these writers have found a system of cosmic order and "created a myth to contain it."

Timelessness, self-sufficiency, and a sense of the numinous are Dr. Wright's ingredients for "mythic quality." By timelessness and self-sufficiency she means stories possessing their own autonomy and not dependent on any outside system. By the numinous she means stories containing superhuman beings of intrinsic merit. In all three writers she finds a strong and similar cosmological element which unites their various realms of myth. In Lewis's case the space world is an original blending of modern science and medieval cosmology. In all three the basic pattern of myth is a hierarchy based on rule, obedience, courtesy, exchange, and correspondence. The very opposite of police states, their kingdoms are filled with life, movement, and ceremony.

In most of these writers, says Dr. Wright, there is a numinous geography, their kingdoms often being located in a remote, mysterious land beyond the sea. Their people are often closely bound together in groups. Their accounts involve in some measure a struggle between good and evil in which evil is concrete, apocalyptic, final, complete, and demonic, and capable of doing actual battle with good. Ordinarily there is some form of a quest or task to be fulfilled through a perilous journey, yet not for personal gain but the good of the kingdom itself. Their myths are replete with symbols of cosmic unity, as the ageless and archetypal Bragdon Wood in *That Hideous Strength* or the magical rings in *The Magician's Nephew*.

Not only is there a mythic geography in these writers, but there is also a mythic history. Dr. Wright considers history both within and without the stories. She gives particular attention to the Arthurian elements in these writers and especially the Logres-Britain symbol. She points out the dangers of allegorical interpretation of their works except in terms of the myth as a whole, not their separate elements. She concludes that truth in fiction consists less in closeness to fact than in the interpretive judgment of the writer. To all these mythmakers, "Christianity is a matter of historical facts and a philosophical interpretation of the universe, as well as a religion" and Christianity "is the great and central historical embodiment of myth." If myth sometimes distorts truth, "it is not because of failure to report history, but because of failure to catch perfectly the outlines of the reality beyond history." All these writers believe that their myths are true to a larger and more universal reality. There is in them also the eucatastrophe or happy ending, yet the ending is for them not so much an end as a beginning.

Dr. Wright concludes her study with an attempt to suggest

the mythic value of these writers, the significance of their appearance at the present stage of literary history, and their reception by the critics of our time. While both Williams and Lewis, she says, derive their material from older myths, they are able to mould and merge it into a cosmos of their own. She notes the difference between such a myth for instance as Lewis's Narnia, which invites expansion, and his Cupid and Psyche myth in *Till We Have Faces,* which does not.

She finds these writers conscious of their times and capable of the realistic "principle of skepticism," especially in religion and politics. Yet they never forget that one of their main purposes is to tell a good story. The amount of explicit Christian content varies with each author and even each story. Christian and didactic elements in Tolkien are far less apparent than in the other two, yet Dr. Wright thinks they are there. The use of eucatastrophe is perhaps the most significantly Christian element common to all three writers.

Criticism of Williams, Lewis, and Tolkien, says Dr. Wright, has been mostly favorable. She notes, as others have, that people tend to be either violently for or against these men, also that their books are propagated less by written criticism than by word-of-mouth enthusiasts.

THE DIALECTIC OF DESIRE: C. S. LEWIS' INTERPRETATION OF *Sehnsucht.*

This doctoral dissertation, submitted by Corbin S. Carnell to the University of Florida in 1960, begins with an attempt to define what Lewis means by *Sehnsucht,* using such words as *longing, melancholy, wonder, exile, isolation, yearning, the numinous, causeless melancholy,* and *the blue flower of longing.* He points out that *Sehnsucht* appears not only in "romantic" works but also in such unexpected works as Dreiser's *Sister Carrie,* Dr. Johnson's *Rasselas,* Voltaire's *Candide,* and the *Tenth Satire* of Juvenal. In *Sehnsucht* the individual feels that he is "becoming one with the universe and desires an even closer union." Both Romanticism and *Sehnsucht* appear to be fundamental in the experience of

Western man, though of course not manifest equally in all times. *Sehnsucht* Carnell believes to be a "given" of experience. He thinks that Lewis, possibly influenced by Joy Davidman Lewis's own preoccupation with *Sehnsucht,* became increasingly interested in the subject.

A long chapter is given to Lewis's biography. His relation to the "Inklings," a discussion circle at Oxford, and particularly his connection with Charles Williams, is covered. The influence of older works, especially those of George Macdonald, is discussed. Among other authors who have influenced Lewis are St. Thomas Aquinas, St. Augustine, Richard Hooker, Thomas Traherne, William Law, Tacitus, Martin Buber, Gabriel Marcel, Rudolf Otto, Coventry Patmore, Owen Barfield, I. A. Richards, Carl Jung, and Edwyn Bevan. "My reading of Lewis," says Dr. Carnell, "shows him to be Thomist, Aristotelian, Platonist, or Neo-Kantian (though rarely the latter) only as something in each of these approaches serves him as a tool of thought."

The main part of this dissertation is given to the manner in which Lewis combines a "tough-minded theology" and the mystical *Sehnsucht* so as to make them compatible and how Lewis's "dialectic of desire" finds expression in his imaginative works. Dr. Carnell finds four dominant images of *Sehnsucht* in Lewis: 1) distant hills, 2) exotic gardens, 3) islands, especially islands of the "Utter East," and 4) a particular kind of music. All four of these images appear in *The Voyage of the Dawn Treader.* After their experience was over, Edmund and Lucy found they could never talk much about the sweet breeze coming out of the East and carrying with it a musical sound. "Lucy could only say, 'It would break your heart.' 'Why,' said I, 'was it so sad?' 'Sad!! No,' said Lucy."

Dr. Carnell observes that Lewis is always more than mere narrator: along with excellence of story there is always message, and this comes about simply because Lewis is deeply convinced that man is a moral creature and that stories which merely entertain can never qualify with those which mirror man in his deeper aspects.

Sehnsucht is closely related to the numinous, which "communicates a sense of disorientation in the face of awesome mystery much as *Sehnsucht* communicates a sense of disorientation in melancholy or questing." The idea of the numinous, says Dr. Carnell, has long been of interest to Lewis and was instrumental in his conversion. The numinous Lewis believes to be expressed in dread and awe, yet in a different dimension from fear. It is a kind of interpretation which man gives to the universe, such as Ransom's feeling on board the space-ship returning to earth that the heavens are not mere black space but rather alive with an excess of vitality that makes earth's puny and our planet an "abyss of death." Logres is the numinous Britain, and when men respond to something from "without" which inspires awe, mystery, and the sense of the holy, then Logres is perceived in Britain. It is the impingement of the supernatural on the natural, and the danger always is that Logres will sink back into "mere Britain" where man becomes the measure of all things and materialism dominates.

All of Lewis's fiction and most of his poetry, especially whenever he wishes to convey *Sehnsucht,* makes use either of allegory or myth. "Allegory to Lewis is more than a sugar coating on the moral pill" but rather is likely to involve profound psychological or metaphysical assumptions. In allegory there tends to be a one-to-one relationship between story and meaning, but in myth the metaphysical or ethical meaning is deeper and more complex, yet both myth and allegory create worlds of their own. Lewis's use of myth is a far cry from escapism, indeed the very opposite.

Dr. Carnell explains Lewis's belief concerning the source and significance of *Sehnsucht* or "Joy." He shows its connections with Tillyard's idea of the growth of man's self-consciousness and gradual ascent over the other animals, Sir Harold Nicolson's explanation in behavioral psychology, and wish-fulfillment theory of Freud, yet points out that it is quite different from any of these, and even from Jung, with whom Lewis is much more sympathetic. Neither is "Joy" to be explained wholly in terms of sex or art.

Although Dr. Carnell sometimes disagrees with Lewis's ideas, his study is on the whole very friendly. He feels very much like Clinton Trowbridge, who said of Lewis's work: "His mythopoeic imagination is so rich in invention, so broad in scope, so sensuously perceptive in descriptive detail that, after we [have read him], we have a difficult time viewing the Cosmos through any but Lewis's eyes."

Dr. Carnell's study is followed by a chronology of Lewis's life and writings, a substantial bibliography that includes Lewis's works, selected critical works on Lewis, and a general list of works dealing with Romanticism, symbolism, aspects of religion, and the like.

ROMANTIC RELIGION IN THE WORK OF OWEN BARFIELD, C. S. LEWIS, CHARLES WILLIAMS AND J. R. R. TOLKIEN.

A doctoral dissertation submitted by Robert J. Reilly to Michigan State University in 1960. Dr. Reilly believes that the two Anglicans Lewis and Williams, the Roman Catholic Tolkien, and the Anthroposophist Barfield have a common interest that may be described as "romantic religion." By the term he means a literary and religious construct which first defends romance by claiming for it a religious significance and then defends religion by means of romanticism.

Because Dr. Reilly considers Owen Barfield as perhaps the intellectual fountainhead of the group, he devotes a long chapter to summarizing Barfield's Anthroposophism. Barfield, a philologist, holds that language is "a window of the soul" and that the history of humanity can be shown from a study of changes in word meaning. He believes that history shows a great evolution from relative unselfconsciousness to relatively complete selfconsciousness. He calls this evolution an "internalization," that is, a process by which objective things are made mostly subjective.

In the beginning there was a great unity of things in which man "participated" far more than he does today. Meaning was then unindividuated. Thinking and perceiving were one, mean-

203

ing and life were one. Reality was self-evident. Language had a living unity that was essentially metaphoric without knowing itself to be such. Early man had an awareness, a kind of extra-sensory link with reality, that by the time of the Reformation had become almost totally lost.

The growing awareness of this loss, and the consequent long-ing to repossess the ancient participation, found its spokesman in Coleridge and Wordsworth and other romantics and especially in Coleridge's enunciation that the imagination is a means of bringing dead objects back to life. For instance, the sun had originally possessed a god-like glory that in course of time degenerated into a conception of it as mere mass, energy, and matter. The sun could regain its status as an object of awe and wonder only by the creative use of the imagination. The romantic poets were overwhelmed with the conviction that something greatly valuable had been lost to man and they therefore longed to revitalize the world. They attempted to reinvest nature, by imagination, with that quality which had been drained out of her by rational abstraction.

Now Dr. Reilly endeavors to show that it is some such romantic conviction which runs through and inspires the works of Lewis, Williams, and Tolkien. Lewis in particular has often acknowl-edged his indebtedness to Barfield. All four of the men are religious and all four are committed to a romantic interpretation of the nature of man and the course of history. Hence Reilly's "romantic religion" and his endeavor to show how it leavens the creative works of the three. For instance, Lewis described the romantic experience as "the baptism of the imagination" and associated it with man's longing for Joy, an experience which he believed to be suffused with holiness and actually representing a calling from God. He concluded that all longing in the soul is finally a longing for God.

The chief objection I find to this penetrating study is that Reilly makes Lewis more indebted to Barfield's Anthroposophy than I judge him to be. "I never came within a hundred miles of accepting the thing," says Lewis in *Surprised by Joy*. Yet Dr.

Reilly is perfectly correct in assuming that Lewis was decidedly influenced by Barfield.

Dr. Reilly's bibliography consists of limited but well-selected primary and secondary items concerning the four men and also a lengthy list of works of general reference.

BOOKS WITH MEN BEHIND THEM

In this book, published by Random House in 1962, Dr. Edmund Fuller gives almost half his space to the triumvirate of C. S. Lewis, J. R. R. Tolkien, and Charles Williams, writers whom he designates as "masters of the fantastic story." Fantasy, Dr. Fuller believes, is often capable of producing greater depths of insight than so-called realistic fiction. In addition to providing brief summaries of their leading imaginative works, Dr. Fuller evaluates the contribution of these three writers to present literature. He gives particular attention to Lewis's space trilogy.

Readers unacquainted with J. R. R. Tolkien and Charles Williams, two men whose works are essential to a full understanding of Lewis, will find Dr. Fuller's book an excellent introduction to these writers. He compares Tolkien's hobbit series with Wagner's ring cycle of operas and points out what strikes every Tolkien reader, that his stories are "astonishingly underivative" and form an autonomous world which can only be experienced not described. Dr. Fuller makes clear that there are large overtones of potential allegorical, even theological, meaning in the hobbit series. He takes exception to a critic who in 1961 reported that Tolkien's books had passed into a "merciful oblivion." On the contrary, he says, these books are selling widely and Sir Stanley Unwin, their British publisher, thinks them more likely to outlast our time than anything else which he has published.

The seven novels of Charles Williams, produced at high speed while their author served as a busy editor for the Oxford University Press, are, says Dr. Fuller, a strange mixture of the detective story and profound religious symbolism. To the thoughtful reader they bring alive a unique spiritual world. Dr. Fuller calls attention to some of Williams's themes, such as the lust for power, substituted love, and the Holy City. He is impressed by the "inexhaustible narrative invention, swiftness of pace, exotic erudition, intellectual penetration, and theological boldness" of Williams's novels.

C. S. LEWIS

This Bodley Head Monograph by Roger Lancelyn Green was published in London in 1963 and is mainly concerned with the Narnia stories and other Lewis books considered suitable for children. It attempts to point out sources used consciously or unconsciously by Lewis. We learn that Lewis had no original plan for the Narnia series and that his first plot for *The Lion, the Witch and the Wardrobe* was greatly different from the finished book; Aslan did not appear in the original plot.

This author thinks *The Magician's Nephew* and *The Silver Chair* are the best of the Narnia books but indicates that *The Horse and His Boy* seems to be the most popular. *Prince Caspian* he considers the least popular, perhaps because the main adventure starts late. Reepicheep and the marsh-wiggle he thinks Lewis's finest Narnian creations, and he points out that the *Dawn Treader* has the qualities of a real ship rather than those of a mere ferryboat with poop and sails stuck on.

Mr. Green thinks *Perelandra* "incomparably more important" than *Out of the Silent Planet* and says that it is impossible either to disbelieve in the enchanting world created in *Perelandra* or to wipe it out of the memory when once it is implanted. He regards *That Hideous Strength* as a novel of sustaining interest and lasting impressiveness. He points out the broad similarity of this story to those written by Charles Williams.

In this monograph we learn of Lewis's love of long, solitary walks in Ulster, Surrey, and the country around Oxford and of his "brief but intensely happy marriage."

Mr. Green believes that many of Lewis's books, particularly the Narnia stories, are likely to take a permanent place in literature. He believes them to be the products of "the mind of a true scholar, of one of the best-read men of his age; of a superb craftsman in the art of letters, with a gift for story-telling; of a thinker, logician and theologian who has plumbed the depths of the dark void of atheism and come by the hardest route on his pilgrimage back to God."

LIGHT ON C. S. LEWIS

This book was published in 1965 by Geoffrey Bles in London and in 1966 by Harcourt, Brace and World in New York. It consists of essays by personal or literary friends of Lewis and contains a definitive bibliography of his writings. Some of the essays are by lifelong confreres such as Owen Barfield and Nevill Coghill. One of the best is by John Lawlor, who beginning his tutorials under Lewis found him "red-faced, bald, dressed in baggy jacket and trousers and obviously in no mood to waste time" but whose hostility finally changed into a "stubborn affection" and eventually into ineluctable admiration. One essay, by Chad Walsh, describes Lewis's impact on America. Walter Hooper's brief introduction to the bibliography is an engaging vignette of Lewis in the last couple of years of his life when Hooper came to know him.

The writers feel that the books by Lewis which are most likely to outlive our time are not his expository studies such as *Mere Christianity* and *The Problem of Pain* but rather his creative works like *Till We Have Faces, Perelandra,* and the Narnia stories. Stella Gibbons describes Lewis as the creator of "a beautiful and dangerous world lit by hope." She is wholly wrong, by the way, in asserting that Lewis did not think highly of his space trilogy. Actually he regarded *Perelandra* as his best book, with *Till We Have Faces* as a close second.

Lewis the writer is regarded by these essayists as superlative in power of imagination, clear rhetoric, and the gift of generalization. Miss Gibbons thinks that some of Lewis's creatures in *Out of the Silent Planet* bear no greatly unfavorable comparison with Shakespeare's Ariel and Caliban and that his *eldila* show much of the same imaginative excellence.

INDEX

Abraham, 185
Absolute, the, 34-35, 162
Adam and Eve, 81, 91-101, 154, 184, 186
Adoration, 159
Adultery, 76, 188
Advertising, modern, 24, 178
Aeschylus, 18
Aesthetics, 59, 198
Affection, 58, 73-75
Alexander, Samuel, 18
Alice in Wonderland, 141
Allegory, 28, 36, 57, 83, 100, 116, 136, 137, 150, 195, 202, 205
Amis and Amile, 75
Anatomy of Melancholy, 24
Angels, 43, 47, 76, 87-88, 97, 98, 104, 105, 110, 160, 166, 192
Anglicanism, 33, 171
Anglo-Catholicism, 25
Anglo-Saxons, 104
Animals, 71-72, 73
Animals and trees, talking, 73, 118, 121, 123, 126, 127, 134, 144, 145
Animal Farm, 115
Anthropology, 163, 175, 203
Anthroposophy, 17, 203-205
Antigone, 153
Apocalypse, 110, 112, 187 (*see also* Christ, His second coming)
Apostles' Creed, 157
Archetypes, 197
Archtype and ectype, 32
Argument, 61
Aristotle, 169, 201
Arnold, Matthew, 16
Art and literature, 43
Arthurian legend, 16, 36, 105, 107, 111-112, 197-198, 199

Arthurian Triptych, 90, 197-198
Art, modern, 179
Athanasian Creed, 157
Atheism, 104, 169, 171, 176, 189
Atlantis, 117, 186
Auden, W. H., 51
Authority, 24
Automata, men as, 65-66
Automobiles, 175

Babbitt, Irving, 33
Bacon, Leonard, 37
Ball, Sir Robert, 15
Baptism, 169
Barfield, Owen, 17, 18, 21, 80, 196, 201, 203-205
Barth, Karl, 33, 147
Beauty, 41, 56-57, 62, 64, 81, 88, 97, 139, 151, 163, 184, 196
Belfast, 13
Belief, 176
Bergson, Henri, 181
Bevan, Edwyn, 201
Bible, as literature, 147-148, 152, 153
Bible, inspiration of, 147, 149, 150, 151-153, 154, 156-157, 166, 191-192
Bible, the, 68, 71, 185
Blood sacrifice, 59, 61
Body, the, 184
Boethius, 5
Books with Men Behind Them, 12, 90, 205-206
Booth, William, 37
Boss, Edgar W., 191-192
Brady, Charles A., 116
Brave New World, 108, 115
Browning, Robert, 16, 62
Buber, Martin, 73, 188, 201

208

Bunyan, John, 28-29, 36, 196
Bush, Vannevar, 108
Business men, 75

Caesar, Julius, 51
Calvin, John, 147, 151
Campbell College, 14, 16
Camus, Albert, 101, 183
Candide, 200
Canon, of Bible, 152
Carnell, Corbin S., 7, 12, 79-80, 90, 144, 155, 191, 200-203
Carpenter, Scott, 84
Carrell, Alexis, 112
Castle, The, 80
Charientocracy, 177
Charity, 38, 77, 179
Chartres, 14, 15, 16
Chastity, 39
Chesterton, G. K., 17, 18, 19, 67, 77, 118
Children, 98
Children's stories (*see* Fairy tales)
Choices, 48, 49-50, 51, 69, 170, 181
Christ, 40, 49, 54, 56-58, 61, 62, 64, 112
    As a Person, 152
    As Benefactor of Man, 94, 128, 132, 138, 142, 148, 169
    As Bridegroom, 151
    As Creator, 157
    As Deity, 157, 165
    As God and Man, 157
    As Guide, 126, 140
    As Reality, 133, 155, 157, 181
    As Sacrifice, 70
    As Savior, 46, 95, 119, 127, 128, 137, 143, 157, 158, 169
    As Son of God, 20
    As Word, 165, 190
    Depth of, 169
    First "Real Man," 171
    His atonement, 191
    His crucifixion, 83, 124, 136, 163
    His incarnation, 41, 82, 90, 156, 158, 163
    His resurrection, 46, 124, 153, 154, 163, 193
    His sacrifice, 63, 137, 154
    His second coming, 98, 160, 192, 193
    His teachings, 152
    His virgin birth, 161
    His wounds, 97, 100
    Not "tame," 136, 137, 144, 157
    Obedience to, 138, 140, 157, 171
    Omniscient, 138
    Only Begotten Son, 157
    Prophesied, 151
    Substitutes for, 51
    Utterly concrete, 159
Christian behavior, 169-171
Christian doctrine, 171, 176
Christian giving, 169
Christianity, as experienced, 154
Christianity, its oddity, 169
Christianity, modern, 174
Christians, called to holiness, 159, 182
Christians, their peace, 113
Christians, to love Christ, 140, 159
Chronological snobbery, 18, 24, 161, 174-175
Church of England, 24-25
Church, the, 35, 41, 158, 171-172, 185
Civic values, 75
Civilization, modern, 177
Classicism, 33
Coghill, Nevill, 18
Coleridge, Samuel T., 42
Collectivism, 24
Commonplace, the, 40, 119, 166, 183-184
Communism, 33, 102
Companionship, 75
Confessio Amantis, 83
Confession, 159
Conscience, 68, 113, 161, 169
Consciousness, 81, 83, 108
Contentment, 179
Conversation, 76
Conversion, 38, 55, 63, 76, 150-151, 152, 159, 164, 179
Correction, by God, 67-68
Courtesy, 73, 74, 121, 142, 199
Creation, 165, 183
Creeds, 154-155

Crisis in Psychiatry and Religion, 68
C. S. Lewis, 206-207
C. S. Lewis: Apostle to the Skeptics,
   114, 160, 192-194
Culture, human, 174
Culture, modern, 177, 180, 197
Culture, stone-age, 86
Cupid and Psyche myth, 54, 200

Damnation, 42, 48, 49, 69
Dante, 51
Darwin, Charles, 72, 175
David and Jonathan, 75
Death, 66, 68, 90, 167, 171
Debunkers, 101
Deep Heaven, 142, 190, 202
De Incarnatione, 162
Demagogues, 179
Democracy, modern, 178, 179, 184
Demons (*see* Satan)
Demythologizing, 166
Depravity, of man, 68, 157-158
De Quincey, Thomas, 6
Descartes, René, 194
De Trinitate, 172
Devil (*see* Satan)
Dictators, 179
Dr. Jekyll and Mr. Hyde, 80
Door in the Wall, The, 80
Doubts, 58, 61, 65, 96
Dreiser, Theodore, 200
Druids, 105, 186
Dryness, 38-39, 42, 76-77
Dyson, H. V. D., 18

Ecclesiastes, 152-153
Eden, Garden of, 32, 68, 73, 93, 98,
   100, 103, 109, 112, 118, 119, 135,
   145, 148, 160, 186, 204-205
Education, modern, 24, 75, 78, 102,
   113, 129, 177, 179, 183
Elias, 112
Eliot, T. S., 33, 144, 174, 194, 197
Emotion, 38
Emperor's Clothes, The, 144, 173,
   194-195
Enoch, 112
Epicurus, 33
Erasmus, 33

Eros, 76-77
Ervine, St. John, 37
Escapism, 170, 202
Essays of Elia, The, 24
Eucharist, 82, 138
Euripides, 18
Evangelism, 157
Everlasting Man, The, 19
"Everythingism," 164
Evil (*see* Satan)
Evolution, emergent, 89, 168
Evolution, theory of, 175, 191
Exclusiveness, 76

Fairy tales, 104, 113, 116
Faith, 171
Fall, of man, 32, 82, 94, 100, 121,
   137, 154, 186, 192
Family, the, 51, 74
Fanaticism, 148
Fantasy, 141, 196, 198
Farinata, 51, 178
"Farther in and higher up," 51, 142,
   167, 187, 188
Fascism, 33
Film-stars, 179
Fisher King, the, 107, 197
Forgiveness, 57, 170
Fra Angelico, 43
Frazer, Sir James G., 19, 163
Freedom, 43, 44, 50, 58, 67, 68, 77,
   90, 94, 95, 97, 111, 164, 167, 169,
   170
Freud, Sigmund, 31, 170, 194, 202
Friendship, 24, 44, 75-76
Fuller, Edmund, 12, 90, 98-99, 205-
   206
Fundamentalism, 193, 194

Genesis, 152, 154, 155, 160
Genghis Khan, 51
Genius, 178
Gilson, Etienne, 12
Glory, 81, 165
Gluttony, 51
God
   As Absolute, 143
   As Beauty, 171
   As Cause, 162

As Creator, 66, 69, 77, 118, 120-121, 144, 149, 164, 165, 167, 168, 169, 190
As Eternal Fact, 51, 155, 164
As Guide, 181
As Legislator, 163
As Maleldil, 86, 95, 97, 98, 100
As Person, 176
As Truth, 190
A "tame," 168
Attributes of, 192
His centricity, 67
His gifts, 76, 78
His glory, 73, 189
His goodness, 66, 189
His greatness, 189
His love, 40, 44, 51, 66, 73, 74, 77, 149
His mercy, 69
His omnipotence, 67, 110-111
His omniscience, 106, 176
His righteousness, 190
His timelessness, 164, 167, 171
His uniqueness, 143
His "vulgarity," 40
Judgments of, 100, 169, 189
Obedience to, 90, 94, 98, 99, 111, 185
Praise of, 150, 165
Goethe, 43, 50, 51
Golden Bough, The, 16
Goodness, 169
Good Works, 42, 48, 95, 111, 159, 169, 170, 178, 185
Gospels, the, 136
Government, modern, 174
Gower, John, 83
Gratitude, 179
Greeks, 56, 164
Greene, Graham, 194
Green, Roger Lancelyn, 206-207
Gresham, David and Douglas, 22
Gresham, William L., 21-22
Griffiths, Dom Bede, 11, 12
Grumblers, 46, 49
Gulliver's Travels, 141

Happiness, 66-67, 169
Harding, D. E., 44, 103, 162

Hart, Dabney A., 11, 12, 36, 64, 100, 191, 195-196
Hartshorne, Charles, 70-71
Hatred, 39, 96, 170
Heaven, 37, 40, 43, 44-52, 69, 70, 78, 82, 122, 135, 136, 137, 140, 145, 149, 156, 159, 160, 167, 170, 171, 180-184, 187, 192, 193
Hebrews, 148-149, 169
Hedonism, 40
Heisenberg Principle, 194
Hell, 12, 37-52, 68-69, 70, 73, 157, 159, 169, 170, 178-179, 181, 182, 185, 192, 193
Henry VIII, 51, 178
Hierarchy, 71, 73, 82, 90, 143, 194
Hierarchy of Heaven and Earth, The, 103, 162
Highet, Gilbert, 79
Hippolytus, 18
Hitler, Adolf, 51, 72, 102, 178
Hoffer, Eric, 114-115
Holiness, 159, 184
Holy Communion, 169
Holy Spirit, 35, 92, 95, 138, 142, 159
Homosexuality, 75
Hooker, Richard, 189, 201
Hooper, Walter, 23, 186
Horace, 33
Howard, Thomas, 136
Hulme, T. E., 194
Humanism, 33
Humility, 39, 179
Humor, 43
Huxley, Aldous, 108, 115
Hypocrisy, 51, 178

Idealism, Absolute, 18
Imagery, Anthropomorphic, 162, 166
Imagination, 156, 195
Immortality, of soul (see Heaven)
Incarnation of the Word of God, The, 162
Individuality, 40, 178
Infancy, 82
Intelligentsia, 15, 26, 30-31, 32, 39, 41, 104, 113
International relations, 178
Ireland, 13, 14
Isaac, 185

Jealousy, 52, 74, 75
Jenkin, A. K. Hamilton, 17
Joad, C. E. M., 65, 70, 72
Job, 22-23, 151, 153
Johnson, Dr. Samuel, 6, 18, 108, 167, 189, 200
Jonah, 153
Joseph, 161
Joy, 14, 16, 17, 18, 19, 29, 47, 48, 50-51, 59, 70, 79, 83, 90, 107, 135, 144, 165, 169, 181, 187, 188, 189, 200-203
Judas, 110, 153
Jung, Carl G., 179, 201, 202
Jungle Books, 116
Juvenal, 200

Kafka, Franz, 80, 141
Kant, Immanuel, 201
Kirkpatrick, W. T., 15-16
Knighthood, 126
Koestler, Arthur, 108

Language, 165
Law, William, 201
Lending at interest, 169
Lewis, Albert James, 13-14
Lewis, C. S.
    As atheist, 14, 15, 16, 30, 66, 207
    As literary critic, 11, 193, 195-196
    As romanticist, 12, 17, 198, 200, 203
    As popularizer, 5-6
    As satirist, 36, 90, 113, 139, 178, 196
    As theologian, 12, 147, 191-192
    As writer, 77, 80, 101, 107, 139, 141, 145, 160, 172, 180, 191-207
    At Cambridge, 21, 23, 174, 186
    At Oxford, 17-19, 21, 34-35, 183, 192, 201
    Charities of, 185-186
    Conversion of, 19-20, 34, 149
    Love of walking, 23-24, 78, 206
    Old Western Man, 180
    Pen names of, 20, 22, 166, 186
    Physical appearance, 12-13, 23, 100, 192
    Prayer life of, 166

Works
    Abolition of Man, The, 72, 79, 101-103, 108, 114, 115, 189
    Allegory of Love, The, 20
    Arthurian Torso, 112
    Beyond Personality, 168
    Broadcast Talks, 168
    Case for Christianity, The, 5, 168
    Christian Behaviour, 168
    Dymer, 20
    Experiment in Criticism, An, 80
    Four Loves, The, 73-78
    George Macdonald: An Anthology, 81
    Great Divorce, The, 37, 44-52, 143, 180, 188, 193
    Grief Observed, A, 22, 71, 166
    Horse and His Boy, The, 131-133, 139, 145, 146, 206
    Last Battle, The, 32, 62, 133-136, 139, 143, 145, 146, 187
    Letters to Malcolm: Chiefly on Prayer, 139, 147, 165-167, 189
    Lion, the Witch and the Wardrobe, The, 73, 117, 123-125, 136, 141, 145, 186, 206
    Magician's Nephew, The, 72, 117-121, 133, 139, 141, 146, 199, 206
    Mere Christianity, 147, 168-171, 180
    Miracles, 60, 147, 160-165, 167, 171, 172, 194
    Narnia stories, 7, 116-146, 181, 196, 200, 206-207
    Out of the Silent Planet, 72, 79, 82, 83, 84-89, 198, 206
    Perelandra, 49, 79, 82, 89, 90, 91-101, 112, 182, 185, 186, 187, 198, 206
    Pilgrim's Regress, The, 20, 25-36, 46, 51, 59, 60, 83, 156, 179, 186, 187, 188, 192, 193
    Poems, 186
    Preface to Paradise Lost, A, 95
    Prince Caspian, 73, 125-127, 206
    Problem of Pain, The, 6, 31, 37, 50, 65-73, 186, 189

Reflections on the Psalms, 147-160, 189

Screwtape Letters, The, 12, 37-44, 51, 157, 178, 180, 193

Silver Chair, The, 99, 129-131, 137, 138, 139, 185, 206

Spirits in Bondage, 20, 23

Surprised by Joy, 13-20, 30, 31, 34, 36, 143, 204

That Hideous Strength, 41, 42, 44, 58, 72, 79, 80, 81, 90, 99, 100, 101, 104-115, 142, 180, 181, 184, 185, 186, 190, 197, 198, 199, 206

They Asked for a Paper, 174

Till We Have Faces, 37, 51-64, 74, 182, 198, 200

Voyage of the Dawn Treader, The, 127-129, 139, 141, 144, 158, 201, 206

Weight of Glory, The, 187

World's Last Night, The, 158, 175, 177

Lewis, Flora Augusta Hamilton, 13, 14

Lewis, Helen Joy Davidman Gresham, 21-22, 166, 201

Lewis, W. H., 14, 23

Life-Force, 93, 168

Light on C. S. Lewis, 207

Lilith, 20, 59, 141, 186

Limbo, 108

Lindbergh, Charles A., 112

Linguistics, 103

Literature, realistic, 116

Livy, 121

Logical positivism, 16

Logres-Britain, 107, 111-112, 197, 199, 202

Longing (*see Sehnsucht*)

Lot's wife, 153

Love, 51, 64, 72, 73-78, 107, 169, 170, 176, 182, 185

Lovelessness, 77

Lowell, James Russell, 6

Lucretius, 15

Lust, 47, 188

Macdonald, George, 5, 16, 17, 18, 20, 48-51, 59, 72, 80, 141, 188, 193

Machines, modern, 174

Macrobes, 99

Maeterlinck, Maurice, 16

Magic, 13, 104-111, 112, 116, 117, 119, 122, 125, 126, 128, 138, 181

Magic, Deep, 124, 136, 137

Managerial class, the, 177-178

Man, as sinner, 87, 88, 90, 111, 157

Man, made for God, 77

Man Who Was Thursday, The, 118

Marcel, Gabriel, 201

Marriage, 74, 76, 170, 188

Mars, 82, 84, 97, 106

Marxism, 33, 194

Mass production, 179

Materialism, 168

Matter, 166, 184

Medieval cosmology, 199

Medieval period, 174

Melchisedec, 112

Melville, Herman, 155

Mephistopheles, 43

Merlin, 104-111, 186, 190, 197

Metaphor, 156, 162, 163, 172, 196, 197

Methodists, 171

Milne, A. A., 141

Milton, John, 18, 43, 44, 50, 51, 69

Miracles, 22, 69, 151, 154, 159, 160-165, 192

Missionaries, 58

Modern Arms and Free Men, 108

Money, 178

Moods, 171

Moorman, Charles, 90, 111, 197-198

Moral order, the (*see Tao*)

Moses, 112, 151, 169

Mowrer, O. H., 68

Music, 41, 59, 97, 98, 118, 120, 177, 184, 201

Music, modern, 74

Myth, 16, 18, 54-55, 57, 60, 63-64, 73, 80-83, 88, 97, 100, 139, 145, 150-156, 163, 166, 169, 173, 183, 193, 195, 196, 197, 198-200, 202, 203

Napoleon, 51

National Anti-Vivisection Society of London, 71
Naturalism, 168
Nature, 39, 41, 42, 58, 60, 66, 73, 75, 77, 102, 108-109, 120, 121, 122, 145, 149, 150, 160-166, 183, 194
New Masses, 21
Newspapers, 24, 113
Nicene Creed, 157
Nicolson, Marjorie Hope, 79, 83
Nicolson, Sir Harold, 202
Niebuhr, Reinhold, 60, 166
Nineteen Eighty-Four, 108
No Exit, 45
Northernness, 16
Nott, Kathleen, 144, 173, 174, 194-195
Novels and movies, modern, 170
Novel, the Victorian, 74
Numinor, 186
Numinous, the, 81, 198-199, 202

Objectivity, 101-102
Odysseus, 141
Oldie, 14
Old Yellow Book, 16
Orthodox faiths, 24
Orwell, George, 108, 115
"Otherness," 41
Otto, Rudolph, 201
Oughtness, 68, 136, 168
Out of My Life and Thought, 72

Pain, 65-73
Pain, animal, 70
Pantheism, 150, 164, 165
Parables, 153, 172
Paradise, 81, 82, 91, 97, 98
Paradise Lost, 95
Parents and children, 78
Patmore, Coventry, 201
Pentecost, 159
People, Places, and Books, 79
Perfection, 67-68, 171, 182
Phantastes, 16-17, 20
Pharaoh Amenhotep IV, 143
Philosophical idealism, 34
Philosophical naturalism, 59
Picon, Gaëtan, 101

Plantagenets, the, 111
Plato, 18, 80, 82, 139, 150, 172, 188, 201
Pleasure, 15, 40, 68, 69, 76, 94, 97, 98, 144, 150, 165, 187, 188, 193
Poetry, 155, 177
Poetry in Bible, 147
Poetry, modern, 174
Politics, modern, 174
Pope, Alexander, 196
Positivism, 104
Post-Christian era, 174
Praise, of God, 150
Prayer, 14, 15, 22, 38, 39, 42, 66-67, 138, 159, 163-166, 171
Prayer, for sick, 159
Preachers, apostate, 46
Presbyterians, 171
Pretense, 47
Pride, 39, 41, 46, 52, 95, 170, 181
Profanity, 105
Prophecy, 67, 150, 151, 155
Prostitution, 88, 90
Protestants, 25
Psychoanalysis, 32, 68, 170, 196
Psychology, 18, 30-31, 102, 103, 139, 165, 193, 194, 202
Purgatory, 167, 191, 192
Puritanism, 13, 25, 28-29, 39, 179, 193
Purity, 111, 181
Pylades and Orestes, 75

Rabelais, 33
Rasselas, 200
Rationalism, 52, 53, 56, 58, 59, 60, 61, 64
Reality, 81, 82, 138-139, 165, 182, 187, 190
Reason, 32, 55, 60, 101, 161, 171, 194, 196
Rebirth, 50
Redemption, 169
Reilly, Robert J., 79, 80, 203-205
Religion, modern, 34, 159
Renaissance, 174
Repentance, 39, 60
Resurrection (*see* Christ)
Resurrection, of body, 60, 167

Return of the King, The, 96
Richards, I. A., 201
Roland and Oliver, 75
Roman Catholicism, 24-25, 171
Royal Air Force, 21
Ruth, 153

Sacramentalism, 191
Sacraments, 82
Sacrilege, 165
Sadism, 105
St. Andrews University, 21
St. Athanasius, 162
St. Augustine, 62, 172, 185, 201
St. Jerome, 151
St. John on Patmos, 187
St. Luke, 153
St. Paul, 49, 153, 157, 159, 160,
    172, 193
St. Thomas, 139
St. Thomas Aquinas, 201
Salvation, 46, 49, 127, 140, 143, 157,
    158
Salvation Army, 24
Santayana, George, 33
Sartre, Jean-Paul, 45
Satan, 38, 43, 49, 50, 66, 70, 76, 82,
    87, 89, 90, 91, 93, 95, 96, 98, 99,
    105, 106, 108, 109, 112, 119, 123,
    130, 136, 137, 140, 142, 144, 149,
    160, 169, 181, 184, 188, 194, 199
Savage, D. S., 6
Sayers, Dorothy, 194
Schopenhauer, Arthur, 16
Schweitzer, Albert, 72
Science, 59, 72-73, 84, 88, 102-103,
    104, 107, 108, 110, 112, 113-115,
    163, 166, 175-176, 177, 193, 194,
    199
Science and the Modern World, 108
Science fiction, 79
Science Is a Sacred Cow, 108
Scientism, 113, 175
Scripture (*see* Bible)
Second Coming (*see* Christ)
Sehnsucht, 14, 29, 35, 36, 40, 60, 61,
    70, 81-82, 144, 151, 155-156, 165,
    170-171, 181, 186, 187, 200-203
Self, 40, 47, 103, 173, 182

Selfhood, 44, 71, 72, 73, 76, 92, 94,
    100
Selfishness, 37, 45, 46, 47, 48, 51, 55,
    56, 58, 61, 62, 64, 68, 69, 70, 74,
    75, 142, 143, 182
Self-righteousness, 41, 170
Senses, the, 156, 166, 184, 188
Sensuality, 188
Sex, 51, 76, 86, 170, 178, 184, 188
Shame, 31, 41, 68
Shaw, Bernard, 72
Siegfried, 16
Siekevitz, Philip, 114
Simons, John W., 194-195
Sin, 68, 89, 90, 110, 121, 148, 152,
    165, 168, 169, 183, 189, 190
Sister Carrie, 200
Slavery, 88, 90
Sleepwalkers, The, 108
Smewgy, 15, 16
Snobbishness, 24, 178
Social conventions, 168
Social good, the, 103
Socialism, 139
Socrates, 150
Sohrab and Rustum, 16
Solitude, 24
Song of Songs, 151
Soper, David W., 11, 12, 21, 25
Space, Time and Deity, 18
Space travel, 84-85, 106, 110, 158,
    177
Space Trilogy, 79-115, 192, 205
Spenser, Edmund, 18, 79
Standen, Anthony, 108
Stealing, 165
Steiner, Rudolph, 196
Stevenson, Robert L., 80
Subject and object, 101-103
Substitution, doctrine of, 64
Superman, 90
Supernatural, the, 46, 58, 60, 61, 159,
    160-163
Survival of fittest, 90
Swift, Jonathan, 90, 178, 180, 196
Symbol, 43, 60, 73, 77, 79, 83, 98, 99,
    100, 108, 136, 138, 145, 150, 158,
    197, 198, 199, 203

Taboos, savage, 175
Tacitus, 201
Tamerlane, 51
Tao, the, 51, 59, 68, 72, 102, 103,
    161, 168, 189-190
Temptation (see Eden)
Theocracy, 177
Theology, 45, 173, 189, 194, 201
Theology, modern, 39, 45, 59, 157,
    166, 179, 180, 191
Theophany, 165
Theosophy, 164
These Found the Way, 21
Tillyard, E. M. W., 202
"Togetherness," 75, 78, 178
Tolkien, J. R. R., 18, 80, 96, 112,
    121, 136, 141, 198-200, 203-204,
    205-206
Tongues, speaking in, 159
Traherne, Thomas, 201
Trinity, the, 90, 157, 171, 172, 192
Tristram Shandy, 24
Trowbridge, Clinton, 203
Truth, 51, 80, 81, 83, 93, 143, 148,
    154, 172, 195, 196, 199
Tynan, Kenneth, 11, 12

Ugliness, 64
Undulation, law of, 42
Universalism, 49-50, 69
Unwin, Sir Stanley, 205
Utilitarianism, 72
Utter East, the, 201

Values, 101-102
Venus (as planet), 82, 91, 97, 106
Venus (as sex), 76

Virgil, 18, 150
Vivisection, 71, 108-109, 139
Voltaire, 200
Voyages to the Moon, 79, 83

Wagner, Richard, 16, 205
Walsh, Chad, 114, 116-117, 160,
    192-194
War, 87, 88, 90
We, 108
Wells, H. G., 15, 80
Whipsnade, 19-20
Whitehead, Alfred North, 108, 114
Willey, Basil, 194
Will, freedom of (see Freedom)
Williams, Charles, 48, 64, 80, 97, 111-
    112, 193, 197, 198-200, 201,
    203-204, 205, 206
Wind in the Willows, The, 12
Wishful thinking, 45
Wolfe, Bernard, 108
Women, modern, 75-76
Worldliness, 42
World War I, 186
World War II, 183
Worry, 185
Worship, 59, 63
Wright, Marjorie E., 7, 64, 73, 100,
    109, 111, 112, 121, 155, 186, 191,
    198-200
"Wyvern" College, 15.

Yahoos, 178, 179
Yeats, William B., 16

Zamiatin, Eugene, 108

216